Speculative Realism

Speculative Realism

An Introduction

GRAHAM HARMAN

polity

First published in 2018 by Polity Press

Polity Press
65 Bridge Street
Cambridge CB2 1UR, UK

Polity Press
101 Station Landing
Suite 300
Medford, MA 02155, USA

ISBN-13: 978-1-5095-1998-9
ISBN-13: 978-1-5095-1999-6 (pb)

A catalogue record for this book is available from the British Library.

Typeset in 11 on 13pt Adobe Garamond Pro by
Servis Filmsetting Ltd, Stockport, Cheshire
Printed and bound in Great Britain by CPI Group (UK) Ltd, Croydon

The publisher has used its best endeavours to ensure that the URLs for external websites referred to in this book are correct and active at the time of going to press. However, the publisher has no responsibility for the websites and can make no guarantee that a site will remain live or that the content is or will remain appropriate.

Every effort has been made to trace all copyright holders, but if any have been inadvertently overlooked the publisher will be pleased to include any necessary credits in any subsequent reprint or edition.

For further information on Polity, visit our website:
politybooks.com

Contents

Introduction

Though barely a decade old, Speculative Realism (SR) is already one of the most influential philosophical movements in art, architecture, and the humanities. A number of books have already been written on Speculative Realism in part or as a whole: those of Peter Gratton, Steven Shaviro, and Tom Sparrow come to mind.[1] But there is still plenty of room for additional treatments of the topic, and so far no such book has been written by any of the original Speculative Realists. Thus, when Polity Press asked my advice as to who should write their planned new survey on the theme, I volunteered for the task myself – the second time such a thing has happened.[2]

Though I relish this assignment, there are two potentially awkward circumstances that should be addressed at the outset. The first is that I am not just the author of this book but also one of its subjects, being one of the four original speakers at the initial SR workshop (along with Ray Brassier, Iain Hamilton Grant, and Quentin Meillassoux), as well as one of the authors most closely associated with the movement. The resulting need to speak about myself from time to time creates a Scylla-or-Charybdis predicament: should I insufferably refer to myself in the first person throughout this book, or even more insufferably in the third person? The solution I have chosen is as follows. When recollecting personal actions such as the giving of lectures or the writing of books, then the first person is the only real option, though I have tried to keep such reminders of authorial presence to a minimum. But when referring to my philosophical position more generally, I will refer to it impersonally as Object-Oriented Ontology (OOO). This entails a certain accidental injustice to my most prominent fellow OOO authors: Ian Bogost, Levi R. Bryant, and Timothy Morton.[3] All three have views that diverge sharply from my own on certain points, and by no means do I claim to speak on behalf of them here. However, since this book concerns not OOO but the looser association of figures found in SR, it should be safe to generalize about the basic assumptions of SR's object-oriented wing as opposed to those of Brassier, Grant, and Meillassoux.[4]

The second awkward question concerns the objectivity of this book. The original SR group did not last very long, and there are sharp philosophical and even personal disagreements between some of its members today. Though a total of two SR workshops were held, Meillassoux did not attend the second; he was replaced capably on that occasion by Alberto Toscano, who had moderated the original Goldsmiths event. As far as I know, the reason for Meillassoux's absence from the second meeting was that he wished to emphasize the *materialism* of his position over the *realism* built into SR's name. A much bigger issue is that there is a stark opposition between Brassier's wing of SR and my own, to the point that Brassier today rejects even the name "Speculative Realism," despite the fact that he coined it himself. His disciple Peter Wolfendale has even published a book of more than 400 pages purporting to demonstrate the intellectual worthlessness of my object-oriented position.[5] I have documented these disputes at some length and will not expand on that exercise here, since this is meant to be an introductory book on Speculative Realism rather than a personal memoir.[6] In any case, the present book aims to provide as fair a summary of Brassier's position as of Grant's and Meillassoux's. While it is inevitable that some of Brassier's devotees will not like my critical presentation of some of his ideas, this is simply a normal occupational hazard of intellectual life.

* * *

On April 27, 2007, an intriguing philosophical workshop was held at Goldsmiths, University of London. Entitled "Speculative Realism," it brought together four authors working in the continental (i.e. Franco-German) tradition of philosophy who each gave an hour-long talk, appearing in alphabetical order according to last name.[7] Ray Brassier of Middlesex University in London went first, followed by Iain Hamilton Grant of the University of the West of England (UWE) in Bristol. After a lunch break I went next myself, unfortunately in terrible pain from a severe throat infection. The fourth and final speaker of the day was Quentin Meillassoux of the École normale supérieure in Paris, the only non-anglophone participant in the workshop. The name Speculative Realism was coined by Brassier shortly before the event as a necessary compromise. I had known him fairly well since our first meeting two years earlier, when he invited me to Middlesex to give a lecture on Heidegger's notoriously opaque concept of the fourfold of earth, sky, gods, and mortals.[8] The following year, as I passed briefly through London as a tourist, Brassier was kind enough to host me for a night at his and his wife's apartment in North London. It was then that he first floated the idea of a joint event involving me and Grant, saying that he found us to be a good intellectual match, though at that point I myself was unfamiliar with Grant's work. A few months later, after he returned from a brief trip to Paris, Brassier recommended a book he had found on the shelves but not yet read: Meillassoux's *Àpres la finitude*, later translated into English by Brassier himself as *After Finitude*.[9] Unlike Brassier, I had enough free time to read the book immediately, and on the basis of my positive report Brassier threw Meillassoux's name into the mix for a joint event as well. Enthusiastic organizer that I am, I quickly emailed both Grant and Meillassoux while on a trip to Iceland, despite knowing neither of them personally; within days I received friendly replies from both. Brassier's longtime friend Toscano quickly got to work organizing the event for us at Goldsmiths the following year; at some point I learned from Brassier that he had also invited Toscano to join our group, though the latter declined for reasons unknown to me. In need of a name for the event, we first considered Speculative Materialism, Meillassoux's term for his own philosophy. But given my own ardently *anti*-materialist positon, Brassier proposed Speculative Realism instead, and obviously that name was eventually adopted.

Is there really such a thing as Speculative Realism, and, if it exists, is it anything new? Various critics have tried to answer "no" to one or both of these questions, though as I see it the answers are clearly "yes" and "yes." Let's start with realism. Though this word can mean different things to different people, its usual meaning in philosophy is relatively clear: realists are committed to the existence of a world independent of the human mind. One easy way to reject realism is to adopt the opposite position – *idealism* – for which reality is not independent of the mind (though we will see that Grant rejects this definition of the term). The most blatant case of idealism can be found in the works of the philosopher George Berkeley (1685–1783), for whom "to be" simply means "to be perceived." Berkeley has few literal followers today, but a more popular contemporary strand of idealism can be found in the so-called German Idealism of J. G. Fichte (1762–1814), F. W. J. von Schelling (1775–1854), and the hugely influential G. W. F. Hegel (1770–1831). In our own time, the prolific Slovenian thinker Slavoj Žižek (b. 1949) is a good example of a philosophical idealist, despite his frequent signs of discomfort with this label. Alongside realists who affirm the existence of an independent world, and idealists who deny it, there are those who claim to occupy a sophisticated middle ground "beyond" realism and idealism. Perhaps the clearest examples of this in the continental tradition of philosophy are the phenomenologist Edmund Husserl (1859–1938) and his rebellious star pupil Martin Heidegger (1889–1976). For both Husserl and Heidegger, the question of an external world is merely a "pseudo-problem." As they see it, we are always already outside ourselves directed at objects (Husserl) or always engaged in the world through pre-theoretical practical activity (Heidegger). From either standpoint there is no possibility of considering thought or world in isolation from each other, since they are always treated as a pair existing only in mutual *correlation*. While analytic philosophy has always considered realism and (to a lesser extent) idealism as live options, continental thought has almost unanimously adopted Husserl and Heidegger's view that the realism vs. idealism question is a clumsy false conflict unworthy of serious philosophical attention. In my debut book *Tool-Being* (2002) I called this doctrine "the philosophy of access," since it is concerned only with our access to the world and never with the world in its own right.[10] Not long thereafter, Meillassoux coined the term "correlationism" for this doctrine and traced it back to the philosophies of Immanuel Kant (1724–1804) and even earlier to David Hume (1711–1776).[11] I prefer Meillassoux's term to my own because of its superior economy and stronger etymological basis, and thus I have adopted "correlationism" for my own philosophical vocabulary as well.

It is safe to say that the original Speculative Realists were united by their rejection of correlationism, though some critics have claimed – wrongly, in my view – that correlationism does not exist. Largely as a result of this disagreement, Speculative Realism is still a minority current in the continental philosophy establishment as represented in the United States by the Society for Phenomenology and Existential Philosophy (SPEP), whose annual conference I have not attended since my graduate student days in 1993. In Britain, there is an analogous group called the Society for European Philosophy (SEP), though my impression has been that this group is more open to SR than is its American counterpart. SEP even invited me to give a keynote lecture at their 2011 conference in York.

There are other critics who do not deny the existence of correlationism but merely dispute that opposition to it is sufficient grounds for a unified philosophical movement; this is especially true in Brassier's circle. Though this attitude strikes me as unjustified, it is a matter of record that the four original philosophical projects of Speculative Realism are so different in kind that they were unable to hold together for more than two years. Žižek has even claimed that the breakup of the band was inevitable: "we can discern the limitation of speculative realism, a limitation signaled in the fact that it immediately split into four orientations . . . Meillassoux's 'speculative realism,' Harman's 'object-oriented philosophy,' Grant's neo-vitalism, and Brassier's radical nihilism."[12] Yet it is far from clear that the split indicates a *limitation* on SR's part. Generally speaking, the stronger a genre of thought or art, the more variations it will generate. Such important twentieth-century currents as phenomenology and psychoanalysis have remained influential largely because of the numerous different ways in which they were practiced, not because they remained rigidly governed by the authority of their respective founders, Husserl and Sigmund Freud. What still interests me in Speculative Realism after a decade of reflection is that four philosophical projects with apparently so little in common – not a single philosophical hero is shared by the group as a whole – nonetheless have a fairly obvious unity compared with the correlationist background of continental philosophy from which they emerged. All four philosophies are *realisms*, though this word means rather different things in each case. And all four are *speculative*, in the sense that, unlike the commonsensical realisms of yesteryear, all reach conclusions that seem counterintuitive or even downright strange.

As part of my effort to be balanced, I will follow the alphabetical order of speakers used at Goldsmiths in 2007. Furthermore, I will make an effort to devote approximately the same number of pages to each of the three SR orientations other than my own. When it comes to OOO, I will deliberately keep my presentation shorter, in part because I wish to avoid too much repetition of ideas I have already published elsewhere. Despite my goal of being objective, I obviously prefer my own philosophy to the three others under discussion, and will therefore make certain criticisms of the others rather than pretending to speak in the disinterested "voice of God." Readers of this book deserve what they came for, which is a candid assessment on my part of the various Speculative Realist positions.

Chapter 1 follows Ray Brassier from his book *Nihil Unbound* (2008) through some more recent articles that hint at a still unpublished new version of his position. At the dawn of SR there was no specific name for the style of thinking pursued by Brassier and his circle, though "Prometheanism" seems to have become their term of choice in recent years, with "Accelerationism" used more often to refer to the strictly *political* thinking of Brassier's disciples Nick Srnicek and Alex Williams.[13]

Chapter 2 turns to Iain Hamilton Grant, beginning with his dense but innovative book *Philosophies of Nature After Schelling* (2006), which reflects his deep indebtedness to the philosophy of Gilles Deleuze (1925–1995). An ostensibly surprising turn occurred with Grant's second book, *Idealism*, co-authored with his talented younger associates Jeremy Dunham and Sean Watson. Yet we will see that what Grant means by "idealism" is not the opposite of realism but refers simply to the role of ideas in the productive power of nature itself, rather than the usual idealism of the privileged human subject. This does not mean that I accept Grant's definition of idealism, as will be seen below.

Chapter 3 takes up the theme of Object-Oriented Ontology, which is most easily described as deriving from the joint influence of Heidegger and Bruno Latour (b. 1947). OOO is without question the strand of Speculative Realism that has had the widest interdisciplinary impact across the globe, and this seems to me an obvious strength rather than a weakness of the object-oriented current.

In chapter 4 we turn to the Speculative Materialism of Meillassoux, a lucid and powerful thinker if not – at least so far – a prolific one. It is important to cover the basic ideas of his landmark debut book *After Finitude*, no doubt the most famous individual work to emerge from Speculative Realism, and hence the one most frequently cited and widely translated. We will also discuss snippets of his strange and important doctoral thesis, *The Divine Inexistence*.

These chapters will be followed by a brief conclusion concerning how the four Speculative Realist thinkers might be divided into sub-groups among themselves. By way of preview: I will claim that Meillassoux and OOO are opposites and that Brassier and Grant are also opposites. The other combinations all entail agreement on one of the two most fundamental issues of Speculative Realism. For the benefit of students and other readers, useful study questions will be found at the end of each section.

1 Prometheanism

Ray Brassier (b. 1965) is of mixed French and Scottish parentage. He completed his PhD at Warwick University, as did Grant. At the time of the Goldsmiths workshop he was employed at Middlesex University in London, which is where I first met him in April 2005. Since 2008 he has worked at the beautiful seaside campus of the American University of Beirut. He has an unusually loyal following, primarily among younger males captivated by his vision of a cold and pitiless cosmos to be probed remorselessly with the instruments of radical scientific enlightenment and radical horror fiction. The chief example of the latter is the American fright lord Thomas Ligotti (b. 1953), for one of whose books Brassier has even written a foreword.[1]

Here as in the other three chapters, I will begin in section A with a brief look at Brassier's presentation at the April 2007 Goldsmiths workshop. After that, we will turn in section B to his difficult but often refreshing book *Nihil Unbound*. Since Brassier's second book has yet to appear, we will attempt in section C to discern his future path by looking at two of his key recent articles.

A Brassier at Goldsmiths

Brassier's presentation at Goldsmiths opened the conference. It runs from pages 308 to 321 in the transcript, followed by an additional twelve pages of audience questions. Though in later years he has denied any important connection between the four participants at the workshop, in 2007 Brassier was more optimistic about the group he had assembled: "The fundamental thing we seem to share is obviously a willingness to re-interrogate or to open up a whole set of philosophical problems that were taken to have been definitively settled by Kant, certainly, at least, by those working in the continental tradition."[2] As for continental philosophy and its difference from the analytic variety, a difference whose very existence he will later deny, the Brassier of 2007 still sees it in terms of two distinct sets of virtues:

> some kind of communication is needed between the speculative audacity which is a characteristic of so-called 'continental philosophy' and the really

admirable level of engagement with the empirical sciences which is a feature of the most interesting work being done specifically in the kind of Anglo-American philosophy of mind that engages directly with, or that sees its project as continuous with, cognitive science. (320–1)

[handwritten margin note: Brassier + cognitive science.]

Although Brassier places great importance on the natural sciences in general, he is especially enamored of cognitive science, which he views as the key to eliminating the modern thought–world dualism. As he put it at Goldsmiths: "I think that arguably *the* most significant philosophical development of the twentieth century is the emergence of a science of cognition: that is, the idea that the process of cognition can be re-integrated into the realm of objective phenomena studied by the empirical sciences" (320). In the years leading up to Goldsmiths, Brassier seemed to place great hope in the philosophy of Alain Badiou (b. 1937) and had even translated a number of the latter's writings into English. Later he began to refer towards Badiou less often. My sense at the time was that this growing coolness to Badiouian philosophy had something to do with disappointment over that author's low regard for any "science of cognition," as revealed in Brassier and Robin Mackay's interview of the French philosopher in the first volume of the journal *Collapse*.[3]

We return to the topic at hand. Brassier's presentation at Goldsmiths consists of a sympathetic summary of the other three Speculative Realist positions that also includes some helpful *objections* to all of our work. In my opinion, his brief overview of Grant is of especial philosophical interest. In the opening pages of the transcript, Brassier goes straight to the core of Grant's thinking: "nature is self-organizing. And the ideal structure of nature produces the structure of thinking. But if cognition is a result, a product – if it's every bit as conditioned as any other natural phenomenon – the question then becomes whether there's any reason to suppose that thought can limn or grasp the ultimate structure of reality at any given moment, any specific historical juncture" (310). The account of Grant here is accurate; we will see that, in his Schelling book and elsewhere, Grant treats thought as just another product of nature rather than as a privileged entity able to transcend reality as a whole. This puts him at odds with Meillassoux in particular, given the high importance granted by the latter to the human subject's mathematical grasp of the primary qualities of things. On this point at least, Brassier sides with Grant: "the structure of material reality generates the structure of thinking. But this means that one must discount any appeal to intellectual intuition, which is to say the idea that thinking can simply transcend its own material, neurobiological conditions of organization and effectuation and grasp the noumenal structure of reality as it is in itself" (310–11). Brassier's primary objection to Meillassoux hinges precisely on the latter's appeal to "intellectual intuition" as a way of gaining direct access to reality. As concerns Grant, Brassier notes the risk that, if we turn thought into a product of nature, we might easily be seduced by the presently fashionable theory that the structure of human thought is simply the result of our evolutionary history: "this is a claim that fuels much of naturalized epistemology, but one that I think is metaphysically problematic, because there is no reason to suppose that evolutionary adaptation would favor exhaustively accurate beliefs about the world" (311). That is to say, "there's no reason to suppose that evolution would infallibly provide human organisms with a cognitive apparatus that can accurately track the salient features or the deep structure of reality" (311). As Brassier notes, Grant's more novel solution is to claim that human thought arises from thought that is already present in nature itself: "the force of Iain's book is to try to propose what he calls a 'transcendental naturalism' – which claims that you can explain the emergence of the structure of ideation from the ideal structure of physical reality," and as a result, "ideation would be capable of tracking the ideal dynamisms, the transcendental dynamisms, that underlie merely empirical or merely somatic reality" (311). And speaking of "merely somatic reality," Brassier seems to endorse Grant's condemnation of the "parochial Aristotelian model of physical reality" (314), whereas Aristotle ranks as one of the great philosophical heroes for OOO.

Brassier's discussion of Grant closes with two more important objections, both of them bearing on Grant's abandonment of the supposedly joint Aristotle–Kant "somatic" model, in which individual bodies are held to be the primary stuff of the universe. What Grant offers instead is a dynamic model in which *force* is primary, with individual entities being merely a derivative configuration of that force. In Brassier's words: "what is the status of dynamism in speculative physics? Is it truly adequate to physical infrastructure? Or might it not be contaminated by certain folk-psychological prejudices?" (314). And further, given that Galileo's mathematization of nature was so critical in replacing the Aristotelean "somatic" view of the universe that Grant disdains, "what is the relationship between the dynamic structure of the idea and the mathematical register deployed for its formalization?" (314). In his response during the question period, Grant does not address this question directly but focuses instead on challenging Brassier's wish to eliminate as many fictitious or folk-psychological beings from the world as possible.

Brassier's final objection to Grant matches one of OOO's own. It touches on whether his unapologetically dynamic model of the universe leaves room for those aspects of the world that seem to be especially *non*-dynamic. As Brassier puts it: "this is a general point related to process philosophy: If you

general problem with process philosophy
how to account for stability.

9

privilege productivity, if these ideal generative dynamisms that structure and constitute materiality can be characterized in terms of the primacy of production over product, then the question is, how do we account for the interruptions of the process? How do we account for discontinuity in the continuum of production?" (314–15). Or even more eloquently: "it seems that you always have to introduce or posit some sort of conceptual contrary, some principle of deceleration, interruption, disintensification or whatever, in order to account for the upsurges of stability and continuity and consistency within this otherwise untrammeled flux of becoming and pure process" (315). We will see that Grant tries to account for such interruptions of process in his Schelling book under the general term "retardation," though his degree of success in doing so remains an open question.

The Brassier of 2007 reacts more warmly to OOO's opposite approach: "Graham turns the question around by showing how the problem consists in showing how discontinuous, autonomous objects can ever enter into relation with one another . . ." (316). But he also poses two objections to my work. The first concerns OOO's distinction between real and sensual properties. Brassier's question on this score runs as follows: "what is the criterion for distinguishing sensible from non-sensible properties for any given object? Is it possible to provide such a criterion without giving it some sort of epistemological slant or formulation?" (316). His second, related question has to do with the implications of allowing existence (as OOO does) to all sorts of real and imaginary things. He worries about the inflationary results of such a flat ontology: "what would be the distinction between a hobbit and a quark here? This is a very serious metaphysical question!" (317). He proceeds to ask how we can distinguish between the real and the sensual, "given that we know that imaginary objects or fictitious entities such as the Virgin Mary or Yahweh or phlogiston seem perfectly capable of producing real effects – it's perfectly possible for these things to generate real effects . . . in so far as people believe in them and do things in the world on the basis of their belief in them" (317).

The root of these objections can be found in the totally different conceptions held by Brassier and OOO as to the purpose of philosophy, and of intellectual life more generally. When Brassier asks for the "criterion" that allows us to distinguish between sensible and non-sensible properties, what he seems to mean is that we encounter a great many properties in our experience of things, some of which turn out to be true and others untrue. Therefore, we need some sort of intellectual tool that allows us to sift our accurate scientific perceptions of, say, a tree from our inaccurate or folk-psychological ones. But this is not what OOO's distinction of real from sensual is about. OOO speaks of real and sensual not in order to distinguish accurate images of the world from impostors: it is an ontological distinction, not an epistemological one. For OOO, *any* perception of or relation to something consists *ipso facto* of sensual qualities. There is no such thing as an "accurate" perception of a thing's real qualities, because by their very nature real qualities are not translatable into something to which we can have access. It is not a question of saying: "I see a horse, and it corresponds to a real horse outside my mind, but I also see a unicorn, which is a mere hallucination because it corresponds to nothing outside my mind." Instead, even my perception of the horse, not just of the hallucinated unicorn, consists solely of sensual qualities. Nor are the real qualities to be obtained by the intellect rather than the senses, as Husserl thinks. The intellect has no more direct access to the real than do the senses — as Brassier would presumably be the first to agree, given his wary attitude towards Meillassoux's intellectual intuition. Nor can we accept Brassier's claim that objects must "know" something about each other in order to interact, at least not if "knowledge" means some sort of direct access to the things. OOO speaks instead of an *indirect* contact with reality, for the same reason that Socrates declares his inability to attain knowledge of anything. As for Brassier's second question, we wonder how he can be so sure in placing Yahweh and the Virgin Mary on the same level as phlogiston. While fully in keeping with the rationalist disdain for religion, this indicates a degree of contempt for religious experience that will always be well received in the circles where Brassier travels, but which cannot do justice to the biographies of such figures as St Teresa of Avila, the Buddha, or Jalaluddin Rumi. While it is always possible that these figures are concerned with merely fictitious entities that "nonetheless" have real effects on their lives, the fragile certainty built into much religious life is a positive ontological phenomenon that Brassier simply ignores on the basis of his own atheist certitude.

We turn in closing to Brassier's interesting remarks on Meillassoux, beginning with his concerns about intellectual intuition as a means of grasping the essence of the world directly. For Brassier, whose major intellectual commitment is to the natural sciences rather than to mathematics, knowledge always remains *fallible* because of its lack of "resemblance" to reality. Though at Goldsmiths Meillassoux tries to downplay the necessary role of the mathematical in understanding the world, in *After Finitude* he explicitly tells us that the primary qualities of things are those that can be mathematized. And furthermore, as Brassier notes: "[Quentin] explicitly wants to rehabilitate the Cartesian project, where mathematical ideation accurately describes the objective structure of reality as it is in itself, against the Kantian one, which would limit the scope of scientific cognition to the phenomenal realm" (319). This leads Brassier to puzzle over how to square

11

the purported ability of mathematics to grasp the absolute with the fact that thought arises through processes of nature. But to understand this perplexity in more detail, we must turn to the development of Brassier's arguments in *Nihil Unbound.*

Study Questions for Section A

1 What is the philosophical importance for Brassier of a science of cognition?
2 In his Goldsmiths talk, Brassier speaks against the notion of "intellectual intuition." What does he see as philosophically dangerous in the claim that such intuition exists?
3 Why is Brassier wary of the recent trend of saying that the structure of human thought is the end product of our evolutionary history?
4 What are the reasons Brassier gives for caution against Grant's heavily *dynamic* conception of nature?
5 Why does Brassier ask OOO for "criteria" to distinguish between the real and the sensual? What might OOO say in response?

B Brassier's Nihilism

Brassier is well aware that nihilism sounds like a passé topic from the era of post-World War II existentialism. Yet he also rightly notes that, outside professional philosophy circles that merely laugh at such claims as "existence is worthless," the topic still captures a good deal of interest from the lay philosophical public. As Brassier tells us in his straight-to-the point preface: "this apparently banal assertion [that existence is worthless] harbours hidden depths which have yet to be sounded by philosophers, despite the plethora of learned books and articles on the topic."[4] On the second page of his preface Brassier approvingly cites Jonathan Israel (b. 1946), the historian and author of *Radical Enlightenment*, further indicating his view that nihilism is not an adolescent indulgence but the proper outcome of full commitment to the Enlightenment project. Brassier's sworn enemies are those contemporary thinkers who seek to moderate or redirect modern rationalism. The rationalist must be a nihilist precisely because he or she is a realist: "nihilism is . . . the unavoidable corollary of the realist conviction that there is a mind-independent reality, which, despite the presumptions of humans, is indifferent to our existence and oblivious to the 'values' and 'meanings' which we would drape over it in order to make it more hospitable" (xi). But note that the conclusions Brassier draws from the existence of a mind-independent reality are not the only possible ones. From the fact that there is a reality outside the mind, it need not follow that the reality *inside* the mind has no role other than to be eliminated by science, as Brassier seems to hold. At times his rhetoric about the worthlessness of life strays beyond the bounds of purely logical argument and veers into emotional assertion: "Philosophy should be more than a sop to the pathetic twinge of human self-esteem" (xi). As we will see in the next chapter, Iain Hamilton Grant's philosophy draws an entirely different conclusion from realism, arguing that ideas and perceptions are products of Nature just like anything else and therefore need to be accounted for by philosophy rather than eliminated. In contrast to Grant's relatively flat ontology in which everything is equally real, Brassier's tendency is to celebrate all mind-independent reality while treating all realities internal to the mind as merely provisional and ultimately contemptible. This aspect of his philosophy is in my view especially dubious.

Nihil Unbound is divided into seven chapters, each of them organized as a response to one or more prominent thinkers. For our purposes it will be useful to pay attention instead to Brassier's grouping of these chapters into three specific parts. Many of his readings of important philosophers are highly original and worth exploring in their own right. But here we will need to be selective and focus solely on those aspects of each chapter that develop his own philosophical position. When I first met Brassier in 2005, what was most refreshing in discussions with him was his openness to science and analytic philosophy, both quite rare in the continental philosophy world – though somewhat less rare these days, thanks in part to his own efforts. This balancing act is still visible in *Nihil Unbound*, though in more recent years Brassier seems to have lost patience with continental thought as a whole.

"The Destruction of the Manifest Image" is a fitting title for Part I of Brassier's debut book. For it is not only an accurate description of the content of his first three chapters but a fitting introduction to his entire philosophical project. It is often possible to identify a thinker's major commitments by detecting those opposing positions that they most viscerally loathe. Based on my past conversations with Brassier as well as his own writings, it is safe to say that he roundly detests the phenomenology of Edmund Husserl and the actor-network theory of Bruno Latour (both of them pivotal influences on OOO). Though Husserl and Latour are not often grouped together, there is at least one major similarity between them: their commitment to the non-eliminability of merely apparent beings. For Husserl, the objects given to consciousness need to be taken seriously as intentional objects even if they later prove to be delusional: to be an object is to be present to some intending mind. Latour's criterion is different, though equally false from a Brassierian standpoint: to be an "actor" (Latour's term for object) means to have an effect on other actors. For both Husserl and Latour, Donald Duck and a blurry ghost seen in your grandmother's attic are both legitimate personae for philosophy no less than are chemicals and atoms, to be explored on their own terms no matter how unreal they turn out to be. Brassier is a nihilist because his first reaction when encountering such claims is to attempt to *eliminate* such unreal entities, to demand that they be expelled altogether from the recognized universe. Like most philosophical attitudes, this one has its upside and its downside. The upside can be found in Brassier's unshakeable commitment to fact and his deference – so rare in continental philosophy – to the tangible results of the modern physical sciences that have contributed inestimably to human knowledge over the past four centuries. While this point in isolation would merely qualify him as just another foot soldier in analytic philosophy, with its congenital addiction to science-worship, in continental thought it is enough to provoke a potential revolution. The downside of Brassier's position was noted in an early review of *Nihil Unbound* by the intellectual historian Knox Peden, who on the whole is sympathetic to his fellow rationalist Brassier. As Peden sees it, one of the vices of *Nihil Unbound* is a tendency towards "premature refutation."[5] Though any reader of Brassier's book will see that he is perfectly capable of offering balanced accounts of the virtues and vices of most philosophers, there are other thinkers – generally those who deny the privileged cognitive status of natural science – who seem to provoke his outright dismissal. Sometimes this applies in sweeping fashion to entire disciplines: I once heard Brassier denounce the whole of sociology as a non-science, and one searches his writings in vain for any significant concession to the cognitive value of the arts. While Meillassoux has sometimes been accused of fetishizing mathematics, in Brassier's case natural science is always the court of final appeal. It needs to be said, however, that continental philosophy has long been in need of provocation from a figure of this sort. Heidegger's infamous claim that "science does not think" is simply one of the most blatant continental attempts to degrade the speculative role of the sciences, and Brassier is even firmer than Meillassoux in denouncing such attitudes.[6]

It should be said that *Nihil Unbound* is not an easy book to read. Brassier shows independent speculative talent in this work as elsewhere, and for me at least, the best portions of the book are those where he speaks in his own voice and gives us his unremittingly pessimistic vision of the world. This vision can be summed up in Brassier's signature phrase: "we are already dead." Not only do phenomenology, actor-network theory, and other phi-losophies with a liberal conception of what exists fail to heed the eliminative lessons of natural science; more radically than this, science itself teaches merciless lessons about the ultimate incineration of the Earth, the burning of stars into dismal brown husks, and a final fireworks display of subatomic particles before even atoms themselves vanish without a trace. Yet the chal-lenge this poses to Brassier is at least twofold. First, given the purported ultimate meaninglessness of everything, he will need to show why we should devote ourselves to science and nihilistic philosophy (which he explicitly advocates) and political revolution (which he recommends more vaguely) rather than to a hedonistic spirit of *carpe diem* or to passing the time with a charming enjoyment of sunsets and flowers. A second, related prob-lem strikes even closer to the heart of Brassier's philosophical ambitions. Although he agrees with Grant and OOO (and against Meillassoux's "intel-lectual intuition") that there is a permanent rift between reality itself and the scientific image of reality, he is nonetheless committed (unlike Grant and OOO) to the notion that one particular privileged discourse – that of natural science – demands our full-blown commitment. Brassier does this by way of the phrase "adequation without correspondence" (238), which occurs most prominently on the final page of *Nihil Unbound*, and whose ultimate source is his unorthodox reading of the French "non-philosopher" François Laruelle (b. 1937). Traditionally, philosophical realism has walked hand in hand with a correspondence theory of truth, which generally means that truth is that which "resembles" reality in some way. This notion is retained in Meillassoux's mathematicist vision of primary qualities but is roundly rejected by Brassier (as by Grant and OOO). Having foresworn correspondence as the basis of truth, Brassier nonetheless claims that we can still speak of "adequation," which effectively means that natural science gives us a closer, more adequate link to the real than does any other type of human thought. Aesthetics, which OOO takes to be the very pillar of cognition, is repeatedly dismissed throughout *Nihil Unbound*, seemingly because it deals with eliminable phenomena that lack science's particular form of adequation to the real. While it seems to me that Brassier's solution fails, there is no denying that he has gained a sizable following, though the interdisciplinary reach of his work has been curtailed by his dismissal of most disciplines outside the hard sciences.

Part I of *Nihil Unbound* is lengthy, rich, and complex. Chapter 3, on Meillassoux (49–94), is required reading for anyone interested in Speculative Realism, and is especially strong in its challenge to Meillassoux's ability to reconcile rationalism and materialism by way of intellectual intuition. Chapter 2, which covers the Frankfurt School theorists Theodor Adorno

(1903–1969) and Max Horkheimer (1895–1973), nicely foreshadows the themes of death and extinction that play such a major role at the conclusion of Brassier's book. But we will focus on chapter 1, which in my view contains the nucleus of his philosophical position to this very day. Though the chapter is ostensibly about the discussions of the "manifest image" found in the works of Wilfrid Sellars (1912–1989) and Paul Churchland (b. 1942), we learn more about Brassier's thought by reading his lengthy attack on the phenomenological notion of the manifest image and on Heidegger's non-conceptual way of claiming to give us a glimpse of Being itself.

Sellars makes an appearance at the beginning of *Nihil Unbound,* though in a cameo role hinting at his future centrality in Brassier's thought. Most important here is Sellars's distinction between the "manifest image" of everyday experience and the "scientific image" so often called upon to correct our everyday views. Sellars has at least two important points to make about the manifest image. Many philosophers treat this image as obvious and immediate, a human birthright in which everyone timelessly dwells prior to any theoretical work. But Sellars, quite correctly in my view, sees the manifest image as always already woven through with theoretical inference and cognitive achievement. As Brassier puts it: "The manifest image is not the domain of pre-theoretical immediacy. On the contrary, it is itself a subtle theoretical construct, a disciplined and critical 'refinement or sophistication' of the originary framework in terms of which man first encountered himself as a being capable of conceptual thought, in contradistinction to creatures that lack this capacity" (3). It follows that the manifest image is simply a crude version of the scientific image available at any moment in history, and it follows further that our current commonsense manifest image is subject to possible radical revision in the light of current and future cognitive achievement, which for Brassier means primarily the findings of natural science. In addition, though the manifest image is in this respect inferior to the scientific image, it also "enjoys a *practical,* if not theoretical, priority over the scientific image, since it provides the source for the norm of rational purposiveness . . ." (6). What the last part means is that the manifest image for Sellars has a *normative* status pointing to the status of "*persons* as loci of normative agency" (6). In its own right, the manifest image has no ontological status, merely a "functional" one. OOO would call this an "overmining" strategy, since the manifest image is regarded as nothing in its own right but only as having a socio-cultural-normative purpose. Yet Brassier, much like Sellars's eliminativist disciple Churchland, simultaneously has an "undermining" take on the manifest image, since it can be replaced by an account of human experience in terms of subpersonal neurocomputational components. This is where Brassier breaks with "much contemporary philosophizing" (6) that continues to take the manifest image on its own terms, whether this be phenomenology, existentialism, critical theory, hermeneutics, and post-structuralism on the continental side or ordinary language philosophy among the analytics. For Brassier emphatically *does not* wish to take the manifest image on its own terms. Instead, the manifest image ought to be reduced in both directions (downward to physical explanation and upward to cultural/normative explanation), with everything in the middle to be eliminated. In OOO terminology, Brassier proposes nothing less than the "duomining" of everyday experience, where duomining refers to the act of undermining and overmining a phenomenon simultaneously, reducing it out of existence in both directions at once (see chapter 3 on OOO below).

Brassier goes on to note, again correctly, that partisans of the manifest image often try to reduce science to their own favored domain of everyday human experience, by giving an "instrumental" or "pragmatic" interpretation of what science does: in OOO terms, such authors *overmine* science by treating it solely as a human practice. While this might seem to create a mere deadlock between two equally inadequate approaches, Brassier finds the scientific attitude to be clearly preferable to the manifest one. Why so? Because the partisans of the manifest image "conspicuously avoid delineating the conceptual criteria in accordance with which the structures of the scientific image might be reduced [in instrumentalist and pragmatist theories of science] to the workings of the manifest image" (6). Given that science seems to offer a plethora of such "conceptual criteria," it is therefore the superior approach. This leads Brassier to an initially sympathetic account of Churchland's greater willingness than Sellars to eliminate the manifest image by scientific means, though Brassier later goes on to subject Churchland to severe criticism. The details of that critique need not concern us here, but the conclusions Brassier draws from it are of interest. His first conclusion is that naturalism – the sort of philosophy that tries to ground everything in natural or scientific explanations – is not sufficiently coherent in its metaphysics, even though its "vague talk of rendering philosophy consistent with the 'findings of our best sciences' remains entirely commendable . . ." (25). Speaking of his own ambitions rather than Churchland's, Brassier contends that "the goal is surely to devise a metaphysics worthy of the sciences," and the enemy on this point is not just pragmatism but also "empiricism's enthronement of experience . . . [as well as] naturalism's hypostatization of nature" (25). The alternative, Brassier holds, is to focus on "science's *subtractive* modus operandi . . . [in which] science subtracts nature from experience, the better to uncover the objective void of being" (25). Here Brassier strays far from mainstream philosophies of science. Drawing on Badiou's concept of subtraction, he envisions a nothingness rather than a hidden being as what lies behind appearances, a model that fits nicely with the deep cosmic pessimism of *Nihil Unbound*'s final pages. The mission of philosophy, Brassier holds, "consists in expediting science's demolition of the manifest image by kicking away whatever pseudo-transcendental props are being used to shore it up or otherwise inhibit the corrosive potency of science's metaphysical subtractions" (26). For this reason Churchland, who is often portrayed by his enemies as a grim scientistic liquidator of everything that makes human life worth living, is depicted by Brassier as a humanist sell-out to those merely functional aspects of knowledge that enable the evolution and survival of our species.

Nonetheless, Brassier praises both Churchland and Daniel Dennett (b. 1942) for "having driven an irrecusable wedge between our phenomenological self-conception and the material processes through which that conception is produced" (26). It should therefore come as no surprise when Brassier directs his ire against Husserl, who drives a similar "irrecusable wedge" between the material and phenomenal worlds while reaching the opposite conclusion. For whereas Churchland, Dennett, and Brassier all wish to disintegrate the pretensions of the manifest image, Husserl treats it as the homeland of all existence and *a fortiori* of all knowledge. Brassier quotes Husserl's famous passage on phenomenology's "principle of principles," which states that reality can be directly intuited in experience, and that such intuition is the ultimate authority in cognitive matters, given that all knowledge is grounded in our direct encounter with the world. Stated more simply, Brassier treats Husserl as a philosophical *idealist*, an assessment in which I happen to agree with Brassier against the phenomenologists. What Brassier fails to grasp is that there is a lot more going on in Husserl than idealism. As OOO has often argued, the real virtue of Husserl consists not in his admittedly lamentable idealist ontology but in his discovery of a strife *within* the ideal or phenomenal realm between objects and their qualities. Let's say that we encounter a mailbox, one of Husserl's classic examples. It is true that Husserl "brackets" or "suspends" the question of whether the mailbox exists in the outside world in order to examine it as a phenomenon in its own right. Husserl's idealism stems from the fact that he rejects any possibility of a mailbox-in-itself; he holds instead that the existence of the mailbox lies solely in its being, in fact or in principle, the object of attention by some mind. On this point Husserl is merely Berkeley with an alibi, no matter how loudly his disciples claim that he is a sort of "realist" since we are "always already outside ourselves" in encountering objects in the world. The point is that these objects never encounter *each other* in Husserl's world; to be an object is to be the correlate of a mental act.

Here, despite my phenomenological background and ongoing passion for the contributions of that movement, I agree with both Brassier and Meillassoux that Husserl leaves us trapped within the circle of human thought. Yet there is more to Husserl than this, even if the point is generally missed. What we find in Husserl that is nowhere in Berkeley or the empiricists is the notion that what comes first in experience is an *object*, not sense data molded arbitrarily into objects by the human mind. This is a crucial step forward in the history of philosophy, one that Brassier misses in his haste to drive the manifest image towards the outer darkness without giving it a hearing. What Husserl notices – and here is the lasting insight of all phenomenology – is that I encounter an object as a unit, and it remains the same object for me even as its outer appearances or "adumbrations" (*Abschattungen*) shift wildly from one moment to the next. Thus, there is an important tension between objects and their qualities, which OOO will call *sensual* objects (SO) and *sensual* qualities (SQ), since they exist only as correlates of some observer. But we are not yet finished, for there is another kind of quality present in Husserl's philosophy, since not all qualities of the experienced object belong to a swirling sensory kaleidoscope of passing accidents. Instead, some qualities of the object are *essential*, since we would no longer regard the apple as an apple if we determined that certain apple-features were not present after all, as when for example we determine that we are really looking at a pear rather than an apple. When Husserl talks about the "intuition of essences," his most unfairly derided concept, all he means is that with appropriate theoretical work we can come to understand those qualities that make the apple the very apple that it is. This involves mentally scraping away the accidental features of the apple and coming face to face with its essential ones, which Husserl claims can be done only by the intellect, never by the senses (though OOO holds that even the intellect is unable to do it). What we have, then, is not simply an idealism that merely replaces perceptions with perceived objects, though this would already be a great deal. More than this, we have a sensual object engaged in tense relations with both its sensual qualities ("adumbrations") and its real ones ("essence"). Husserl's *ideal* objects have the strange property of consisting of *real* qualities. But none of this can be seen if one holds, like Brassier, that the only job of the manifest image is to be exterminated by science.

Returning to Brassier's own argument, he condemns both Husserl and the analytic philosopher John Searle (b. 1932) for holding that when it comes to appearance, appearance is all there is, so that it must be taken on its own terms. Brassier complains that this attitude "harbors an inbuilt circularity. [For] this appeal to the self-evident transparency of appearance conveniently dispenses with the need for justification by insisting that we all already know 'what it's *like*' for something to appear to us" (25). This is not exactly true. Husserl always remained perplexed by the various contours of phenomena and spent his career developing a massive technical apparatus to verify and confirm his findings. What Brassier really means here is a point he had already made more clearly elsewhere: Husserl assumes that we should not reduce phenomena downward to their material underpinnings. This is true, but it is only relevant if one agrees in advance with Brassier that the manifest image is merely a crude scientific image that needs to be replaced, rather than a genuine portion of reality that needs to be accounted for, just like the entities of natural science. In this connection it is not reassuring that Brassier calls on the aid of the German neurophilosopher Thomas Metzinger (b. 1958), whose work I hold in lower esteem than Brassier does.[7] As Brassier puts it: "Thomas Metzinger has pointed out [that] it is precisely the simplest most rudimentary forms of phenomenal content that cannot be reliably individuated from the phenomenological perspective, since we lack any transtemporal identity criteria to identify them" (29). Metzinger proposes to obtain such criteria by identifying the "minimally sufficient neural and functional correlates" of various phenomena so as to determine scientifically if they are *really* identical. In other words, we should not trust Husserl's report that he is seeing the same apple as it passes through many different constellations of qualities while being rotated in his hand. What we should do instead is analyze Husserl's brain to determine if all of the adumbrations of the apple are neurally and functionally similar enough for us to conclude that he is truly experiencing the same object as it shifts its appearance in the evening air. Yet there are at least two major problems with this approach. The first is that the neurologist who carries out this experiment will still have to assume the identity of each wire, each meter reading, and each notebook entry over time in order to verify via neuroscience that the apple is in fact the same one. And here the neurologist is in the same position as Husserl, trusting her own sense of identity over time as the appearances of phenomenal objects and scientific instruments subtly shift. It would do no good to add a second set of wires and meters to the neurologist's brain to ensure that we have the correct "transtemporal identity criteria" to verify her findings about Husserl, because now we are on the road to a vicious infinite regress of wires monitoring the brains of those who use the wires, and so forth. The identity criterion used by Husserl is the same as that which any scientist must use. Here is the apple, the same one I saw five seconds ago, though it looks a bit different now; here is the scientific apparatus, the same one I saw five seconds ago, though it looks a bit different now. No neuroscientist can escape this same provisional trust in one's own immediate experience. The second problem is that Metzinger's appeal to "minimally sufficient neural and functional correlates" does not work out very well in his colossal book. In chapter after chapter, as documented in my critical article on his work, Metzinger is forced to admit with comical regularity that we still have no idea what the minimally sufficient correlates are for this or that phenomenon. In short, there is no reason to turn to Metzinger against Husserl unless one is viscerally committed, like Brassier, to a program in which science must have the final word on every topic under the sun, including those topics where it has less to offer than phenomenology itself.

Before moving on, we should mention that Husserl's famous former student Heidegger also comes under fire in Brassier's opening chapter. Unlike Husserl, Heidegger does not believe in the transparency of appearance, since his entire philosophy is based on the opposite view: that presence to consciousness means a mere presence-at-hand that hides the deeper being of any entity. What offends Brassier is that, for Heidegger, it is not science that can lead us into these depths, since science is merely another way of converting things into presence-at-hand by objectifying their qualities and ignoring their concealed reality. Inevitably, this requires the use of non-literal, non-discursive language, which Brassier always treats with open contempt: "much post-Heideggerian phenomenology has been engaged in an ongoing attempt to deploy the figurative dimension of language in order to sound sub-representational depths, which, it is claimed, are inherently refractory to any other variety of conceptualization, and particularly to scientific conceptualization" (28). It is unclear why Brassier should be so hostile to this, even in light of the fact that Heidegger's ventures into poetic language often degenerate into cringe-worthy Black Forest *kitsch*. For it does not follow from Heidegger's own excesses that the discursive, conceptual, propositional use of language is the only one with cognitive value. Here Brassier forgets that Socrates never arrives at a definition of anything, that *philosophia* does not mean knowledge, and that Aristotle tells us in the *Poetics* that metaphor is the greatest gift. He also leaves no room for any cognitive prowess in the arts, an important realm of human experience about which Brassier has nothing helpful to say. Instead, he busies himself in calling for the expulsion of figurative language from philosophy altogether: "It might be better to concede that the aims of phenomenological description *stricto sensu* are better served through the artifices of literature, instead of hijacking the conceptual resources of philosophy for no other reason than to preserve some inviolable inner sanctum of phenomenal experience" (28). While such views have always been common in analytic philosophy, Brassier is probably the first author from a basically continental background to utter them. Notice, however, that the same professional question can be posed in reverse: if Brassier is so convinced of the cognitive superiority of the sciences, then why are his concerns not better served by a career in the sciences, rather than by hijacking Socratic *philosophia* to serve a naturalistic pseudo-knowledge that Socrates always held at arm's length? I ask again, without irony, why Brassier thinks philosophy has any value if, when pursued in optimal form, it is to be nothing more than flattery of what the sciences have already found for themselves without philosophical assistance? In chapter 3, section D, I will explain why OOO regards metaphor in particular as such an important component of philosophy. More important here is that Brassier's allergy to figurative language also results in his rejection of Heidegger's most famous word: *Sein*, or Being. Rather than join Heidegger in holding that being is an unobjectifiable and unconceptualizable residue behind all experience, Brassier says it behooves us "to grant that this non-manifest dimension is perfectly amenable to description from the third-person point of view characteristic of the sciences . . ." (30). In effect, Brassier is asking philosophy to become the handmaid of the natural sciences, just as it was once the handmaid of religion.

This can be seen again in Brassier's following chapter, on Meillassoux, when he remarks in passing that philosophy should aspire to provide "an appropriate speculative armature" (63) for science. Granted, what Brassier is attacking in this passage is the familiar but dreary "division of labor" in which science handles the empirical domain and philosophy the transcendental. But rather than let philosophy out of its prison to explore the extra-human domain as it did before Kant, Brassier wants philosophy to adopt a submissive role, merely supplementing what science has already done. This project has gradually become less appealing even to working scientists, many of whom expect better things than this from philosophy. To cite just one example, we have the following words from the prominent Italian physicist Carlo Rovelli: "I wish that philosophers who are interested in the scientific conceptions of the world would not confine themselves to commenting [on] and polishing the present fragmentary physical theories, but would take the risk of trying to look ahead."[8]

Nonetheless, Brassier's chapter on Meillassoux is strong, and his objections to the French thinker's Speculative Materialism ring true. The central problem Meillassoux faces, according to Brassier, is "trying to square the Galilean–Cartesian hypothesis that being is mathematizable with an insistence on the speculative disjunction whereby being is held to subsist independently of thought" (88). We will see that Meillassoux defends himself against such charges by drawing a distinction between Descartes and Pythagoras: Meillassoux insists that he and Descartes are not claiming (as Pythagoras seems to have done) that *being itself* is mathematical, only that mathematics indexes or points to a reality outside thought, which Descartes famously calls *res extensa* and Meillassoux "dead matter." But Brassier thinks there are bigger fish to be caught than dead matter. As he sees it, both Badiou and Laruelle (the subjects of his chapters 4 and 5) go further than Meillassoux. Speaking of the former case, Meillassoux "has not provided us with a non-metaphysical and non-phenomenological alternative – such as we find, for example, in Badiou's subtractive conception of the void" (88). Expanding on this point, Brassier adds that "Badiou's subtractive conception of ontological presentation effectuates a scission in being as such which precludes its intuition in terms of presence, whether phenomenological or metaphysical" (88). As for Laruelle's contribution, Brassier holds that it comes from a similar direction: "we shall redefine the diachronicity which Meillassoux takes to be definitive of ancestral time in terms of a structure of 'unilateralization' . . . which ultimately accounts for diachronicity understood as the separability of thought and being, their non-correlation" (84). We also find Brassier's usual assertion that the march of scientific progress will eventually render portions of Meillassoux's philosophy obsolete: "Admittedly, [cognitive science] is still in its infancy; nevertheless, its maturation promises to obviate the Cartesian dualism of thought and extension – and perhaps also the residues of the latter which subsist in Meillassoux's own brand of speculative materialism . . ." (89).

We turn now to the chapters on Badiou and Laruelle, the French thinkers from whom Brassier draws his own most important weapons. He knows the two authors personally, and at various times has had a reputation for being one of the leading experts on the work of both. This combined interest is somewhat unusual, given the apparently low opinion that Badiou and Laruelle hold of each other. Laruelle has actually published a book entitled *Anti-Badiou*; Badiou has not gone quite that far in return, though he is known to regard Laruelle's work as unintelligible. But, as mentioned, Brassier finds both authors useful in bringing a new form of negativity into philosophy, something he finds missing in the work of Meillassoux.

Among other things, Brassier sees Badiou as providing an anecdote to the Heideggerian excesses of continental philosophy. This occurs through Badiou's demystification of ontology by way of equating ontology with mathematics. In Brassier's bold summary: "Since ontology is now the province of mathematical science, and since (contra Heidegger) being is neither inherently meaningful nor the harbinger of truth, meditative rumination upon being is no part of the philosophical remit" (98). In this way, Brassier tries to erase the importance of what Heideggerians consider the unsurpassable profundity of the question of the meaning of Being. Now, we saw earlier that Brassier is aware of the danger of treating philosophy by too close an analogy with mathematics, since he criticizes Meillassoux for allying so closely with the mathematism of Descartes and Galileo that he runs the risk of losing realism altogether. And indeed, Brassier will end his chapter 4 by accusing Badiou of idealism, just as he accuses almost everyone else of that same defect. But before reaching that point, he tries to draw some lasting resources from Badiou's work.

One of Badiou's most famous sayings is that "the One is not"; among other consequences, this leads him to distinguish himself from Deleuze, whom he treats as essentially a philosopher of the One.[9] Yet it is important to note that Badiou means "the One" in two different senses, both of which he rejects. The first meaning of the One is the unity of the cosmos as a whole. Badiou rejects this kind of One on account of his commitment to the transfinite mathematics of Georg Cantor (1845–1910), who discovered that infinity comes in many different sizes, with no greatest infinity able to encompass all the others. In this first sense, there is no One because the world cannot be totalized. But the second sense of the One that Badiou rejects is perhaps even more fateful for his philosophy. Here I refer to the *many* Ones known as individual entities. In the Aristotelian tradition a dog is one dog, a star one star, a song one song, and so forth. Leibniz tells us in the "Monadology" that to be is to be one; hence his use of the term *monad*, drawn from the Greek word for "one." For Badiou, however, there are no independently existing entities that count as "ones." What we call "one" thing is for Badiou the retroactive result of a "count." All the entities that result from a count belong to what he calls "consistent multiplicity," and since they result from a count they cannot be identified with individual things in their own right. What comes before this is what Badiou calls "inconsistent multiplicity," and, despite the fact that he calls it a "multiplicity," it does not really contain any exact number of individual things at all. Badiou's inconsistent multiplicity is utterly anti-object-oriented; his treatment of objects comes in *Logics of Worlds*, the sequel to *Being and Event*, where objects are treated as belonging solely to the world of appearance. In Brassier's words: "For Badiou, ontology cannot be coordinated around a 'concept of being' because the very idea of a 'concept of being' is incompatible with the claim that being is inconsistent multiplicity" (99). And furthermore: "The necessity of structure is a nomological feature of discursive presentation, not an ontological characteristic of being itself" (101).

This might make it look as if Badiou were deploying inconsistent and consistent multiplicity as his own version of the classic opposition between "in-itself" and "for-us," or noumena and phenomena. Brassier denies this: "For in fact, the split between counted consistency and uncounted inconsistency, or structure and being, is an index of the underlying identity between the inexistence of structure (i.e. counting) and the inexistence of inconsistency (i.e. being itself)" (101). For this reason, "the non-being of the One, the merely nomological status of structure, converges asymptotically with the being-nothing of inconsistent multiplicity . . ." (101). For Brassier, this is the sense in which Badiou adopts the dictum of Parmenides (c. 515–450 BCE) that thinking and being are the same: "Thinking and being are both nothing" (101).

For Badiou, in Brassier's reading, "the law of presentation is the guarantor of a literally vacuous isomorphy between thinking and being . . ." (102). And this has serious consequences: "the price [Badiou pays] is a peculiar variety of discursive idealism wherein even the supplement of inconsistency invoked as a real interruption of the ideal order of ontological discourse is itself merely an instance of unstructured thought: the event as aleatory *deciding* of the undecideable, wherein thinking itself comes to embody inconsistency" (102): in other words, as an "event." For Badiou, who draws this result from set theory, any situation *includes* more than officially *belongs* to it. One obvious example would be the proletariat in politics: though they are not officially taken into account by the current state of affairs, they are included in it nonetheless, and hence they may erupt unexpectedly in a revolutionary event that qualifies as an event only insofar as the subject retains retroactive *fidelity* to it. Not all humans count as "subjects" for Badiou as they do in most modern philosophy. Instead, to be a subject is to wager one's whole existence that an event has occurred in one of the four areas that Badiou recognizes as evental: politics, art, science, and love. The echoes of Søren Kierkegaard (1813–1855) are unmistakeable.[10] Fidelity to an event requires absolute devotion to it, regardless of the consequences. Fidelity to revolution may require imprisonment, exile, or death in the streets of Cairo, just as fidelity to love (which Badiou treats solely in heterosexual terms) may mean the end of longstanding marriage and family life. Brassier is no great admirer of Badiou's concept of the event, and later in the chapter (114) he expresses his disappointment that *Logics of Worlds* de-emphasizes the subtractive concept of being in favor of a lengthy and often beautiful meditation on how specific concrete events are structured. Brassier calls out Badiou for ultimately being unable to push the negative aspects of his philosophy all the way, for "a philosophy that chooses to relinquish worldly plenitude in favor of subtractive ascesis must be prepared to take the plunge into the black hole of subtraction" (100–1). This extreme subtractive ascesis is apparently how Brassier understands his own philosophical work.

Where Badiou and Brassier are very much in agreement, we have seen, is in their claim that there is no hidden, mysterious dimension of Being to be gotten at in some indirect fashion, as if "being [could] only be presented as 'absolutely Other': ineffable, un-presentable, inaccessible via the structures of rational thought and therefore only approachable through some superior or initiatory form of non-conceptual experience . . ." (107). Brassier suggests that Badiou's remedy for this mistake, an error the French thinker calls the Great Temptation, is his principle that "there is no immediate, non-discursive access to being" (107). But the conjunction of the words "immediate" and "non-discursive" gives rise here to an important ambiguity. Does Brassier mean these two words as synonyms or as separate terms? And if as separate terms, does the problem arise only when the two are illegitimately combined? I make this point because it is not clear that the passage above criticizing the "ineffable, un-presentable, [and] inaccessible" works against Heidegger in the way Brassier presumably wishes. For while it is clear that Heidegger, especially the late Heidegger, has a very high opinion of non-conceptual experience, it is far from clear (I would even say *false*) that Heidegger thinks Being can be accessed *immediately*. This sounds more like Plotinus (204–70) and his Neo-Platonic school than like Heidegger.[11] In any case, even if it could somehow be proven that Heidegger claimed a direct, mystical experience of Being itself, this would not be a necessary consequence of *every* philosophy that made room for non-conceptual experience. But Brassier's main point here is about Badiou: "The law of presentation conjoins the authorization of consistency and the prohibition of inconsistency in an unpresentable caesura wherein the deployment and subtraction of structure coincides" (107). Although this is a mouthful for any reader from outside the Badiouian tribe, its meaning is relatively straightforward: there is nothing hidden from presentation, as if a secret were sleeping behind the visible phenomenon. Badiouian presentation, for Brassier, is an "anti-phenomenon," a site where the apparent opposites of consistent structure and inconsistency meet without entirely meeting. Brassier also calls it a "split noumenon," though it fails to recede from us in the manner of the Kantian noumenon. It is actually an *immanent* noumenon, just as Laruelle's One will prove to be. In this way, Brassier is getting very close to the result he wants. There is a noumenon deeper than the crude manifest image, but it is not hidden, and therefore it can be explored in principle by the explicit conceptual tools of mathematics and natural science.

Which is not to say that Badiou would agree. We have seen that he has little interest in the incipient "science of cognition" that so fascinates Brassier. For Badiou, as for Descartes before him and Meillassoux after, thought is a distinct piece of the furniture of the world and cannot be directly explained in terms of its physical underpinnings. More generally, Brassier proceeds near chapter's end to criticize Badiou for his idealism. This idealism is said to be visible in Badiou's excessive commitment to "the event." While Brassier wants to conceive of the unconceptualized surplus in any presentation as an "immanent hiatus," Badiou's event turns it into "a transcendent irruption of ontological consistency" characterized in Brassier's opinion by "inherent gratuitousness" (113). This leads Brassier to his final critical verdict on Badiou: "his philosophy simply stipulates an isomorphy between discourse and reality, logical consequences and material causes, thinking and being. Thinking is sufficient to change the world: such is the ultimate import of Badiou's idealism" (113). But while I do not share Brassier's low regard for Badiou's theory of the event, which in my view contains insights of lasting importance, I agree wholeheartedly as to the *limitations* of the Badouian event. For Badiou, all four types of event involve not just human beings, but human beings in their capacity as thinkers: "Accordingly, the Big Bang, the Cambrian explosion, and the death of the sun remain mere hiccups in the way of the world, in which he has little or no interest" (114). Brassier adds that it is a question less of anthropocentrism than of *noocentrism*, since Badiou is interested in humans only insofar as we happen to be the entities that think. He also rightly adds that Badiou's philosophy "conflicts with the realist postulates of the physical sciences, which assume that objects exhibit causal properties rooted in real physical structures that obtain quite independently of the ideal laws of presentation" (116). Badiou therefore runs the risk of an even more dangerous mathematism than we find in Meillassoux. "But can one maintain," Brassier asks rhetorically, "that being is mathematically inscribed without implying that nothing exists independently of mathematical inscription? This would seem to be one of the more nefarious consequences of the Parmenidean thesis . . . [of] a pre-established harmony between thinking and being" (117). Nonetheless, Brassier accepts Badiou's demystification of hidden Being even while rejecting his unmistakable streak of idealism.

In chapter 5 Brassier turns to Laruelle, an extremely difficult philosopher to read, though one with a sort of international cult following that sees his work as a bridge to the intellectual future. I almost wrote "to the future of philosophy" but worried that this might be confusing, given that Laruelle does not see his own work as philosophy at all. His name for what he does is "non-philosophy," though Brassier will discount this self-description and read Laruelle as simply a non-correlational philosopher. Brassier's attitude towards Laruelle is complex and interesting. On the one hand, he admits that Laruelle's work is covered by a "rebarbative carapace" (118) of nearly impenetrable jargon, and agrees that he seems to join two frequent vices of recent French thought: "a tiresome preoccupation with non-philosophical alterity coupled with an indulgent penchant for terminological obscurity"

(119). At the same time, Brassier sees Laruelle's philosophical achievement as "nothing short of extraordinary" (118) and even contends that his "conceptual depth (if not extensive breadth) at once equals and challenges that of Hegel's dialectical logic" (148). High praise indeed! Let's take a closer look at what Brassier finds so intriguing in Laruelle.

One of Brassier's most consistent complaints about Laruelle is that he is too hasty in claiming that all of "philosophy" has a single essence, when really there are just a number of individual philosophies, each with its own characteristics. Brassier notes that, while Heidegger and Derrida might well be accused of making similar over-generalizations, they at least do their historical homework with thousands of pages of close readings, which Laruelle does not (121). The point about there being no essence of philosophy as such is somewhat odd coming from Brassier, who normally shows distaste for this sort of Rortyan hyper-nominalism. Nowhere, for instance, does Brassier contest the use of the single word "science" to cover the multitude of various scientific disciplines and practices; indeed, he often indulges in a kind of scientific essentialism in which science = true cognition = good. In any event, Laruelle sees philosophy *tout court* as made up of a structure of "decision" that "conjoins three basic terms: immanence, transcendence, and the transcendental" (122–3), just like the philosophy of Kant. The alternative he proposes is one of "radical immanence," which he often describes as an immanent "One," a term guaranteed to annoy Badiou. Unfortunately, Laruelle develops his vision of non-philosophy in convoluted prose so painful to read that it can *literally* cause headaches if one focuses on it intensely for several days in a row. As Laruelle sees it, philosophy makes a cut between what counts as transcendent and what counts as immanent: "it is the reality peculiar to transcendental synthesis as what unifies and constitutes the possibilities of thought and experience . . ." (126). The task of non-philosophy, on the contrary, is to "[show] how the decisional complex of transcendence, immanence, and the transcendental is ultimately determined by the unobjectifiable immanence which Laruelle identifies with 'the real'" (127).

We can already sense why Brassier is interested in Laruelle, and why he claims a close link between Laruelle and his ostensible enemy Badiou. Both French thinkers remove the in-itself from the hidden domain so beloved by the likes of Heidegger and Emmanuel Levinas (1906–1995) and replant it in the domain of immanence, where it is both real and accessible in a manner that Brassier can easily render compatible with the scientific image. And in fact, Brassier's personal frustrations with Laruelle are most visible whenever the latter veers too closely towards Heidegger. For instance, "despite [Laruelle's] claims to non-philosophical radicality, he remains all too beholden to Heidegger's radicalization of the post-Kantian pathos of finitude" (127). Above all, "Laruelle insists on identifying the unobjectifiable immanence of the real with 'man' or 'the human' in person: 'Man is precisely that real which is foreclosed to philosophy'" (127). And again: "notwithstanding the now familiar claim that subject–object dualism has been left behind, the unobjectifiable immanence of Laruelle's 'One' seems to be situated squarely on the side of the subject rather than on the side of the object" (127). Brassier will eventually tell us that "this ultimately arbitrary identification of the real with the human individual threatens to reduce Laruelle's vaunted non-philosophical radicalism to a transcendental individualism . . . which is all too redolent of Fichtean solipsism to be convincingly described as non-philosophical" (137).

Nonetheless, Laruelle remains valuable for making certain points that Brassier finds useful. For instance, Laruelle's claim that the real has "no contraries or opposites" (137) makes him the close ally of Badiou's subtractive conception of "being-nothing" (137). Ultimately, Laruelle is important not for the non-philosophical gesture that Brassier finds so tedious, but because he "[defines] conditions under which thinking does not intend, reflect, or represent its object but rather mimes its unobjectifiable opacity insofar as the latter is identical-in-the-last-instance with a real which is 'foreclosed' to identification. This is what Laruelle calls 'determination-in-the-last-instance'" (138). Brassier tries to clarify this by explaining that "[thought] becomes non-thetic and is thereby turned into a vehicle for what is unobjectifiable in the object itself. The object becomes at once the patient and the agent of its own determination" (139). This amounts to a "unilateral duality" between thought and thing that "manifests a non-correlational adequation between the real and the ideal without incorporating the former within the latter . . ." (139). In fairness to Brassier, we should point out that, as difficult as his explanations of Laruelle are to understand, Laruelle's original argumentation is expressed in even cloudier fashion. But perhaps the following is a clearer formulation of the point: "instead of being objectively manifest as the correlate of an objectifying act, the object becomes the subject which determines its own objective manifestation; it is taken up *in* and *as* the agent of thinking which unilateralizes its own transcendent objectification" (141). Whether or not the reader can easily follow this line of thought, its usefulness for Brassier should be evident. For it allows him to extract an independent object from the thought–world correlate without following the Heideggerian claim that the way to escape correlationism is to look for a mysterious real object hidden beneath it. Just as Brassier always claims in the case of the scientific image, the object for Laruelle becomes adequate for the purposes of knowledge even though it does not correspond to some hidden, deeper reality. And here, as with his reading of Badiou,

Brassier is able to saturate the phenomenal and scientific world with non-being, all the better to call into question the meaning and ultimate value of human existence.

Brassier closes the chapter by affirming his view that "the account of unilateralization which we have extracted from the work of Laruelle consolidates and deepens the logic of subtraction we examined in Badiou" (147). It should be remembered that this connection is by no means obvious, and that Brassier has to do a tremendous amount of work to make the link seem feasible. Laruellean unilateralization, as he sees it, is "a surgical intervention upon the body of transcendental synthesis, severing terms from relations, amputating reciprocity, and sharpening one-sidedness. Every synthesis is double-edged and hence reversible, but to unilateralize synthesis means to endow it with a capacity for achieving an irreversible, one-sided cut" (147). In *Logics of Worlds*, Badiou boasts about having achieved an absolutely new conception of the object, which he confines to the logic of appearances, or – as in the title of the book – to "logics of worlds." As Brassier sees it, Laruelle also offers a new conception of the object, which is "no longer conceived of as a substance but rather as a discontinuous cut in the fabric of ontological synthesis" (149). In parallel with this, "it is no longer thought that determines the object . . . but rather the object that seizes thought and forces it to think it, or better, *according* to it. As we have seen, this objective determination takes the form of a unilateral duality whereby the object thinks through the subject" (149). Though I do not think the realist cause is well served by Brassier's turn to Badiou's being-nothing and Laruelle's unilateralization, he clearly engages in heroic efforts of interpretation to synthesize these two concepts in an unprecedented way.

Chapter 6 of *Nihil Unbound* is entitled "The Pure and Empty Form of Death," though it consists mostly of close readings of Heidegger and Deleuze, yielding the predictable result that both are idealists. But before we get to that topic, it is interesting that Brassier also critiques both philosophers for a type of aestheticism that we already know he detests. In Heidegger's case, the hermeneutic need to *interpret* ever-hidden reality rather than simply stating direct true propositions about it predictably annoys Brassier. Heidegger's allegiance "is to the requirements of appropriate or 'authentic' interpretation, rather than to those of impartial stringency. In matters of interpretation, talent outweighs rigour and finesse overrules stringency" (163). It strikes me as odd that Brassier sees no positive role for finesse and talent in philosophy, though this attitude is often found among arch-rationalists, who see thinking as a matter of following rules and criteria with remorseless rigor in a way that even a machine could be programmed to do. As for those areas of human intellectual life that are obviously not just a matter of the rigorous following of rules, such as art criticism or the translation of foreign languages, such rationalists generally respond by denying that these are cognitive activities of the same stature as the "impartially stringent" sciences, already an unhealthy account of how science itself reaches its results. Brassier follows this up with the additional unjustified claim that Heidegger merely "stipulates" the ontological difference between Being and beings without arguing the point (164). Heidegger is not central enough for us at the moment to make a refutation of Brassier's claim worthwhile, though the point is worth mentioning as further evidence that Heidegger is perhaps Brassier's most significant foil.

In the case of Deleuze, Brassier offers curmudgeonly complaint about a passage in *Difference and Repetition* that praises brilliant colors and precious stones. In person I have even heard him denigrate the paintings of Henri Matisse (1869–1954) for their pretty colors, though the status of Matisse as one of the pivotal figures of modernist painting is justly beyond question. This is worth mentioning, because Brassier seems to find the very notion of beauty repellent, at least in a philosophical context. As he sees it, "beauty, brilliance, preciousness, and vibrancy are aesthetic rather than cognitive qualifications. The transfiguration envisaged here betrays the perspective of a transcendental aestheticism" (189). The philosophers Fichte and Nietzsche both made famous statements to the effect that, beyond all claims of objective argumentation, the philosophy each of us chooses depends on what sort of person we are. In this respect, it is perhaps impossible to persuade Brassier to see the cognitive significance of beauty, brilliance, preciousness, and vibrancy, not to mention talent and finesse. His objection to such phenomena seems to be based on a doggedly *literal* approach to the world, grounded in turn on his hostility to the notion that anything might be incapable of paraphrase in discursive propositional language. This strikes me as a desolate conception of what should count as real, though sometimes the limitations of philosophers produce subordinate virtues of their own, as when Husserl's regrettable idealism allows him to make important new discoveries about the phenomenal world. Yet something about beauty and optimism seems to make Brassier angry, for reasons I find mysterious.

Otherwise, the chapter is concerned mainly to demonstrate the idealist tendencies of Heidegger and Deleuze. In Heidegger's case this is fairly uncontroversial, with Brassier focusing on the straightforward way in which Heidegger reduces time to *time for human beings (Dasein)* at the expense of objective clock-time (156, 159). With Deleuze, the claim is slightly more conflictual, given that many fans of the renegade philosopher view him as a materialist, and in Manuel DeLanda (b. 1952) we have at least one prominent expert who sees Deleuze as an outright realist.[12] Brassier could hardly disagree more. Perhaps even more than with Badiou, Deleuze's philosophy "seems to harbour the fantastic implication that physical qualification and partitioning, as well as biological specification and organization, can simply be eliminated though an act of thinking" (188). Not only is Deleuze not a realist, but his lack of realism leads him to "[leave] vast tracts of reality completely unaccounted for" (199). He includes "muscles and water within the ambit of actual experience, but not galaxies and electrons" (199), though we might just as well complain that Brassier includes galaxies and electrons within the ambit of reality, but not artworks, Santa Claus, or eloquent funeral orations. At any rate, Brassier may be right to contend that "the speculative audacity with which Deleuze upholds the rights of virtual ideality should not blind us to the curiously conservative nature of [his] empiricist premise" (200). Brassier concludes more broadly that, "for Deleuze, . . . being is nothing apart from its expression in thought; indeed, it simply *is* this expression" (203).

We come at last to the concluding chapter 7 of *Nihil Unbound*, where Brassier unveils the full extent of his dark vision. What he gives us in these pages is probably the most thoroughgoing pessimism in Western philosophy since Arthur Schopenhauer (1788–1860) and Eduard von Hartmann (1842–1906). This is the chapter in which Brassier shifts from discussing the non-existence of any hidden being behind the nullity of the manifest and scientific image to proclaiming the inevitable *physical destruction* of such images. He begins the chapter with a long epigraph from Nietzsche, not usually one of his favorite authors, about the utter insignificance and transience of the human intellect within the cosmos. As Brassier sees it, the passage from Nietzsche "perfectly distills nihilism's most disquieting suggestion: that from the original emergence of organic sentience to the ultimate extinction of human science 'nothing will have happened'" (205).

We are already dead. This is the central claim of Brassier's philosophy. To this end he cites Jean-François Lyotard (1924–1998) in *The Inhuman*: "as Lyotard points out, [the] terrestrial horizon will be wiped away, when, roughly 4.5 billion years from now, the sun is extinguished, incinerating the 'originary ark' [Husserl's term for the Earth], obliterating the self-secluding [Heidegger], and vaporizing 'the deterritorialized' [Deleuze]" (223). For those inclined to argue for interplanetary colonization as a way of saving us from the eventual destruction of the sun, Brassier will answer that they are simply postponing the day of reckoning. For even further down the line, Brassier tells us in one of his finest passages, "the stellar corpses littering the empty universe will evaporate into a brief hailstorm of elementary particles. Atoms themselves will cease to exist," and the still inexplicable force called dark energy "will keep pushing the extinguished universe deeper and deeper into an eternal and unfathomable blackness" (228). There is no question that such dark cosmological thoughts can serve to put our relatively trivial personal problems in perspective. But Brassier draws a more sweeping and paradoxical conclusion: since the thought–world correlate will eventually be exterminated, it already *is* exterminated (229). Whatever you hope to leave behind on Earth in the wake of your brief existence, it will all eventually come to naught in the degenerate breakdown of the universe as a whole. This puzzling result is asserted most clearly on the preceding page, when Brassier writes that "cosmic extinction is just as much of an irrecusable factum for philosophy as biological death – although curiously, philosophers seem to assume that the latter is somehow more relevant than the former, as though familiarity were a criterion of philosophical relevance . . ." (228).

Yet the problem with Brassier's deployment of the eventual death of the universe as a factor in present-day philosophizing is not so much its "unfamiliarity" as its irrelevant remoteness. Brassier is insisting that philosophy should ground itself on a purported cosmic extinction event billions of years in the future, proposed by cosmological theories that are no more than a century old, at a time when we are only four centuries into the Scientific Revolution. Already there are questions on the scientific margins as to whether the Big Bang really happened, whether it is really inevitable that the universe will die out, and even whether there might not be a completely new universe inside of each black hole, as the physicist Lee Smolin (b. 1955) suggests in his intriguing book *The Life of the Cosmos*. Though the universe may indeed become extinct in the distant future, and though it is interesting to contemplate what the implications of this might be for human life, we face far more immediate threats to our survival. This not only includes our current biological mortality, which is an observable daily fact in a way that cosmic extinction simply is not. It also includes the possible near-term obliteration of humans by a destabilized climate, a super-plague, an asteroid collision, or artificial intelligence run amok. Even if none of these apocalyptic incidents should occur, there are more inevitable and immediate threats. Somewhere in his correspondence, H. P. Lovecraft makes the best case for embracing mortality that I have ever read: to the effect that, as we age, reality continues to change in ways increasingly uncomfortable to those of our generation, until finally a world arrives in which we would no longer care to live. For my own part, I have no wish to live into a future that witnesses the extinction of tigers and elephants, widespread consumption of insects as a major protein source, or the possible nuclear destruction of one or more cities that I know and love. These near-term prospects horrify me and challenge my existence in a way that the hypothetical distant decay of all atoms simply does not.

One might also question whether Brassier's vision of an immanent negativity in presentation, with no hidden meaning behind it all, leads as neatly as he thinks to pessimistic conclusions. Berkeley was no pessimist, although he held that everything we experience is simply a set of images coordinated by God. Badiou seems far from resigned in his outlook on the human race, even though he indirectly provides Brassier with some of his key pessimistic tools. The consequences of a subtractive approach may indeed be, as Brassier holds, that even our scientific images ultimately rest upon the emptiness of a void. But the link between this inherent void and the eventual emptiness of cosmic destruction is not so clear. It seems to me that this link works only if one is *disappointed* in the claim that there is nothing but empty presentation, only if one had ever *demanded* that the world provide them with more. While Brassier basks in the unspeakable grimness of cosmic extinction, Nietzsche's eternal recurrence is actually a far more horrifying idea, just as Nietzsche meant it to be. Brassier's endless sleep for the extinguished universe sounds far preferable to the endless repetition of every stubbed toe, boring meeting, painful surgery, heartbreak, and canker sore we have ever had to endure. In any case, the fact that we will someday be dead obviously does not mean that we are *already* dead. This claim assumes that immediate experience has no value unless it somehow leaves a preserved trace in whatever follows. Many Stone Age incidents are permanently lost to history, but it would be wrong to say that they therefore never happened at all or never had any value or meaning.

Study Questions for Section B

1　Give a brief summary of Brassier's critique of phenomenology.
2　Alain Badiou accepts Parmenides' thesis that "being and thinking are the same," while Brassier rejects it. What does Brassier think are the negative consequences of this thesis for Badiou's philosophy?
3　Give a brief explanation of François Laruelle's concept of "unlitateralization." Why does Brassier find it so promising?
4　What does Brassier mean when he says that we are "already dead"?
5　On the one hand, Brassier insists that scientific theories are always fallible; on the other, he is so convinced of the eventual extinction of the universe − itself a relatively recent scientific theory − that he thinks it proves the meaninglessness of human existence. Is there a contradiction between these two points, or can they somehow be reconciled?

C The Path Ahead

Until the successor to *Nihil Unbound* is published, we have to look to Brassier's articles of the past decade to gain a sense of the direction in which he is headed. It is safe to say that, whereas the Brassier of 2007 was attempting a unique synthesis of contemporary French philosophy (Badiou, Laruelle) with analytic philosophy of mind (the Churchlands, Metzinger), the post-Speculative Realism Brassier sounds more like a mainstream analytic philosopher, despite his ultra-pessimistic cosmology. The French references have diminished, and his attention has focused with increasing intensity on the work of Sellars. In fact, the new visibility of Sellars in continental philosophy circles owes almost everything to Brassier's strong influence in certain quarters. It seems to me that two of Brassier's recent articles are the key to understanding who he is intellectually today. I will discuss each of them briefly, though in thematic rather than chronological order. Let's begin with his "Prometheanism and its Critics" (2014), since Brassier and his circle have been floating "Prometheanism" as a possible brand name for their group. We will then turn to Brassier's polemical but informative "Concepts and Objects" (2011), no doubt his most important piece of work published since 2007.

We have seen that Brassier considers his philosophy to be a radical extension of the project of the Enlightenment, which aims to replace tradition and superstition with the liberating discoveries of Reason. One important aspect of Enlightenment is its focus on the future as the horizon onto which indefinite improvements can be projected. While this project has always been challenged by conservatives, in recent decades it has become more common even for political progressives to wonder whether modernism is still a viable option. The challenges of modernism bear on any number of topics, though the one Brassier cites first in "Prometheanism and its Critics" is politics. The new progressive critics of political enlightenment "have insisted that the best we can hope for, via a radical scaling down of political and cognitive ambition, is to achieve small-scale rectifications of universal injustice by establishing local, temporally fleeting enclaves of civil justice."[13] At the root of these reservations is a specific historical experience: "these narratives, whether on the left or the right, draw a direct line from post-Galilean rationalism, and its advocacy of the rationalization of nature, to the evils of totalitarianism" (469). The implied reference here is not to Hitler, whom no one would call an Enlightenment figure, but to Stalinism, the great unhealed wound of the twentieth-century political Left. We could also speak of Maoism, which Badiou has openly tried to rehabilitate. The

excesses of these movements aside, Brassier urges us "to defend the normative status of the claim that *things are not as they should be*" (470). This leads
him to a definition of the key word in his title: "Prometheanism is simply
the claim that there is no reason to assume a predetermined limit to what
we can achieve or to the ways in which we can transform ourselves and
our world" (470). Needless to say, for Brassier this means that scientific
rationality must point the way forward. Echoing Metzinger, he also says
that Prometheanism requires "a subjectivity without selfhood" (471).

Brassier is not shy about naming those thinkers who stand in his way.
His ultimate target is Heidegger, with his "critique of subjectivist voluntarism" (471). More specifically, Brassier is critical of the appropriation
of Heidegger found in the liberal political philosopher Hannah Arendt
(1906–1975) and her admirer Jean-Pierre Dupuy (b. 1941), whose essay
"Some Pitfalls in the Philosophical Foundations of Nanoethics" is dealt with
at some length. Dupuy insists that the problems concerning nanotechnol-
ogy, biotechnology, information technology, and cognitive science (NBIC
for short) have been misread "epistemologically," in terms of our *ignorance*
about the eventual effects of these developments. He argues instead that
NBIC points to an "ontological" situation in which such technologies are
both good and bad. Heavily dependent on Heidegger and Arendt, Dupuy
sees humans as having less a *nature* than a *condition*, one defined by our
unique transcendence. This makes us absolutely different from animals and
from everything else. Hence, as Brassier describes Dupuy's position: "the
levelling of human existence onto a fixed catalogue of empirical properties
blinds us to the existential difference between what is proper and what is
improper for human beings to become . . ." (473). For Dupuy as for Arendt,
"the human condition is an inextricable mixture of things given and things
made" (474). This mixture is characterized further as a fragile balance or
equilibrium that is disturbed only at our peril. As for Brassier, he "[takes]
this claim that we *ought* to respect the 'fragile equilibrium' between what is
made and what is given to be fundamental for the philosophical critique
of Prometheanism" (474). Whereas the Promethean joins Marx in seeing
humans as free and conscious artificers of the world and of themselves,
Dupuy's deep Heideggerian streak leads him to view this attitude as "a
metaphysical reification of human existence, which is properly understood
as finite transcendence" (477), and therefore as the shepherd of balance
between what is given and what is made. This balance is threatened when
the Promethean "[destroys] the equilibrium between the made and the
given . . . The Promethean trespass resides in *making the given*" (478).

To the extent that calls for "balance" often take the reactionary form of
wanting to leave the main aspects of civilization as they are, Brassier has

a strong case to make. He refers in particular to the view of the philosopher Ivan Illich (1926–2002) that pain, disease, and death are ineradicable features of the human condition, and that "it is 'unreasonable' to want to extend life or improve health beyond certain pre-determined limits" (479). Prometheanism is surely worthy of support insofar as it means that horrific diseases ought if possible to be eradicated. Those who argued against anesthesia in the nineteenth century now rightly strike us as ridiculous, as would someone today who longed for the return of rampant smallpox or polio as a way of teaching steadfastness to children. The permanent risk run by partisans of "balance" is that they wish arbitrarily to freeze progress at the very point where they happen to be standing. Those of us living in 2017 who still face mortality have learned to deal with that prospect in various ways; projecting ourselves towards our eventual deaths may even help us to gain a more authentic sense of our potentiality for being, as Heidegger contends. Yet it does not obviously follow that physical death *ought* to be preserved as an essential element of the human condition. Most of us would be overjoyed to learn that the indefinite medical extension of life and health would be available in the near future. Even if we were to reject such technology and face our deaths bravely like all other humans up to the present, many or most of our fellows would accept the new life-extending technology and find ways to enjoy fruitfully their additional centuries or millennia of existence. The ardent atheist Brassier blames religion for the widespread inappropriate attitude to Promethean possibilities: "At the root of all religion lies the claim that suffering is *meaningful* . . . in the sense that suffering is something to be interpreted and rendered significant" (481). This is surely true, insofar as one of religion's functions is to offer solace in the face of unbearable pain. It is of course equally true that religion is often the basis for a reactionary insistence that what happen to be the conditions of the present day (or one's favored time in the recent past: say, the 1950s) are the natural equilibrium from which we should never depart. Nonetheless, religion would surely find a place even in a fully Promethean future as a way of dealing with ultimate uncertainties, however badly Brassier might wish it to be erased by the forward march of civilization.

In any case, Brassier is right to be suspicious of the implicitly Heideggerian position of Dupuy that "once being human is no longer another kind of difference – existence – but just another kind of being, a particularly complicated natural mechanism, then the danger is that we will lose the meaning-making resources through which we were able to project a point or purpose orienting our attempt to explain and understand ourselves" (483). We need only recall Heidegger's bizarre hostility to *typewriters* to see how appeals to the essential finitude of Dasein might be used to treat certain devices as forbidden transgressions, even if they merely make life more convenient and pleasurable. But we should disagree with Brassier's attitude towards a hypothetical anti-Promethean who might say that "Marxism . . . is guilty of eliding the difference between what is made and what is known. Only what is humanly made is humanly knowable" (484). Brassier seems to be arguing that both the human-made and the given are equally knowable, and therefore that both ought to be subjected to free conscious manipulation by humans. I would argue instead that *neither* the human-made nor the given are knowable, but that both – under certain conditions – may be subjected to manipulation anyway. For this reason I happen to agree with Brassier's skeptical reaction to the anti-Promethean claim that, "even if we have acquired the power to create life, we shouldn't do it" (484). The lesson of Mary Shelley's *Frankenstein* is not that we should avoid creating what is beyond the normal human province of creation, but simply that creation has consequences that no human being, Promethean or otherwise, can predict or prevent. When the anti-Promethean intones that "you have introduced a disequilibrium into existence" (485; emphasis removed), we should calmly respond that every creation induces disequilibrium. Even within recent memory, newspapers, postal services, and video rental stores have been laid waste by new technologies, a kind of destruction that Marx celebrated but that too many contemporary Leftists habitually bemoan. Brassier approvingly quotes J. G. Ballard's remark that "all progress is savage and violent." He adds that "there is indeed a savagery recapitulated in rationality. But there is a kind of sentimentalism implicit in the insistence that all savageries are equivalent . . ." (486). And he goes on to attack, rightly enough, "the frequently reiterated claim that every attempt to circumscribe, delimit, or manipulate phenomena is intrinsically pathological . . ." (486). He ends by saluting the Marxist and Badiouian "project of re-engineering ourselves and our world on a more rational basis" (487).

There is a sense, however, in which Brassier provides Prometheanism with targets that are too soft and too easy. It is not hard for an author with Brassier's sort of readership to take shots at religion, nor is it difficult to challenge the claim that suffering or mortality are inherently meaningful and therefore must not be removed by the hubris of human beings. Nonetheless, there are some very good reasons why modernism has encountered bumps in the road, and in this essay at least, Brassier has not quite faced up to them. Since he is quick to salute Badiou as an icon of political Prometheanism, it is fair to ask him about Badiou's ongoing support for the apparently ultra-modernist and ultra-Promethean Chinese Cultural Revolution, which led to countless atrocities. To make this point is not necessarily to fall into some sort of tepid prudence that demands that humans not risk the greatest good for fear that it will reverse into the greatest evil, as many critiques of totalitarianism go. It is simply to note a possibility of excess that is inherent in Enlightenment itself, and which entails at least three dangers.

The first danger is one that I would call *extrapolationism*. Brassier looks back admiringly at modern history and watches the Enlightenment sweep away a corrupt clergy, a deceitful religion, an inferior science, an oppressive *ancien régime*, a legion of horrific illnesses, and an openly institutionalized slavery. The results of these struggles seem so obviously favorable that Brassier simply extends the series in his imagination, projecting it forward. "Things are not as they should be" means, for him, that we did not go far enough when we should have pushed it all the way. We need ever more radical Enlightenment to cut down even more naïve, unscientific beliefs than anyone has ever dared to demolish in the past. We already *know* the model for progress, Brassier thinks, and now we simply need the courage to push it further despite all reactionary objections. The problem is that history never works this way indefinitely, and thus cannot be extrapolated in the manner that Brassier proposes. There are admittedly periods – in philosophy, politics, and elsewhere – when the radical extrapolation of previously timid, half-hearted measures is precisely what we need. But eventually a point is always reached when the exciting new idea presses against its limits and begins to confront that which *rightly* resists it. Modern philosophy becomes increasingly daring in its idealism, before reaching the point where – Brassier would be the first to agree – it is no longer a liberating idea. Global exploration revolutionizes the self-conception of European societies, until the globe is completely mapped and empire becomes bogged down in its own victories and exploitations. Industrial development radicalizes the economies of the world, until warming skies and brutal hurricanes teach us the limits of the environment in which we live. Modernist housing projects become unlivable and crime-infested; planned cities turn into traffic nightmares; People's Revolutions become mass extermination projects. One of the things I miss in Brassier's work is any sign that lessons have been learned about those moments when ideas crash against realities; instead, his tendency is tacitly to dismiss such issues as pseudo-problems posed only by fearful religious capitalists with vested interests in stasis.

This brings us to a second danger faced by Brassier: his tendency to view politics as a form of *knowledge*, despite his awareness that knowledge might somehow be "adequation" but cannot be a form of "correspondence." That is to say, Brassier ought in principle to be well aware that our political ideas are not an exact match for political realities, yet he somehow seems confident that political "adequation" to reality is possible. It is especially worrisome that he sees his recent political model in Badiou, who endorses absolute fidelity to a universalizable revolutionary event, despite the fact that Brassier sees Badiou as a "noöcentric" idealist who has a hard time grasping that which differs from every effort of thought. Any political doctrine that does not incorporate our fundamental ignorance of politics into the picture, with the appropriate dose of caution that this implies, runs the risk of becoming a political idealism, however gallant it may sound to the adoring young.

Third and finally, when Brassier speaks about politics, it is always in terms of the voluntarism of a freely constructing *human* subject. But politics does not consist just of human subjects; it also consists of countless inanimate objects that act as stabilizers for human society. For all of Brassier's some-times warranted attacks on the notion that we must pay heed to the "fragile balance" of the world, there is the glaring reality that at the moment we do face an especially fragile balance, one that is mostly *not* under human control. It will not do simply to blame capitalism or "neoliberalism" for the situation, given the horrible environmental damage wrought even by the Marxism that Brassier professes to admire. Any political theory that speaks only of humans shaping the world indefinitely as they please must at least deal with the question of our environmental limits, even as it hypotheti-cally boasts about promoting the end of death, illness, and all meaningless suffering.

We turn now to the 2011 "Concepts and Objects," which is Brassier's most frequently cited article other than the co-authored Goldsmiths transcript, and no doubt his most significant piece of work since *Nihil Unbound.* The principal merit of the article lies in its blunt claims about the basic question of philosophy: "Thought is not guaranteed access to being; being is not inherently thinkable. There is no cognitive ingress to the real save through the concept. Yet the real itself is not to be confused with the concepts through which we know it. The fundamental problem of philoso-phy is to understand how to reconcile these two claims."[14] Herein we find the central paradox of Brassier's thinking. There is no isomorphy between thought and being, such as we find in Meillassoux and most scientific real-ists. Nonetheless, "it falls to conceptual rationality to forge the explanatory bridge from thought to being" (47). Brassier does not tell us why it is solely *conceptual* rationality that must bear this burden, though there is little else available in his toolbox; ultimately "conceptual rationality" for Brassier is not just one kind of rationality among others, but the only kind. We start to understand this phrase better through observing that current of thought from which he most frequently distinguishes it: phenomenology. This includes the hermeneutic phenomenology pursued by Heidegger, which treats reality as something that must be interpreted rather than seen directly, as for Husserl. On this topic Brassier tells us: "The metaphysical investigation of being cannot be collapsed into a hermeneutical interpretation of the being of the investigator and the different ways in which the latter understands things to be" (48). He also urges us to "[avoid] the phenomenological equivocation between meaning and being" (48), a perfectly valid realist rejoinder to the congenital flaw of phenomenology. Brassier counters with a good, basic realist formula, to which he appends the claim that we must pave the way for realist ontology by way of a preliminary assessment of our ability to know the real: "we must attain a proper understanding of what it is for something to *be* independently of our conceiving, understanding, and interpreting its being. But this will only be achieved once we possess a firm grip on the origins, scope, and limits of our ability to conceive, understand, and interpret *what* things are" (48). But conceptual reality does not have hermeneutic phenomenology as its sole enemy, as Brassier proves when he takes a passing shot at Deleuze: "Proponents of a universal conception of being as difference, in which conception is just another difference in being, would effectively supplant the metaphysical question 'What differences are real?' with an affirmation of the reality of differences: differentiation becomes the sole and sufficient index of reality" (48). Committing oneself to Deleuzean "immanence" and "univocity of being" leads us to pay the heavy price "of a pre-Critical fusion of thinking, meaning, and being" (48), resulting in a panpsychism that absorbs epistemological problems – which Brassier values so highly – into the play of difference as a whole.

Drawing on this preliminary critical discussion, Brassier makes some more general claims, both of them pertinent to the critique of Latour that he will soon undertake. He tells us first that the Deleuzean claim "that 'everything is real' is egregiously uninformative" (48). In fact, although such a claim can be only an opening move in any philosophy, it is by no means uninformative – and certainly not "egregiously" so. If nothing else, starting off with a flat ontology that places everything on the same footing is a way of attacking the usual classifications of the world handed down to us from rationalist prejudice – above all, the distinction between thought and world that Brassier insists upon against Deleuzean univocity. Though Brassier would surely be annoyed at this, I can think of no better term than "folk-taxonomical" for philosophies that start out with an absolute difference between thought and world rather than doing their job and first identifying the deeper layer of which both of these poles are modifications. Brassier has no shortage of nasty things to say about those opponents who treat thought as just another event in the world among many others, and yet he never successfully clarifies why there must be such an incredible gap between these two realms in particular. Once again anticipating his critique of Latour, he tells us that "knowledge is not information: to know is to endorse a claim answerable to the norm of truth *simpliciter*, irrespective of ends. By way of contrast, the transmission and transduction of information requires no endorsement; it may be adequate or inadequate relative to certain ends, but never 'true' or 'false'" (49). What we find here is simply the *assertion* of an ontological difference in kind between information and knowledge. No doubt there is an important difference between Einstein struggling with his equations for gravity and a palm tree bending in hurricane winds. Everyone will agree with that. But Brassier is arguing for more than a *difference* between them: he is arguing for a difference so fundamental that it needs to be built into the very foundation of ontology. Yet he never provides a good reason for this inherited modernist prejudice, and is content simply to ridicule those (including Deleuze and Latour) who view the matter differently. There is the added complication that, unlike most scientific realists, Brassier rejects any notion of a correspondence theory of truth, and therefore he needs to clarify the special ontological status of "knowledge" by way of a non-corresponding adequation; this topic is evoked in key passages of *Nihil Unbound* but, again, never really clarified. Brassier's only real argument here – and it is not much of an argument for a philosopher to make – is that science is widely recognized as giving us a privileged sort of truth about the world, and that this truth would be threatened if there were not an abyssal gulf between knowledge and every other sort of transmission of force.

Two other points are in order before we turn to Brassier's critique of actor-network theory. The first concerns his incorrigible naturalist bias, as when he tells us that "meaning cannot be invoked either as originary constitutent of reality . . . or as originary condition of access to world . . . it must be recognized to be a conditioned phenomenon generated through meaningless yet tractable mechanisms operative at the sub-personal (neurocomputational) as well as supra-personal (sociocultural) level. This is a naturalistic imperative" (48–9). It may be a *naturalistic* imperative, but that does not make it a philosophical one, unless we assume in advance that naturalism is true. Note also the bi-directional reductionism that makes this passage a good case of what OOO critiques as "duomining" – simultaneously reducing a thing downward to its components and upward to its effects, while assuming that the thing itself is nothing outside of these.[15] Brassier asserts that meaning is not what Heidegger thinks it is, but that meaning is a combination of subpersonal neurocomputational processes *and* supra-personal sociocultural processes. There could be no clearer proof that naturalism is not a genuine realism, but simply a folk-reductionism that privileges neurons and societies over anything falling in between. This needs to be mentioned, given what I regard as the unearned reputation of continental naturalism (as represented by Brassier and his circle) for peerless philosophical rigor. On the positive side, it is worth applauding Brassier's tip of the hat to Kantian noumena, as when he bemoans how "the liquidation of the in-itself . . . marks correlationism's slide from epistemological sobriety into ontological incontinence" (49).

We now turn to Brassier's critique of Latourian actor-network theory, which runs for five highly polemical pages (51–5). It is important to note the context of Brassier's engagement with Latour, whose philosophy he seems to know only from "Irreductions," the admittedly crucial appendix to his book *The Pasteurization of France*. Brassier's critique of Latour can only be understood as a proxy attack against the Latour-influenced OOO (though the latter is mentioned only in the sarcastic footnote 8 on page 51). Given both his lack of serious engagement with Latour and his hidden aim of a flanking critique of OOO, Brassier's remarks end up being a mix of various useful and not-so-useful things. At some moments there are legitimate accounts of the drawbacks of Latour's philosophical position, while at others we find a speculative critique of the secret motivations said to be hiding behind his work. At some points Brassier tacitly lumps together Latour and OOO, or even Latour and "postmodernism," on topics where they are in explicit and open disagreement. Other portions of these pages show Brassier nakedly proclaiming the importance of scientific epistemology against the "sophistry" of actor-network theory, though his defense of the former is so assertoric that it seems to be meant only as free red meat for the already converted.

Brassier's critique opens with a point on which the otherwise pro-Latour OOO is partly in agreement. In Latour's philosophy, Brassier holds: "The metaphysical injunction to know the noumenal is relinquished by a postmodern 'irreductionism' which abjures the epistemological distinction between appearance and reality the better to salvage the reality of every appearance, from sunsets to Santa Claus" (51). There is no question that Latour rejects the noumenal (though Brassier's claim to "know" it is a strange way to speak of the noumenal). In Latour's actor-network metaphysics, a thing simply *is what it does*. This reflects the influence not only of American pragmatism and Alfred North Whitehead (1861–1947) but also of the semiotics of Algurdas Greimas (1917–1992). OOO has repeatedly criticized Latour for his rejection of the thing-in-itself. What is unclear is why Brassier finds Latour's refusal of the noumena any more repugnant than similar gestures by, say, Hegel or Badiou; this is presumably on account of aspects of Latour's philosophy other than his anti-noumenal attitude *per se*. In any case, the reason there is no noumenal realm in Latour is because he sees the world as consisting entirely of actors tied together in networks; none of these actors contain any surplus over and above their current actions. This exaggerated ontology of actions does provide Latour with a powerful method for the social sciences, where he is currently one of the world's dominant researchers. When looking at any situation, simply "follow the actors," without making any prior decisions about what is important or unimportant. Nonetheless, this method runs afoul of critiques of "actualism" in philosophy that go as far back as Aristotle's refutation of the Megarians in Book Theta of the *Metaphysics*.[16] It remains the case that Latour's anti-noumenal view is a respectable philosophical position (though I happen to think it fails); it needs to be critiqued on its merits rather than simply dismissed as a frivolous rhetorical ploy. The latter, unfortunately, is a good description of Brassier's account of Latour: "Far from trying to prove anything, Latour is explicitly engaged in persuading the susceptible into embracing the irreductionist worldview through a particularly adroit deployment of rhetoric. This is the traditional modus operandi of the sophist" (53). This comes just two pages after Latour's famously lucid and witty prose is described as "suave and unctuous" (51). There are at least two problems with this. The first is that Brassier is simply not a reliable judge of good prose style, given that his frequent jeers at "aesthetics" show his failure to understand the important cognitive role of vivid (and not just "clear") writing in philosophy. The second problem is that Latour's fabulous style may sometimes be "suave," but it has so little of the "unctuous" about it that this term feels as if it came from a random insult generator. Brassier sees great importance in the work of Sellars, whom I would call one of the worst prose stylists in analytic philosophy, whatever his other merits may be. And absolutely no one in continental philosophy is a worse writer than Laruelle, who by Brassier's own admission might reasonably be dismissed as "combining the worst of Derrida and Deleuze, deconstructionist sterility with constructivist extravagance."[17]

As for calling Latour a "post-modern," this remains a dishonest tactic unless Latour's own devastating critique of postmodernism is taken into account. This can be found in his best-known work, *We Have Never Been Modern*, a book that Brassier conspicuously fails to cite and has possibly still not read. Latour's basic idea here is that the postmoderns are simply moderns with a minus-sign added: just like the moderns, the postmoderns uphold the modern purification of subjects from objects (as does Brassier himself). A more substantive philosophical problem arises from Brassier's complaint that Latour wants to preserve absolutely everything, from sunsets to Santa Claus. Nonetheless, sunsets do exist in human experience, even if Brassier wishes to eliminate them in favor of a duomining replacement: a mixture of subpersonal neurocomputational processes and supra-personal sociocultural contexts. The same holds, of course, for Santa Claus. The fact that Brassier has a specific temperamental interest in sifting relatively true appearances (scientific images) from mostly false ones (manifest images), despite his admission that the mind's correspondence with the world is impossible, does not mean that ontology as a whole needs to exclude all personal experience of beauty and Christmas-time characters. If philosophy has any trait that distinguishes it from the specific sciences and other fields, it is surely that it is in a position to cast the widest possible net, covering literally everything. There is more to be said about sunsets than the fact that they involve brain processes, and more to Santa Claus than his "socio-cultural" aspects, given – among other things – that both societies and neurons are shaped by Santa Claus in turn.

This brings us to the aforementioned sarcastic footnote, which despite its unearned condescension is in some ways the most helpful passage in the article for understanding Brassier's philosophy.

> It is not enough to evoke a *metaphysical* distinction between appearance and reality, in the manner for instance of "object-oriented philosophies," since the absence of any reliable cognitive criteria by which to measure and specify the precise extent of the gap between seeming and being or [to] discriminate between the extrinsic and intrinsic properties of objects licenses entirely arbitrary claims about the in-itself. (51)

As we will see in chapter 3 of this book, OOO draws an absolute distinction between what it calls the "real" and the "sensual." Real objects and qualities are those that exist quite apart from any relations in which they might currently or ever be involved, while sensual objects and qualities exist only as correlates of someone or something that experiences them. For all intents and purposes, OOO's real objects are the *noumena* that Brassier claims to value so highly. Now, insofar as Brassier admits the impossibility of correspondence and thereby concedes a permanent asymmetry between concept and object, he rides in the same boat as OOO. It is true that the real/sensual distinction in OOO is "metaphysical," but the same holds for Brassier's own preferred distinction: the Sellarsian rift between manifest and scientific images. Despite Brassier's admission that the world is not isomorphic with our concepts of it, and that the world itself is therefore somehow "noumenal," he leaves no room for the noumenal at all when he embraces a mere distinction between two kinds of *image*. However deeply the Sellarsian conflict between manifest and scientific may be thought to run, *both are images*. For this reason, any "criteria" given to distinguish one from the other will still leave us at the level of images – no less than in *Matter and Memory* by Henri Bergson (1859–1941), a thinker Brassier detests as a "spiritualist." Yes, Brassier will add the proviso that the scientific image is "fallible," but whatever new scientific image we put in the old one's place, it is still nothing more than an image. Hence, even the *scientific* image is still – by Brassier's own admission – incommensurable with the real. But this means that Brassier's rift between object and concept is every bit as "metaphysical" as OOO's analogous distinction between real and sensual. Insofar as Brassier makes an additional demand for "criteria," these will simply allow us to sift good images from bad ones – *Santa Claus bad, quantum theory good* – even though quantum theory is admitted not to be isomorphic with the reality it describes. And while Brassier asserts that OOO will be left with "arbitrary" claims about the in-itself, his own claims would appear equally arbitrary if not that he subcontracts all statements about the in-itself to various scientific disciplines, in which he himself is no licensed practitioner.

There is also the matter of Brassier accusing Latour of a performative contradiction for denouncing reductionism but engaging in it "wantonly" anyway. Brassier again: "Latour has no qualms about reducing reason to arbitration, science to custom, knowledge to manipulation, or truth to force: the veritable object of his irreductionist afflatus is not reduction per se . . . but *explanation*, and the cognitive privilege accorded to scientific explanation in particular" (51). The first thing to note is that, contra Brassier, Latour's term "irreduction" does not mean "non-reduction." This is simply incorrect. Latour's point is not that nothing can be explained in terms of anything else (since of course this happens all the time) but that any reduction carries a price. Latour does treat one kind of reduction as preferable to others, and his philosophy openly pays a price for it: the reduction of everything in the universe to *actors* or *actants*. In the world of Latourian ontology, sunsets and Santa Claus both act on other things no less than science does, and therefore all are equally real. I can understand why Brassier is concerned to protect the social prestige of quantum theory in comparison with tarot cards and witchcraft, but I am not sure why this prestige entails that we must be forbidden to reinterpret science in terms of actants. This very move is what allows Latour and his colleagues to ask valuable questions about the production of scientific facts, questions that need not be embargoed just because they sometimes stray into an indefensible social constructionism. Brassier and I are both ardent realists, and thus we would both disagree with Latour's claim that Ramses II could not have died of tuberculosis since it had not yet been discovered.[18] But this shows us nothing more than an excess in Latour's ontology that needs correction, and Brassier's own ontology – like every other – has excesses of its own.

The primary excess of his ontology, in my view, can be found in its obsession with policing the distinction between good and bad images, despite its having little to say about how any image at all can be adequate to the reality beyond images. Brassier takes Latour to task for dismissing this relationship, "which has preoccupied an entire philosophical tradition from Frege through Sellars and up to their contemporary heirs" (52), as well as for attempting to "liquidate" the "unfolding epistemological problematic from Descartes to Sellars" (52), and finally for "[writing] to reassure those who do not really want to know" (52), forgetting that Socrates knew nothing and was *for this very reason* a philosopher rather than a scientist.

To some extent, Brassier conflates Latour with OOO when he accuses the former of "[supplanting explanation] with a series of allusive metaphors whose cognitive import becomes a function of semantic resonance: 'actor,' 'ally,' 'force,' 'power,' 'strength,' 'resistance,' 'network': these are the master-metaphors of Latour's irreductionist metaphysics . . ." (51). It is hard to see what is superfluously metaphorical about any of these terms. Even the most cursory grasp of etymology shows that most if not all words have meta-phorical roots, including such everyday terms as "window" ("wind-eye"). There is nothing especially imprecise about Latour's technical vocabulary; it is perfectly clear what he means when he says, for example, that actors engage in alliances through a network and thereby increase their ability to withstand trials of strength. To repeat, there are things that can be said *against* such a metaphysics – for example, its actualist inability to account for future changes in actor-networks – but there is nothing the least bit unclear about it. It may well be that Brassier has a puritanical allergy to the "anthropomorphism" of metaphors such as "ally" and "negotiate" when ascribed to inanimate beings, but there is nothing of the panpsychist about Latour, and these terms are as good as any. Thus Brassier loses his way when he declaims Latour's "paltry metaphorics that occludes every real distinc-tion through which representation yields explanatory understanding" (53). There is nothing "paltry" about it: Latour's model has brought about some-thing of a revolution in the social sciences by focusing new attention on local actors rather than fuzzy abstractions such as "society" and "capitalism," and by defending the social agency of inanimate objects. When Brassier complains about Latour using *allusive* metaphors, he seems to be taking a misdirected stab at OOO, which uses both "allusion" and "metaphor" as technical terms. But on this point OOO has nothing in common with Latour at all, since its sense of allusion and metaphor refer exclusively to the withdrawn thing-in-itself, a notion that Latour banishes altogether.[19]

To close these remarks, we should address the most flagrant case of *ad hominem* in Brassier's article: "there is nothing to prevent the cynic from concluding that Latour's politics (neo-liberal) and his religion (Roman Catholic) provide the most telling indices of those forces ultimately motivating his antipathy towards rationality, critique, and revolution" (53). The fact that Brassier admits his cynicism hardly makes it more palatable. But I happen to disagree with Meillassoux's view that these sorts of reflections on motives are always out of place in philosophy. It is *in fact* useful for understanding Latour's philosophy to know that he is a practicing Roman Catholic, though not in Brassier's cynically dismissive way. Readers of Latour (especially supportive ones) have often noted that his fascination with *mediators* owes much to the spirit of the Catholic Church, with its confessors, its intervention by saints, and a number of indirect liturgical acts so foreign to the direct-to-God outlook of Protestantism. The real problem with dismissing someone's philosophical views with cynical biographical explanation is not that there is never anything to it, but that one's own biography is rarely beyond equivalent scrutiny. It would be equally easy to trace Brassier's philosophical views to biographical accidents and idiosyncratic temperamental quirks, though there is a limit to how fruitful such explorations would be. As for the claim that Latour is a "neoliberal," this is a typically sloppy use of the term, which ought to refer to the free market policies of Austrian and Chicago School economics but these days is used to mean little more than "jerk."[20] It would be fair to call Latour a political *liberal*, but he is certainly no unrestrained free-marketeer, as becomes clear from his attempted decomposition of economics in the closing chapters of his book on the various modes of existence.[21] Hence, the description "neoliberal" is off the mark. As for the passing praise of "revolution," at present this is nothing more than virtue-signalling: one reads Brassier's works in vain for any sustained meditation on politics.

Though Brassier's engagement with Latour is too unsympathetic to be very fruitful, there are moments when his disagreements do give us a clearer picture of his own position. For example, it is perfectly fair when he complains that "Latour's reduction of things to concepts (objects to 'actants') is of a piece with his reduction of concepts to things ('truth' to force)" (55). Yet contra Brassier, this gesture does not qualify Latour uniquely as some sort of "sophist," but is simply the unfortunate price paid by any philosophy that excludes the noumenal and thus equates entities with their appearance or their relations to something else. Brassier is right to insist on a gap between reality and our concept of it, yet it seems to me that he badly underestimates that gap: "We need to know what things are in order to *measure* the gap between their phenomenal and noumenal aspects as well as the difference between their extrinsic and intrinsic properties" (55; emphasis added). It is hard to see how such a gap could ever be "measured," given the striking incommensurability between concept and object: "To know (in the strong scientific sense) what something is is to conceptualize it. This is not to say that things are identical with their concepts" (55). Surely Brassier is correct in his intuition that some images are more adequate than others in guiding us towards how things really are. What must be questioned is whether we can conceive of the distance between concept and object as lying along a measurable continuum of "you're getting warmer" and "you're getting colder." So far, Brassier does not even seem very interested in developing a theory of how one concept could be "closer" than another to a reality that is incommensurable with both. I suspect that this is because he is interested less in the metaphysical problem of knowledge than in enforcing the function of science in silencing people he considers irrational. Even Brassier's best formulations of the problem are inadequate, and seem more like a wish list based on wordplay than a genuine solution. For instance: "The gap between conceptual identity and non-conceptual difference – between what our concept of the object is and what the object is in itself – is not an ineffable hiatus or mark of irrecuperable alterity; it can be conceptually converted into an identity that is not of the concept even though the concept is of it" (55). With the puzzling phrase "not of the concept even though the concept is of it," so reminiscent of the figurative and rhetorical language he claims to despise, we again see Brassier's dependence on Laruelle's concept of unilateralization. It is hardly more helpful when Brassier adds that "the difference between the conceptual and the extra-conceptual . . . can be presupposed as already-given in the act of knowing or conception. But it is presupposed without being posited. This is what distinguishes scientific representation and governs its stance towards the object" (55). A promising starting point for a new theory of science? Time will tell. But this is hardly convincing enough to put Brassier in position to dismiss others as "sophists" who write merely for "those who do not care to know." The same holds when he adds, tantalizingly, that "there is an immanent yet transcendental hiatus between the reality of the object and its being as conceptually circumscribed . . ." (55). Here again, "immanent yet transcendental" is just the first step of an uncompleted fishing expedition. Such fishing is always underway at the borderlands of any philosophy, since no philosophy ever gains mastery of everything within its reach. Yet even Brassier's fairly rudimentary conception of how science ties together the manifest image, the scientific image, and the object that is never adequately expressed by either would seem to advise more caution and patience in sizing up his opponents than he generally shows, given his tendency to what Peden called "premature refutation." The fact that science has enjoyed "remarkable cognitive achievements" (65) does not mean that the philosopher should borrow the glory of these achievements to pillory others too hastily. The cognitive achievements of science are not the cognitive achievements of Ray Brassier himself, any more than they are the achievements of Bruno Latour, and thus it is not clear why Brassier considers himself their authorized spokesman.

Yet in passing, I do want to note the refreshing moment when Brassier goes behind post-Galilean science to find interesting precursors for his ideas in medieval thought: "The distinction between the object's conceptual reality and its metaphysical reality has an analogue in the scholastic distinction between objective and formal representation" (57). Yet towards the end of the article, Brassier shies away from this use of Scholastic terminology, for reasons that strike me as wrong but still enlightening: "How can we acknowledge that scientific conception tracks the in-itself without resorting to the problematic metaphysical assumption that to do so is to conceptually circumscribe the 'essence' (or formal reality) of the latter? For we want to be able to claim that science knows reality without resorting to the Aristotelian equation of reality with substantial form" (64). Brassier does not tell us why substantial forms are "problematic"; one suspects it is merely because modern science found it easy to dispense with such forms, replacing them with quantifiable extension and motion. Yet there is no inherent reason why successful methods in natural science should equate to truths in metaphysics, unless scientism has become an end in itself. In any case, Brassier glosses his statement on substantial forms as meaning that "the structure of reality includes but is not exhausted by the structure of discretely individuated objects" (65). While in one sense this is obviously a tacit critique of OOO, it also points to Sellars's upholding of *process* against objects, despite Brassier's earlier worries at the Goldsmiths workshop about the processualism of Grant.

We should also say something about "Stove's Gem," named after the cantankerous Australian philosopher David Stove (1927–1994), to whom Brassier often skillfully refers.[22] For here we see another point in common between Brassier and OOO: their shared rejection of the correlationist circle, which Meillassoux claims to surmount only following a deep appreciation of its supposed conceptual rigor. Though the Gem need be only a correlationist argument rather than an outright idealist one ("you can't think something outside thought without thinking it"), Berkeley's master argument remains the clearest example: since we cannot think or perceive something without thinking or perceiving it, therefore it cannot exist without being thought or perceived. As Brassier notes: "Berkeley's premise is a tautology, since the claim that one cannot think of something without thinking of it is one that no rational being would deny. But from this tautological premise Berkeley draws a non-tautological conclusion, viz., that things *depend* for their existence on being thought or perceived and are *nothing apart from* our thinking or perceiving them" (57). Nonetheless, the Gem is widely accepted to this day, serving as "the trusty adjutant for almost every variety of late 20th Century correlationism, from Goodman and Rorty at one end to Latour and Foucault at the other" (59), despite Stove dismissing it as the worst philosophical argument ever made. Yet however wrong the Gem may be, Brassier goes too far in calling it so bad that its wide acceptance can be explained only by "emotional," "psychological," and "political" factors (59). As Latour of all people has taught us, if we use these factors to explain the views of our opponents, then we must also be prepared to use them in explanation of our own, and it is not clear that Brassier could pass such a test any better than anyone else. Moreover, even if the Gem is wrong, that does not make it *ridiculously* wrong. Thinkers as diligent as Fichte and Meillassoux have made use of the Gem, and though I share Brassier's dismay at Meillassoux's fondness for it, his defense of the correlationist circle is not lacking in a certain formal rigor: it can hardly be explained by "emotional" factors stemming from something gone amiss in Meillassoux's personal psychology. Here once more we encounter the frequent Brassierian vices of an impatient rush to ensure that science retains sweeping authority and a zealot's tendency to demonize the psychology of his opponents, while Meillassoux at least patiently works out the tension between correlationism and the ancestral data of the sciences. That said, it is nonetheless true that Brassier's arguments against the Gem have an admirable clarity and power. For instance: "It is certainly true that I cannot think about the Empty Quarter without thinking about it; but it does not follow from this that the Empty Quarter is populated by my thinking about it" (63). And even better: "Once one realizes that Fichte's intimidating Teutonicisms mask flimsy Berkeleyan Gems, it becomes no more impossible to refute Fichte than it was to refute Berkeleyan immterialism" (63).

Near the end of the article is a passage that strikes me as an excellent statement of Brassier's philosophical position as a whole: "For those of us who take scientific representation to be the most reliable form of cognitive access to reality, the problem is one of granting science maximal (but not, please note, incorrigible) authority to the scientific representation of the world while acknowledging that science changes its mind about *what* it says there is" (64). So-called structural realism tries to square this circle by claiming that a certain *mathematical core* remains invariant even when scientific theories are abandoned for better ones over time. But while Brassier has occasionally flirted with the structural realists, something so far has prevented him from openly joining their ranks; one suspects it is because he sees the structural realists as guilty of the same over-fondness for mathematics that he finds in Meillassoux.[23] In the meantime, it is fair to give Brassier the space he needs to develop his theory of how science manages to track the in-itself despite being unable to correspond or coincide with it. Yet it does seem to me that his wish to grant "maximal authority" in the meantime to science sheds considerable light on what I find to be the most unpleasant aspect of his philosophy: a tendency to excessive science-worship of the sort usually found among analytic rather than continental philosophers. This is not without consequence for the style and content of his philosophy, as seen by his expressed contempt for aesthetics, rhetoric, and metaphor, and seems to explain the fact that interdisciplinary readers – so important to a philosopher's sphere of influence – have not flocked to Brassier in great numbers. To expand beyond his natural readership base of aggressively scientistic and Leftist young males, he will need to show more sympathy with other types of cognitive performance than those that are showcased in the hard sciences.

Study Questions for Section C

1 How does Brassier respond to criticisms that Prometheanism endangers the "fragile balance" between what is given to humans and what they make?
2 In the article "Concepts and Objects," Brassier appeals to "conceptual rationality" against three different adversaries: phenomenology, Deleuze, and Latour. What are his different – though related – complaints about each of these three currents?
3 What is Stove's Gem? How does Brassier employ it against Meillassoux's defense of the correlationist circle?
4 What exactly are the philosophical stakes of Brassier's insisting on a key role for *epistemology* (theory of knowledge)?
5 At one point, Brassier makes positive mention of the scholastic distinction between formal and objective reality. What aspect of his own thinking does this distinction resemble?

2   Vitalist Idealism

Iain Hamilton Grant (b. 1963) is Senior Lecturer in Philosophy at the University of the West of England (UWE) in Bristol, the same institution where he was employed at the time of the 2007 Goldsmiths workshop. Like Brassier, Grant did his doctoral work at Warwick University. There he was associated with the Cybernetic Culture Research Unit (CCRU), which was led by Sadie Plant (b. 1964) and, later, the controversial Nick Land (b. 1962). During the 1990s Grant also translated two of the most charismatic books of French postmodernism: Jean-François Lyotard's *Libidinal Economy* and Jean Baudrillard's *Symbolic Exchange and Death*. Grant has devoted his philosophical career to developing a vitalist philosophy that draws, above all, on the philosophy of Schelling and the more recent French thinkers Gilles Deleuze and Félix Guattari (1930–1992), the latter two being dominant influences in 1990s Britain as Grant and Brassier came of age intellectually. But especially important for Grant is Schelling, a colorful prodigy who matured more quickly than his older and more famous classmate Hegel. In what follows we will discuss Grant's interpretation of Schelling as a philosopher of nature and follow the consequences he draws from this for contemporary philosophy. But first, let's consider what Grant had to say in London on April 27, 2007, at the first meeting of the Speculative Realists.

A Grant at Goldsmiths

Grant's remarks at Goldsmiths were brief, covering pages 334 to 345 of the meeting transcript, followed by a much longer set of responses to audience questions. Yet those eleven pages are enough to sample the nectar of Grant's intellectual work, while unifying in advance his otherwise two rather different books to date: *Philosophies of Nature After Schelling* (2006) and the co-authored *Idealism* (2011). As we will see in more detail when discussing his Schelling book, Grant's worry is that philosophy has not advanced much at all during the post-Kantian period, which began with the various important reactions in the 1790s to Kant's three great works of the previous decade.[1] As Grant sees it, Schelling's vast output is a permanent philosophical beacon guiding us away from Kant's limitations, if only we would learn to take it seriously. Grant is hardly the first to make such a claim: Schelling is perpetually regarded as a "philosopher of the future" filled with untapped minerals, much like Maurice Blanchot (1907–2003) or the later writings of Maurice Merleau-Ponty (1908–1961). The special interest of Grant's version of Schelling is to be found in the details.

The standard account of the post-Kantian period in philosophy goes roughly as follows. Kant proclaimed an unbridgeable gap between appearances and the thing-in-itself, or between "phenomena" and "noumena." Since there is no way for humans to perceive anything directly outside our pure intuitions of space and time and the twelve categories of the human understanding, philosophy must content itself with discussing things as they appear to finite human cognition. Beginning with the brilliant alcoholic vagabond Salomon Maimon (1753–1800), continuing through the pugnacious genius Fichte, and running on up to Hegel, Kant's most gifted followers developed his philosophy by belittling the role of the thing-in-itself to an increasing degree. For how can Kant say that the thing-in-itself "causes" the appearances when he holds that causation is merely a category of the understanding which, like all of the categories, cannot be applied to the noumenal world? And more generally, if we claim to know the existence of a thing-in-itself beyond thought, this claim is itself a thought, and therefore it collapses because of internal contradiction. The only consistent response, it is said, is to bite the bullet and accept that everything we can speak of is saturated by thought rather than lying somewhere beyond it. With this step, we have entered the world of German Idealism. Fichte's response to Kant's double world of phenomena and noumena is to absorb nature entirely into what is for him the dominant theme of philosophy: an ethics based on human freedom. Later, Hegel makes an effort to treat both "nature" and "spirit" on equal terms, though this effort still presupposes the abandonment of Kant's thing-in-itself, making the distinction between phenomena and noumena internal to the phenomena. Hegel's book title *Phenomenology of Spirit* is a claim to speak about the whole of reality, not an admission that there are noumena lying beyond spirit that need to be discussed elsewhere; he could never have written a companion book called *Noumenology of Nature*. How Schelling fits into this story depends on whom you ask. For most Hegelians and mainstream historians, Schelling was an unruly Romantic rendered philosophically unsound by his excesses, a transitional figure superseded by Hegel and his more mature system. For defenders of Schelling, who include figures as important as Heidegger, Hegel's dialectic enclosed him in a man-made prison, while Schelling guides us beyond those prison walls towards the magnetic, electrical, and chemical forces of nature, the essence of human freedom, and the blind rotary drives of a tormented god.[2]

Grant is among those who find Schelling to be the most important and most futuristic of the post-Kantian philosophers. Moreover, he opposes the usual view of scholars that the prolific Schelling went through multiple phases in his career, classified somewhat differently by each historian. For example, Andrew Bowie splits Schelling's career into (1) Transcendental Philosophy, (2) Philosophy of Nature, (3) Philosophy of Identity, (4) Philosophy of the Ages of the World, and (5) Positive Philosophy.[3] Yet Grant is uncompromising in his contrary view that Philosophy of Nature was Schelling's one and only phase. Anyone who wishes to escape our era's ongoing philosophical imprisonment in Kant's two-world ontology can escape it, Grant holds, only by pursuing something like a philosophy of nature.

We now turn to Grant's own remarks at the Goldsmiths workshop. Like all of the Speculative Realists (each in a different way), Grant is keen to escape the perpetual focus on how humans gain access to knowledge about the world in favor of a return to philosophizing about the world itself. As he puts it: "if philosophy of nature is followed consistently it entails that speculation becomes necessary, as the only means not of assessing the *access* we have, but of the *production* of thought."[4] That is to say, rather than simply beginning from the usual modern opposition between thought and world, Grant wants to show how thought is *produced* by the world. Viewed superficially, this might sound like just another form of scientism: after all, cognitive science and neurophilosophy also try to strip away the special modern status of thought in favor of a scientific discourse that explains its origins. But Grant does not see it that way, as can be gathered from his responses in the question period to Toscano (345–8) and Brassier (364–6). Grant seems uncomfortable with Toscano's notion of thought as a formal pattern that does not need a substrate in some biological individual, and he appears to reject outright Brassier's view that speculative philosophy needs to become involved in eliminating non-existent entities and revising metaphysical concepts on the basis of empirical research. Perhaps more importantly, Grant's conception of nature differs from that of others in two important respects. He is unlike most idealists in viewing nature as a multi-layered kingdom rather than just a monolithic Other of thought. In Grant's words: "we [must] accept that there's something prior to thinking, and that there are several layers of dependency amongst what is prior to thinking. It's not just one thing, it's an entire complex series of events" (334). Mainstream philosophers with scientific inclinations, or "naturalists" as they are often called, would also agree with the passage just quoted. But they would quickly desert Grant with his next step – a far more speculative one. For even if we try to draw direct causal links between the sub-cognitive processes of nature and their outcomes on the level of thought, we find that, for Grant, "such a task is inexhaustible in principle, not merely in fact. It's inexhaustible in principle because the conditions that support the event that's produced also support the production of other events" (334). If I read this passage correctly, Grant is speaking not of causal links in the mechanistic and linear sense that many naturalists prefer, but of causes as concealed potencies that might have taken many other paths in nature than the ones they actually did. This approach to causation has a whiff of the Deleuzean "virtual" about it and parallels the anti-empiricist views of causation found in such authors as Roy Bhaskar (1944–2014) and Manuel DeLanda.[5] Though some readers of Grant insist on his compatibility with "naturalizing" positions in the philosophy of science, this can be done only if we ignore a crucial difference between them. For Grant, nature is not a basis to which everything must be *reduced* but a basis from which everything is *produced*. There are too many complex layers of reality lying between quarks and human emotions for Grant to have any interest in dismissing our everyday talk of moods as "folk psychology." Nor, in a Grantian intellectual universe, is there any straightforward way to reduce effects to their ultimate physical causes, given the number of things that could have unfolded differently at every causal layer. Grant is not a naturalist but a speculative philosopher of nature. Though he holds that everything emerges from a chain of natural production, there is no easy way to reverse this chain and ascend to initial explanatory causes so as to "eliminate" the more derivative layers such as those of so-called folk psychology.

Grant now raises the second major topic of his Goldsmiths talk, the one he discusses at length in his later co-authored book on idealism. One might expect Grant, as a Speculative Realist, to oppose any form of philosophical idealism. After all, "idealism" in philosophy has traditionally meant the view that the existence of the world is dependent on those who observe it, and this would surely spell doom for Grant's ambition to address nature directly. The solution to the paradox is simply that Grant gives a different meaning to idealism from the usual one. In fact, idealism in this new sense is something he cherishes: "I'm very concerned to show that idealism, as it were, doesn't look like we think it does. I'm very concerned that we see and acknowledge this to be the case, because the speculative tools that it has built into it are immense" (336). Grant sees idealism not as a doctrine about the non-existence of a world outside the mind but simply as a broader form of realism: "it seems to me that idealism is committed to a realism about all things, a realism that applies equally to nature and to the Idea" (338). Continuing the thought, he asks: "does this or does this not, as it seemed to at the turn of the nineteenth century [i.e. in Schelling's time], provide an exit from the strictures of Kantianism? Clearly, I think it does, and it does so by denying that interiority plays any role whatsoever" (339).

What is at stake in Grant's rejection of "interiority"? The easiest example of interiority can be seen in the belief that I am having a thought, and that therefore the thought belongs to me and is contained by me. Grant rejects this notion in favor of a model in which my production of thoughts is of the same type as nature's production of forces, species, animals, and flowers. There is no way to reduce any product – whether physical or mental – to what came before it, since, even if everything requires a cause, that cause is not sufficient to determine what shape its products later take:

> The Idea is external to the thought that has it, the thought is external to the thinker that has it, the thinker is external to the nature that produces both the thinker and thought and the Idea. There are a series of exteriorities between thinker, thought, Idea, the various strata of the nature necessary to produce that event – necessary but not sufficient, it should be stressed. (339)

One of the more stirring implications is that "we no longer have a series of interiorities within which it's possible for anyone to recognize themselves in the production of their thoughts. It's simply a banal accident that we know what it feels like to have thoughts. That is not particularly significant. What's significant is the thought" (340). There is some resonance here with Latour's metaphysics of translation, which lies at the basis of his widely deployed actor-network theory (ANT) and has provided inspiration for Object-Oriented Ontology as well.[6] Latour gives us a memorable and practical example: "when . . . a student of industry insists that there have been a multitude of transformations and mediations between the oil trapped deep in the geological seams of Saudi Arabia and the gas I put into the tank of my car from the old pump in the little village of Jaligny in France, the claim to reality of the gas is in no way decreased."[7] In the face of the traditional dispute between "correspondence" and "coherence" theories of truth, Latour offers an alternative "industrial" model. There is not some essential "form" existing in both the crude oil in Saudi Arabia and the gas in Jaligny, only a series of transformations at each step of the process. The difference, of course, is that Latour is a philosopher of science and technology who is concerned mainly with how *humans* do the transforming, while Grant is a philosopher of nature for whom humans are a relatively late stage in comparison with all the sub-human processes that precede us. Nonetheless, Grant is much closer to Latour than he is to someone such as Meillassoux, who holds that the mind can neatly extract mathematical forms from the world and thereby know the primary qualities of things. In Grant's own words: "there's a necessary asymmetry, if you like, between thought and what precedes it, and it's this asymmetry which means that thought is always different from what precedes it and always at the same time requires what precedes it as its necessary ground – necessary, but not sufficient" (343). For Grant, as for ANT and OOO, the intermediate stages of production or translation are much too numerous and too transformative to guarantee any sort of correspondence or identity between one stage and another. This is why Žižek correctly observes that Brassier and Meillassoux belong to the "scientific" wing of Speculative Realism, with Grant and OOO in opposition.

We spoke earlier about the difference between Grant's position and mainstream naturalism. He takes up the theme once again near the end of his Goldsmiths talk, when praising the spirit of *speculation* that is so often missing from mainstream naturalism: "I would like to make the claim that speculation is entailed by natural productivity" (343). By speculation, Grant means a type of thinking that explores the obscure gap lying between grounds and products, a gap that Kant finds himself unable to explore. Grant again: "We don't have . . . that comfort zone to slip back into, and to say to ourselves, 'Ah, look, we have recovered the totality of the conditions under which thought is possible, and *only* possible'" (343). Nor is the problem merely hypothetical, since it challenges our usual conception of the relation of thought and world. Grant continues: "[This] also means something very bizarre epistemically at a quite mundane level, at the level of reference. What is it that happens when we have thoughts about things? Two things happen: there are things and there are thoughts. What's the basis of their relation?" (344). It is not the thinker who bears the burden of the relation, since the thinker and her thoughts are produced by nature itself. In this respect it is the world that speaks in this relation, not we ourselves. For Grant, countless strata are interspersed between the world and the entity which thinks it. But again, for Grant (unlike most modern philosophers) there is nothing special about thought. In a passage that might well have come from one of the ecological works of Timothy Morton (b. 1968), Grant argues that "if nature thinks, then it follows that nature thinks just as nature 'mountains' or nature 'rivers' or nature 'planetizes,' or what have you. These things are the same to all intents and purposes. In other words, there are new products every time there are thoughts, which creates the problem of ground" (344).[8] We will encounter this problem of ground once more in Grant's book on Schelling, since it bears on his rejection of the priority that OOO grants to objects or entities, criticized by Grant under the name of "somatism."

Before ending this summary of Grant's rather streamlined talk at Goldsmiths, it is worth raising the question of his political views, since politics is paramount in the mind of so many readers these days. Late in the question period following his talk, Grant bucks the recent trend by citing some of the negative aspects of recent political materialism. As he puts it: "a *critical* materialism is *not* a materialism. Fundamentally, it's a materialism oriented, driven, steered, designed, by critique. In other words, it's a theory of matter held by people with some use for certain bits of it and none for others" (360). Though Grant's dig at "critique" obviously has Kant as one of its targets, at the workshop I also sensed some misgivings about Leftist critical theory. For this reason I tried to draw him out on his position towards Marxism, long a powerful presence in the intellectual life of the United Kingdom. Grant responded with an exuberant attack on this school:

> Love [Marxist materialism]! No, it's simply wrong. The idea that it's possible to invoke a diminished realm, as it were, for matter and to condemn whatever does not fulfill the economic, teleological purposes of certain types of agents to a sphere of "merely crude matter," where it has absolutely no effects whatsoever, where it's left to one side of the philosophical and the political problem, seems to me a recipe for political disaster. (360)

Grant shares this suspicion of the philosophical basis of Marxism with OOO, whereas Meillassoux expresses overt sympathies for Marx, and we have seen that Brassier – though his political philosophy has so far been expressed only in vague statements of allegiance or dismissal – speaks positively of "revolution" in at least one passage.[9] This difference is best explained not by some basic difference in political instinct (both Grant and OOO are somewhat left of center) but by what Žižek noted in his early remarks on SR: Brassier and Meillassoux's open embrace of rationalism, coupled with Grant and OOO's enduring suspicions about it.

Study Questions for Section A

1 What does Grant mean when he says he is interested in thought as *production*, not as *access*? What are the implications of this?
2 In what ways does Grant resemble philosophical naturalists, and in what ways does he differ from them?
3 Why is it so important for Grant to say that there are many different layers of nature that precede thought?
4 Grant tells us that there is a "series of exteriorities" between nature, thinker, thought, and idea. What are the philosophical implications?
5 Why does Grant think that *speculation* about nature is so important and necessary?
6 How does Grant's notion of "idealism" differ from the usual philosophical meaning of the term?

B Grant's *Philosophies of Nature After Schelling*

Grant's book on Schelling, originally published in 2006, is both an important work of German Idealism scholarship and the outline of an original philosophical program. Though Schelling is clearly the focus of the volume, Grant's reading of Schelling as a career-long philosopher of nature is possible only on the basis of novel interpretations of Kant, Fichte, and Hegel. Grant also reinterprets Plato by placing a large bet on the *Timaeus* as the key Platonic dialogue, a notion common many centuries ago but less so today. He also brings into the discussion a number of philosophers of nature who were rough contemporaries of Schelling and Hegel, such as the Norwegian-Danish thinker Henrik Steffens (1773–1845). Guiding the whole discussion is Grant's fondness for the works of Deleuze and Guattari, who seem to be his favorites among contemporary philosophers. For our purposes, it is not practicable to follow all of the important historical claims in Grant's book. We will focus instead on digging out his most important philosophical theses, like diamonds shoveled from the crater of a volcano.

Though the Speculative Realists are not quite as anti-Kantian as is sometimes said, all agree that Kant still defines the horizon of contemporary philosophy, and hence the one that must be overcome if a new era of philosophy is to emerge. Grant puts it somewhat depressingly in the opening chapter of his book: "postkantianism marks the horizon of contemporary philosophy exactly as it did in the nineteenth century."[10] It is post-Kantian "not merely in the historical sense of succeeding Kant, but philosophically, in that it is defined by the coordinates set by Kant for philosophical activity" (9). By excluding the thing-in-itself as a topic of direct investigation, Kant turns all questions of nature into questions of *science* as a type of human knowledge. Consider the second part of his *Critique of Judgment*, which in typical Kantian fashion abandons all hope of knowing whether nature has a purpose and converts this question into the narrower one of what humans can *know* about such purpose. While many contemporary readers are dazzled by the way in which German Idealism eliminated the thing-in-itself, Grant is openly appalled by what this did to the philosophical status of nature, other than in Schelling's case. For the most part, nature has been left to the natural sciences, while philosophy has been reduced to an increasingly narrow preoccupation with ethics, language, or intersubjective communication. While Hegel is often the target of choice for those who think German Idealism took the wrong fork in the road, Grant reserves his especial ire for Fichte. For this key post-Kantian thinker treated the "not-I" as something posited by the "I," and his ventures beyond the human realm stopped at animals without daring to enter the vegetable or inanimate realms.

This leads us to an important side issue concerning Grant's disappointment with contemporary philosophy, a disappointment that OOO shares. Too often, those contemporary philosophers who boldly claim to have escaped the walls of the human subject end up going no further than the concepts of "embodiment" or "life," while still leaving inorganic reality out of the picture. DeLanda has described this situation humorously by describing "the body" as "a kind of token material object, invited to ontology just to include at least one member of a minority."[11] Grant has a zinger of his own at the ready: "Life acts as a kind of Orphic guardian for philosophy's descent into the physical. This is because life provides an effective alibi against accusations of philosophy's tendency to 'antiphysics,' while centralizing ethico-political or existential problematics as philosophy's true domain" (10). This is what makes Schelling such a key figure for Grant, since Schelling argued that "the perimeter dividing organic from 'anorganic' nature be eliminated as naturalistically untenable and philosophically vicious, in order that organization become not an exception to a mechanistic natural order, but rather the *principle* of nature itself" (10).

From here Grant goes on to reject Badiou's false dichotomy of "number or animal," identified by Badiou with the difference between Plato and Aristotle. In linking nature with the animal, Badiou repeats what Grant regards as Fichte's primary mistake. Grant wishes to avoid the usual post-Kantian alibi of working on "animality," "embodiment," or the "organic," in favor of a place where "deep, geological time" (6) has an autonomous existence far from any human gaze, human practical-embodied handling, or even sheer animal behavior. The philosophy of nature, a discipline almost killed off by the success of the natural sciences, must be able to cover the inorganic and the organic by the same stroke; Grant holds this to be of crucial importance, since it is nature alone that enables us to break free from the still post-Kantian philosophical coordinates of our era. For Schelling, the point of philosophy is to carry us *beyond* the finite representations that Kant bequeathed as the ruins of human knowledge and which now infect "the bedrock of most phenomenological and all ethico-political philosophy, alongside the linguistic idealism that represents 'nature' as determined solely in and for language" (15). In view of these foul consequences, Grant urges that "an exposition of Schellingianism therefore entails the systematic undoing of [Kant's] critical revolution" (6).

Not everyone agrees with Grant about Schelling, and for at least two different reasons. Above all, we have seen that the orthodox reading of Schelling treats him as a philosopher who went through many distinct phases: the philosophy of nature is said to be the second of these phases, quickly overcome by the so-called philosophy of identity and philosophy of freedom that ensue. Throughout the book, Grant returns repeatedly to his claim that Schelling was *always* a philosopher of nature, thereby swimming against the current of scholarly consensus. Yet Grant's verdict is clear: "commentators' reluctance . . . to consider the naturephilosophy *core* to Schellingianism, rather than just a *phase*, vitiates any coherent conception of that philosophy . . . [and therefore] the periodizing tendency found in virtually every account of Schelling's philosophy is therefore at best misleading" (3). The other conflict results from the widespread tendency to go in the *opposite* direction from Grant's interpretation and find Schelling's main significance in ethics, politics, or "existential" themes. The main target here is Heidegger's contemporary Karl Jaspers (1883–1969), who, according to Grant, "provides the basic type of the frequently reiterated and erroneous proposition that naturephilosophy amounts to an extension of Kant's or Fichte's critical philosophies" (14). Nor are more recent examples hard to come by, as seen in Grant's critical reference to the translator Keith Peterson as holding that "[Schelling's] philosophy of nature is an explicitly ethical project" (61). *Au contraire*, says Grant: "Schelling is not extending but undoing Kant" (61). And whereas Jaspers faults Schelling for having no followers and having generated no movement or school, Grant contends that, in fact, *everyone* is a follower of Schelling, or at least everyone who is on a worthy philosophical mission: "Schellingianism is resurgent every time philosophy reaches beyond the Kant-inspired critique of metaphysics, its subjectivist-epistemological transcendentalism, and its isolation of physics from metaphysics" (5; emphasis removed). Until this resurgence prevails, we will be trapped in the endless reign of practical reason and the prioritizing of language found in Heidegger and others: "naturephilosophy accordingly rejects . . . the logico-linguistic or phenomenal determination of nature [and] rejects the primacy of the practical" (19).

A careless reader might glance at Grant's opening pages and assume that he argues for placing philosophy entirely in the hands of science. After all, he quotes Schelling as saying that nature itself is prior to everything that the human species has *thought* about nature, and he clearly approves of "Schelling's hypothesis . . . that there is a naturalistic or physicalist ground of philosophy" (2). Yet, as we will soon see, Grant views nature as a disembodied personal force, not as a realm of discrete individual things in the manner of science (or of OOO, though in a different manner). For he agrees with Schelling that naturephilosophy should waste no time "in the 'pitiful, mundane occupation' of 'apply[ing] philosophy to natural science'" (11). Grant goes on to express his contempt for the advice from Karl

Popper (1902–1994) that "philosophical interventions in nature [should be reduced] to a theoretical resource to be raided as and when the natural sciences deem it necessary, stripping the usable core of naturephilosophy from the 'neomedievalizing obscurantism' of its metaphysics" (11). Grant upholds the rights of metaphysical speculation against any claim that, unlike contemporary naturalism and full-blown scientism, it ought to be the handmaid of contemporary scientific disciplines. In fact, Grant wants to treat nature not just as a bodiless primal force swelling up into everything visible but as a *subject* rather than a gigantic object. This would be additional grounds for most practicing scientists to expel him from the ranks of respectable thinkers. Of course, nature for Grant is not a subject in any familiar sense of this term: rather, "the unconditioned I has a nature which, rather than empirical consciousness, corresponds to the self-acting of a *subjectnature* [or *subjectobject*]" (16), a notion he traces as far back as Plotinus. On the basis of this deeply impersonal sense of the subject, Grant denies his position is vulnerable to "the general clichés surrounding Idealism: that it *anthropomorphizes* nature, or that it consists solely in the determination of nature by intellect" (16).

This brings us to two important issues that will resurface when we consider Grant's surprising interpretations of Plato and Aristotle. The first is his hostility to treating nature as a sum of the actions of individual bodies – a doctrine he calls "somatism," after the Greek word *soma* (body). In particular, he rejects Heidegger's "determination of nature in terms of '*beings* as a whole'" (7), along with Kant's similar definition of nature as "the sum total of all things" (7). More interesting for Grant, as for his contemporary hero Deleuze, is the idea of nature as a productive force that generates individual bodies as a derivative byproduct. The process of individuation – just as for Deleuze's intellectual cousin Gilbert Simondon (1924–1989) – is more interesting for Grant than already fully formed individuals.[12] He puts this in a fine phrase: "the philosophy of nature itself . . . is no longer grounded in [the properties or accidents of bodies], but in the dynamics from which all ground, and all bodies, issue" (8). The second important issue to consider is the way Grant drives a wedge between Kant and Plato, though both are usually viewed as "two-worlds" thinkers, despite Kant's focus on the phenomena and Plato's opposite focus on what Kant would call a noumenal world of perfect forms. Grant does this by turning to Plato's *Timaeus*, whose cosmology fascinated ancient and medieval readers, but whose stock fell in modernity after the rise of mathematical physics, though the dialogue has made a comeback recently through the attention of Jacques Derrida (1930–2004) and his students. As Grant notes, "Schelling's naturephilosophy begins with a study of the one-world physics presented in Plato's *Timaeus*, set against the background of problems from Kant's critical philosophy" (10). Whereas orthodox readings of Plato see the *eidos* of each thing as a perfect form – the perfect horse, color white, justice, or virtue – that is copied by all the imperfect examples we see in the material world, Grant reads the *eidos* as being a natural cause of each thing, one that does not "resemble" its products in the least. This is what Grant means when he reads Plato's philosophy in terms of a "one-world physics" rather than the two-world metaphysics of perfect forms and imperfect copies that one normally finds in the textbooks. This leads him to make common cause, albeit briefly, with Badiou's rejection of the perpetual "overcomings of Platonism" that have long been a stock figure of postmodernism: "we accept Badiou's counter-Deleuzian view that philosophy ought to have done with overturning Platonism (although not for the same reasons), and must reject Kantianism in its stead . . ." (8). This may be the only time that Grant ever sides with Badiou against Deleuze on any philosophical issue, and even here he thinks that Badiou misses the real point of Platonism. Whereas Badiou's Plato is a mathematician who guides us towards formalization as the true path of philosophy, Grant's Plato is a champion of nature (*physis*), a domain that plays no significant role in Badiou's system at all.

We turn now to the question that proves so central to Grant's divergence from OOO, despite our agreement on many other points: how does nature relate to the numerous individual beings that seem to exist in the world? The relation between the One and the Many is, of course, one of the most important themes in Ancient Greek philosophy. For Parmenides, Being is essentially One if we follow reason, while the numerous different beings merely belong to the realm of opinion (*doxa*). For those pre-Socratic thinkers who defend the parallel notion of a formless, boundless *apeiron* that precedes all individual beings, it is simply a matter of giving a causal account of how this *apeiron* was originally broken up into individual things. Anaximander (c. 610–546 BCE), who came first among them, held that justice would eventually destroy all opposites, with a final *apeiron* being the result of this strife. Pythagoras (c. 570–500 BCE) and Anaxagoras (c. 510–428 BCE) both saw the *apeiron* as existing in the past before some catastrophic event created a multiplicity in the being: for Pythagoras because the *apeiron* inhaled void or vacuum from its surroundings, and for Anaxagoras because a powerful mind (*nous*) caused the *apeiron* to rotate so quickly that vibrations broke it up into the countless individual things we see today. We are right to expect that Grant, a twenty-first-century man, will offer no such creation myth as an account of the passage from unified nature to the many individual beings. Nonetheless, he continues to downplay such individual beings. Anyone who follows OOO in placing discrete objects at the center of philosophy will soon reach the purported dead end of what Grant calls "somatism." But still, as Brassier asked at Goldsmiths, how does Grant aim to account for the passage from the One to the Many?

The main technical term Grant uses to account for this passage is "retardation." Nature is a force somehow retarded or blocked in its flow, thereby giving rise to what we think of as individual objects (apparently including our individual selves). This term first appears later in the book, when Grant describes *two* forces at work in Schelling's philosophy of nature: "[the] first force is the 'principle of all motion,' while the second or negative force *retards* the first, [and] their necessary union slows infinite becoming to the point of phenomenal production" (143). In other words, if not for the second or "retarding" force, nature would be nothing more than a splurge of infinite becoming, lacking in any of the individual selves, perceptions, objects, or events that normally seem to populate the cosmos. But since both forces are ubiquitous, Grant holds that the two extremes of pure becoming and pure retardation are never reached. There is a further interesting dualism at work in Schelling, and apparently in Grant as well: along with the infinite becoming that accounts for half of every entity (its retarding side provides the other), there are also the forces that "perpetuate the wholesale transformation of phenomena" (145). The basic "cell" where these forces are found is the world-soul, one of the most familiar concepts of Neo-Platonism: "The world-soul, the primary diversifying antithesis in the [sequence of levels] of nature, is so-called precisely because, while not *being* body, it is nonetheless matter; it is the 'darkest of all things' precisely insofar as it generates phenomenality" (145). With this appeal to matter as the dynamic home of all oppositions, Grant – like Schelling himself – comes into proximity with the thought of the colorful Italian thinker Giordano Bruno (1548–1600) – the most comical of philosophers, though ultimately crushed by the most tragic of fates, when burned at the stake in Rome after a decade of imprisonment and torture. As for Schelling, rather than speaking – like Plotinus – of an "emanation" or – like Nicholas of Cusa (1401–1464) – of a "contraction" from infinite force down to more local, retarded ones, he speaks in terms of "decomposition." Schelling's work "moves from the decomposition of infinite forces as matters, followed by the further decomposition of matters into the varieties of matter – calorific, gaseous, electrical, magnetic, organic, and so on" (148). It is a "serial decomposition that is never finished" (148). For Grant as for Schelling, infinite productivity comes first: all individual *products* are phenomenal; conversely, everything phenomenal is only a product and cannot be identified with productivity itself. Each individual product counts as a "recapitulation" of identity. Returning to Nicholas of Cusa's language, Grant reports that "there are . . . identities wherever there are products. We may therefore define identity as the contraction or retardation of the infinite in the finite, or productivity in the product" (175). Sounding somewhat like Deleuze, Grant adds that we should speak not of static oppositions but of "antithetical '*trajectories*' across the absolute, which is by definition open territory since if it had boundaries and limits, it would not be absolute, but relative to those limits" (173).

How successful is Grant's solution to the old dilemma of the One and the Many? Given that I am a OOO theorist who takes individual objects to be the starting point of philosophy, it will come as no surprise that I think Grant proceeds in the wrong order. As we will see, he criticizes both Kant and Aristotle for sharing at least three separate failings: phenomenalism, logicism, and somatism. On the first two points I am in agreement with Grant philosophically, if not with his reading of Aristotle. If we commit ourselves ardently to "phenomenalism," to the view that appearances are what primarily exist, then we are condemned to end up in a position like Berkeley's (though we will see that Grant reads Berkeley differently), in which it makes no sense to speak of anything other than appearance. Or perhaps we will fall into a more watered-down idealism such as Hegel's, which tries to implode the phenomena/noumena distinction entirely into the side of accessible phenomena. Event Kant's philosophy, though it provides some room for realism by conceding the existence of the thing-in-itself, leaves us with such sparse opportunities to discuss that thing-in-itself that "phenomenalism" is almost as fair a description of Kant as it is of Berkeley. Yet we should also note that Grant has a somewhat ambiguous relation to the thing-in-itself; I emphasize the singular here, since Grant could never allow for a multitude of *things*-in-themselves. In one sense he celebrates Schelling's overleaping of Kantian finitude since, after all, he agrees with Schelling that philosophy is supposed to allow us to escape the finite boundedness of everyday experience. Nonetheless, Grant is also no rationalist like Meillassoux, who thinks that by mathematical means we can reach the primary qualities of things as they really are. Instead, in Grant's matter there is darkness and in his world-soul there is darkness too. Furthermore, given that thought is just a *Scheinprodukt* (phenomenal product), it cannot hope to gain a direct vision of the unconditioned and infinite productivity that both bubbles in the heart of every entity and stands beyond all entities in order to guide all bubbling from beyond.

For the same reason it is easy to understand Grant's opposition to logicism, the notion that reality can be adequately captured in logic or language. For these too are phenomenal products, incapable of digging as deep as the place where the world-soul can be found. Though Schelling is able to tell us a few things about that powerful cosmic psyche, how could we ever fathom the depths of what the world-soul conceals in its heart? *Physis* or nature is where the action is for Grant, and both thought and human individuality more generally are products of nature rather than constituents of it, despite a few stray passages where Schelling speaks so highly of human beings that *medicine* is treated as the crown jewel of the sciences.

I find it harder to understand Grant's opposition to somatism and suspect that this comes from his partiality to Deleuze's notion of "sterile surface-effects" opposed to a virtual power residing in the depths. The obvious advantage of positing a deeper unified force behind all individual things is that, from here, it is possible to reach a more interesting model of how things interrelate with each other: through descent from a common origin rather than through the everyday causation mocked by some philosophers as "clunk causality." Yet Grant pays a high price for going along with Schelling's monistic conception of nature. Given that any notion of onefold Nature so obviously contradicts our experience of a multitude of things, and given the obvious inadequacy of Parmenides' dualism between reason (which tells us that all is One) and mere opinion (which falsely tells us that the world is Many), Grant is left with no other option than a "physical" explanation of how individuals arise. The primary productive force must be opposed by a second, retarding one in order to give rise to the individuals we encounter. But given that the primary force is the same everywhere, this places the entire burden of individuality on the back of retardation. Why should there be different retarding forces in different parts of the cosmos, giving rise here to a star, here to a statue of the Buddha, there to a raucous German drinking song, here to a lonely proton, and over there to a Franciscan monastery? And if this diversity of retarding forces needs to be assumed as belonging to the cosmos in advance, then no ontological parsimony has been gained, and one might as well have accepted the existence of individual objects in the first place. We will return to this dispute soon enough. For now, we turn to Grant's unconventional readings of Plato and Aristotle.

The recent wave of interest in Plato's *Timaeus* among contemporary continental philosophers should not obscure the many centuries during which this dialogue was out of fashion, no doubt because the theory of nature it presents looks primitive and even a bit crazy by comparison with modern European physics. This makes Schelling, and even Grant, somewhat unusual for their respective eras. However, "by singling out the *Timaeus* for a commentary, Schelling joins company with the ancient and pre-Thomist traditions of commentator-philosophers for whom Platonism as a whole simply was 'the theory of the universe presented in the *Timaeus*'" (26). Grant complains that even most contemporary readers of this dialogue "continue to present the *Timaeus* as an ethico-political allegory . . ."

(28). Even Schelling's own commentary leaves Grant exasperated, since it "remains unable to resolve the problems stemming from the Aristotelian settlement that Kant inherited" (29). And still worse, "excruciatingly, the commentary ends by conceding everything . . . [since] its concluding sentence repeats the isolation of physics from metaphysics – and thus of matter from the Idea – that are the hallmarks of Aristotle's critique of Platonism . . ." (29–30). In some measure, therefore, Grant pushes the case for the *Timaeus* even further than Schelling was inclined to do.

Yet by no means does Grant merely follow Plato at Schelling's expense: he quotes a key passage from Schelling that scolds Plato mildly for having such contempt for the visible world that he was unable to grasp "the *form* of the world, its conformity to rule and to law, as *inherent* in matter, or even as *emergent* from matter" (cited 36). Indeed, Grant sees the Platonic ideas as inherent in matter rather than as otherworldly perfections alien to a matter regarded as worldly and therefore base. This is reminiscent not only of Bruno but also of Plotinus, whose "argument for Ideal matter shares with Schelling a rejection of the somaticist grounds of Aristotle's dismissal of the substantiality of the Ideas" (36). It is true, however, that Schelling gives matter a much higher status than does Plotinus, as when the former tells us that "the absolute must be thought purely as matter" (cited 28) and – in Brunonian fashion – that "matter is the general seed of the universe, in which is concealed everything that evolves in later developments" (cited 26).

Another idea of Bruno that wins favor from both Schelling and Grant is the notion that being is simply *power* (28), an idea for which Grant finds additional support in a prominent scientist from the generation after Schelling: "[matter] is *dynamically* conceived as *consisting only* in actions: 'the substance is composed of its powers,' as [Michael] Faraday [1791–1867] put it" (39). Dynamism is among the watchwords of both Schelling and Grant, and in Plato they find a strong ally: "the Platonic Idea of matter itself exerts dynamizing pressures on the Kantian categorical framework" (38). Although there is some ambiguity in Schelling's work as to the priority of production over product, Grant eventually concludes in favor of this principle: "production is what causes being to become" (43). This dynamicist reading of Plato obviously excludes the usual view of how the perfect forms interact with the material world: "the infamous Platonic 'copy' is not a mechanical reproduction" (43). Contrary to "the reciprocal exclusion of the Idea and [nature] that forms the cross by which Aristotle segregates metaphysics from physics" (33), Plato's Idea has everything to do with physics. It is a principle of production, generation, or emergence. An individual horse does not "resemble" the Idea of a horse: "the kind cannot present a *copy* of the Idea, because the Idea has no correlate in nature . . .

The being of the Idea must be conceived in terms that do not invite phenomenal correspondence with natural becomings" (46–7). This leads Grant to formulations that sound a lot like DeLanda's interpretation of Deleuze, as when Grant speaks of the Platonic kind as "a phase space of the Idea in unlimited not-being, that is, the always-becoming, where the Idea acts as the limit-attractor toward which being never ceases to become . . ." (45). A phase space is the totality of possible states that a system can occupy in view of its constraints: for example, if you have three lights in your kitchen, there are eight possible states of these lights in phase space: on–on–on, on–on–off, on–off–on, on–off–off, off–on–on, off–on–off, off–off–on, and off–off–off. In the case of a horse, or justice, or any other Platonic Idea, to view it as a phase space is to treat it as the leeway for a vast number of possible individual incarnations of that Idea. A limit-attractor is a point around which all the individual states of system revolve in phase space. One example is that certain weather graphs show all the actual states of the weather orbiting another state that is never actually reached. There is also the simple case of a marble rolling around a bathroom sink: all of its individual states are guided by the drain at the bottom as their ultimate destination. But even in this case, where the marble finally seems to reach the drain in the end, mathematically considered it never reaches the drain exactly but continues to vibrate around it once it reaches that final point.[13] In any case, all of this dynamism discovered behind philosophical concepts entails, for Grant as for Schelling, that philosophy amounts to "a natural history of our minds" (45), though a far stranger history than would be accepted in cognitive science. It also follows that discussions of what is *a priori* in reality do not have to do with human judgments, as is the case with Kant. Rather, the *a priori* has to do with nature itself rather than our representations of it. Heidegger made a similar point when crediting his teacher Husserl with revising the sense of the *a priori* to mean that which is *a priori* in Being rather than in the mind, with the obvious difference that Heidegger speaks of Being rather than Nature (49).[14]

This is a good moment to turn to Grant's interpretation of Aristotle, which can be described as highly unfavorable. Among other problems: "the damage done to Platonic physics by its flawed analyses in Aristotle's *Metaphysics* is inestimable . . ." (30). More generally, there is the old and apparently well-understood Platonic theme of the "participation" in the forms by material beings, a theme that Grant rereads and turns against Aristotle's more mainstream account of Plato's theory: "Aristotle does not treat the vexed problem of the 'participation' of the Ideas in nature as a problem regarding the physics of the Idea, but considers it merely as . . . lifted from the old Pythagorean problem of the 'imitation' of numbers by sensible things" (32). Grant even holds that Aristotle links Plato with the wrong group of pre-Socratic thinkers, whom he famously – and accurately – divides in the *Metaphysics* into those who think the world is made up of one or more primordial elements (water, air, air/earth/fire/water, or atoms) and those who think these are too specific and therefore appeal to an undivided and limitless *apeiron*, which is an inarticulate or barely articulated blob-like mass. Though Aristotle links Plato with the *apeiron* theorists, Grant instead puts him in the same basket as the atomists, given the strictly physical–causal–natural function he ascribes to the ideas.

Grant interprets Aristotle's own teachings in equally unorthodox ways. This begins with his suspicion of the way that Aristotle categorizes the two kinds of pre-Socratics just mentioned: "it is as if Aristotle sees only two options, not merely for Platonic physics, but for physics itself: whether one all-enveloping body or substrate, or a multiplicity of all-pervading bodies, physics is and remains nothing other than the science of body" (31). We have seen that Aristotle and Kant, two philosophers not often paired by historians, count for Grant as equally guilty of pursuing individual body-oriented philosophy: "the somatism, in other words, [that was] enshrined for Schelling's contemporaries in Kant's mechanistic restriction of natural science to 'the doctrine of body alone' merely reiterates Aristotle's segregation of 'first philosophy' (the science of being *qua* being) from 'physics or secondary philosophy'" (31). Now, even if there is a way in which Aristotle and Kant might be called "somatists," it is hardly obvious that they are somatists in the same way. For Aristotle, "somatism" would refer to his theory of concrete individual things, which under nearly every interpretation of Aristotle are real entities existing independently and in the plural outside the human mind. But for Kant, of course, we can make no firm statement of the nature of entities in the outside world and are not even entitled to assert in the plural that the thing-in-itself is actually *things*-in-themselves, given that "unity" and "plurality" for Kant are just categories of the understanding rather than a way to describe how the world really is apart from us.

This factor alone makes for considerable difficulty in claiming that Aristotle and Kant are philosophical brothers in any significant way. But Grant presses the case boldly, even if not always convincingly. He does so by arguing that Aristotle is guilty not just of "somatism" – even Aristotle's fans would concede his focus on individual things rather than disembodied Platonic–Schellingian–Deleuzian–Grantian becomings and intensities – but of phenomenalism and logicism as well. Here is one especially relevant passage from Grant's book: "Aristotelian physics, as an empirical morphology or *phenomenology*, extracts matter from nature, while metaphysics further supplants matter with form, and reduces 'substantial being' [*ousia*] to the merely predicable subject insofar as this is predicable alone" (34). For this reader at least, these words from Grant go at least two bridges too far. Admittedly, there is no question that Aristotle downplays matter in a way that drives Bruno and other later thinkers crazy, Grant himself among them. It is true that form does the hard labor for Aristotle, with matter playing at best a minimal role in situations such as "the generation of plants and animals" (34). Yet from this it does not follow that Aristotle is left with nothing but "empirical" or "phenomenal" forms. Grant is forgetting the existence of *substantial* forms, the bread and butter of Aristotle's followers for millennia after his death – forms actively at work in entities themselves, making them what they are, and *not* identifiable with any sensibly accessible forms. For this very reason, we also cannot accept Grant's additional claim that forms for Aristotle are nothing more than the correlate of rational linguistic statements, as when he says that "Aristotelian metaphysics is that science concerned with substance not insofar as this is particular, sensible or material, but insofar as it is a *predicable essence*, i.e. only insofar as it is the subject . . . supporting a *logos*" (34). One of the key Aristotelian passages *against* such a claim comes in the *Metaphysics*, when he tells us that individual things cannot be defined, since definitions are formed from universals while individual things are always concrete.[15] Grant quotes a similar passage from Aristotle, though one in which the philosopher takes the opposite tack of saying that substances cannot be defined because they contain *matter*, which is impenetrable to reason. For Grant this counts as yet another denigration of matter by Aristotle. The issue preoccupies Grant so greatly that he misses the other passage just quoted, which makes it clear that substances are incommensurable with any sort of logical or linguistic statement about them.

Though I have made some objections to Grant's book from a OOO stand-point, *Philosophies of Nature After Schelling* gives the outline of a fascinating speculative philosophy. I cannot endorse the blame that Grant heaps on Aristotle for the gradual disappearance of nature from modern philosophy – a rather counterintuitive claim, given Aristotle's diligence and insight in studying natural phenomena, especially in biology. But Grant is certainly right to point to the minimal role of nature in most modern philosophy, and he is also right to disdain the endless alibis produced by mainstream transcendental philosophers to pretend they are advancing boldly into the non-human realm by speaking of "life," "the organic," or "embodiment." His condemnation of the "separation of the Idea from nature" (52) is inspiring, as is his reading of the Platonic Ideas in natural or physical terms. This remains the case even if his heavy reliance on the *Timaeus* leaves too little room for the traditional function of the Ideas as being exemplified in numerous earthly beings. Also of interest is his distinction between at least two different levels of nature. While mainstream naturalist philosophy reveres the same nature pursued by the empirical sciences, Grant is on the hunt for a deeper *virtual* nature, a nature of attractors and phase spaces. He follows Schelling in calling it a "progressive" nature (49) that evolves along all possible paths (52). Though Grant affirms the notion that philosophy should provide us with a natural history of thought, this is not the natural history of mainstream science, but one that sounds like something cooked up by Deleuze and Guattari in 1970s Paris. To close with Grant's own words: "natural history consists in maps of becoming that exceed phenomenal or sensible nature both in the direction of time and in that of the physiology of the senses" (55). We will now have a chance to examine Grant's more detailed application of these ideas to the history of Western philosophy.

Study Questions for Section B

1 What objections does Grant have to the continuing influence of the German Idealist philosopher J. G. Fichte?
2 Explain why Grant is suspicious of the many contemporary philosophers who focus on "life" or "the body."
3 What are Grant's objections to the "phenomenalism," "logicism," and "somatism" he finds in the philosophies of Aristotle and Kant?
4 What does Grant mean by the concept of "retardation"? What are some possible problems with this notion?
5 What does it mean to say that Grant reads Plato's philosophy not as a "two-world ontology" but, rather, as a "one-world physics"?
6 It is safe to say that Grant's interpretation of Aristotle is rather unorthodox. What sorts of objections might an Aristotelian make to Grant's reading? How might Grant respond?

C A New Sense of Idealism

In 2011 Grant published *Idealism: The History of a Philosophy*, a book co-authored with his talented former students Jeremy Dunham and Sean Watson; in what follows I will use the abbreviation DGW as a shorthand for the three authors' names. The multiple authorship of the book raises the general question of whether every contributor in a co-authored piece should be held responsible for every statement it includes. Anyone who has attempted co-authorship is aware of the following features of the process: (1) generally speaking, no one engages in joint authorship without a broad basis for agreement with the other writers working on the project; (2) there are usually moments of compromise where any given author lets certain claims stand despite disagreement, simply because they are not important enough to be worth fighting over. For example, Levi Bryant, Nick Srnicek, and I wrote the editors' introduction to the anthology *The Speculative Turn* (2011). If memory serves, there were two points made by Srnicek with which Bryant and I disagreed and one point to which I specifically objected; none seemed worth a quarrel, and Srnicek got his way in every case.[16] There were no doubt other points on which Srnicek held his tongue and let me or Bryant write things with which he disagreed, simply for diplomacy's sake. In cases where authors or editors have an especially strong disagreement on some important point, the custom is to specify this up front. We note that there is no such disclaimer in the opening pages of the DGW *Idealism* book. And furthermore, the volume contains nothing that contradicts the points made in Grant's *Philosophies of Nature After Schelling*. I would even go further and say that *Idealism* reads very much like the logical outcome of the Grantian philosophical program when applied to the history of Western philosophy.

Nonetheless, though *Idealism* is a feast of a book for any open-minded reader with serious philosophical interests, it has a "neither fish nor fowl" quality that makes it difficult to classify. Although its ostensible topic is idealism, its chapters are broken up survey-style into the proper names of individuals rather than into various structural features of idealism. This gives the book a markedly continental feel despite its obviously competent handling of several analytic philosophers. It also delves regularly into aspects of the various philosophers' systems that have no obvious connection with idealism, which sometimes makes it feel more like a general history of philosophy. Yet that is not quite right either, since a number of major Western philosophers have no chapter of their own and are barely mentioned, presumably because they are not "idealist" enough to fall under the book's stated purview. Aristotle, generally a villain in Grant's view of the history of our discipline, is not covered in any chapter. Neither is any medieval thinker, whether Christian, Jewish, or Muslim; chapter 2 covers "Plato and Neo-Platonism," while chapter 3 jumps straight to "Descartes and Malebranche" in the 1600s. Somewhat surprisingly for someone as Deleuzean in spirit as Grant, there are no chapters on favorite Deleuze forerunners such as Spinoza, Hume, and Bergson. All of this is just to observe that the book falls somewhere between a topical survey of idealism and the extensive summary of major figures that we find in all continental and many analytic histories of the discipline. Despite the mixed genre it represents, *Idealism* succeeds in keeping the reader's interest throughout. It also contains several bonus features difficult to find elsewhere. Foremost among these is a 63-page account of British Idealism, focusing on T. H. Green (1836–1882), F. H. Bradley (1846–1924), James Ward (1843–1925), J. M. E. McTaggart (1866–1925), and Bernard Bosanquet (1848–1923), as well as the more widely admired major thinker who arrived in the wake of them all: Alfred North Whitehead. Given the relative obscurity into which all but Whitehead have fallen after the rise in Britain of the early analytic philosophers Bertrand Russell (1872–1970) and G. E. Moore (1873–1958), these pages alone are worth the price of the book.

But the final two chapters may prove of even greater interest to other readers, since here DGW show themselves to be not only erudite historians of philosophy but also – rare combination – alert observers of contemporary trends in science and philosophy. Chapter 14 considers works on autopoiesis and self-organization in the biological sciences, focusing first on the joint work of the Chilean immunologists Humberto Maturana (b. 1928) and Francisco Varela (1946–2001), and then on the American complex systems theorist Stuart Kauffman (b. 1939). Chapter 15 casts an even wider net in discussing the idealisms – in DGW's sense of the term – still present in contemporary philosophy. First come the influential Pittsburgh Hegelians John McDowell (b. 1942) and Robert Brandom (b. 1950), both dominant figures in recent analytic thought. There follows a long but interesting discussion of a trio of more adventurously speculative philosophers: John A. Leslie of Canada (b. 1940), the late British thinker Timothy Sprigge (1932–2007), and the astoundingly prolific Nicolas Rescher (b. 1928), the German-born Pittsburgh colleague of McDowell and Brandom. The book closes with brief but informative discussions of Deleuze, Žižek, and the two rival Hegel interpreters who polarized French reception of the great German thinker: the Russian emigré Alexandre Kojève (1902–1968) and the French academic Jean Hyppolite (1907–1968).

When writing positively about an unpopular philosophical doctrine, one useful strategy is to begin by showing that it has already had more defenders than one might think. David Skrbina's fine book *Panpsychism in the West* does this for the initially shocking view that everything has some degree of mind, and DGW follow a similar strategy in *Idealism*, arguing for the ubiquity of this less discredited but still widely unloved philosophical position.[17] In order to do so, however, DGW need to restrict and redefine what is meant by idealism, and what emerges is an unexpected portrait of the idealist landscape throughout the ages. For the average reader – myself included – idealism means a form of phenomenalism in which nothing exists behind the appearances of things. For that same average reader – myself again included – the showcase idealist philosopher is therefore Berkeley, so famous for his phrase *esse est percipi*: "to be is to be perceived." DGW's response to this standard picture of idealism is threefold, and it is worth considering each aspect of their response in detail.

Above all, DGW claim that phenomenalism is not the most interesting or useful meaning of idealism. They complain that "six out of eight contemporary dictionaries we consulted presented idealism as the theory that reality is mind-dependent" (4). As they see it, this implies that idealism is motivated by skepticism, when in their view it is actually motivated by the urge for "systematic completeness" (4), which means that ideas ought to be included in our conception of reality along with metal, rocks, and wood. If it turns out that, say, panpsychism is true, then this thesis of universal mindedness would simply expand our conception of reality rather than corrode it. Just as we saw in Grant's Schelling book, the two-world ontology that is usually ascribed to Plato assumes that thought and what lies outside thought (the perfect forms, in his case) are so utterly different in kind that serious philosophy has no choice but to orbit around this distinction. But once we treat thought as just another reality, as DGW do, we have something completely different from the typical understanding of Plato: namely, "we arrive at a conception not of the two-worlds idealism beloved of interpretations of Plato, but of a one-world inflationary idealism. The world of change, birth, and decay is a not a world causally isolated from that of the Ideas, since, as the *Phaedo*, for instance, makes clear, the Idea has as its nature to be causal in respect of its becomings" (6). This fondness for the causal power of Platonic Ideas makes DGW a natural match for the often neglected Neo-Platonists, who read Plato in precisely this way. It also allows DGW to avoid the usual nominalist critique of the Platonic Ideas, a critique that presupposes the mainstream reading of Plato as holding that the Ideas or forms are otherworldly perfections copied by degenerate earthly beings. As DGW put it: "there is no 'red in itself,' such critics hold, but only red things. How could anyone argue that universals are *more* real than the world of particulars, and that they occupy a separate and eternal realm?" (7). Instead, DGW reintroduce the Neo-Platonic version of the problem, emphasizing "the One that is the source of all things, with matter as its lowest ebb of productivity; the One whose power is augmented by production, while its productions lack sufficient power to return to it. These Platonists share a commitment to the causal dimension of the Idea, integrating it into the world as its immanent reason for being what it is . . ." (7). More generally, DGW close their Introduction to the book with a threefold idealist platform distinguishing them from many other so-called idealists:

"*first*, that the Idea is causal in terms of organization; second, that this is an organization that is not formal or abstract in the separable sense, but rather concretely relates part to whole as the whole; and third, therefore that such an idealism is a *one-world* idealism that must, accordingly, take nature seriously" (8). When idealism is redefined in such a way, it is not incompatible with the platform of Speculative Realism as introduced at the Goldsmiths workshop. For this reason, Grant's involvement in a book called *Idealism* that praises that ostensibly anti-realist trend does not entail a secession from Speculative Realism. This does not mean, however, that DGW's decision to define idealism in this way ought to be emulated. More on this issue shortly.

A second reason for DGW downplaying the usual "phenomenalist" sense of idealism is that they wish to deny that anyone was ever a phenomenalist in the first place. We will see momentarily that they do not even regard Berkeley, usually the textbook idealist philosopher, as an idealist in the usual sense; later in the book they will even call him a "*common-sense realist* who follows this common-sense realism as far as it will go" (203). Yet even if we play along with this controversial reading of Berkeley for a moment, DGW still seem mildly conflicted about whether anyone is guilty of denying the existence of reality. For instance, they assert that even among the German Idealists (who were idealists, after all), "only Fichte [rejected] any form of naturalism as philosophically important" (3). This rather understates DGW's view of the degree of mischief Fichte inflicted on all honest realism, given the Fichtean ethico-practical dogma they see lurking in such later thinkers as Marx (105) and Žižek (295), and their complaint that "contemporary idealisms tend overwhelmingly to leave nature behind" (8–9). Despite these counterexamples, DGW assert in their Introduction: "philosophers committed to the mind-dependent existence of entities cannot maintain, it is held, the existence of a physical reality. We know of *no idealist* for whom this is true" (5; emphasis added). But DGW face a tall order in their claim that Berkeley or even Fichte upholds the existence of a physical reality in any meaningful sense, and even in our own time Žižek can fairly be said to deny the existence of a physical realm in the absence of any human subject. DGW's justification for saying that even apparent idealisms often do not deny the physical world is as follows: "Kant's transcendental idealism, for instance, is premised on Newtonianism having the nature of the physical universe fundamentally right . . ." (5). But this is to conflate nature itself with the *science* of nature, a distinction that Grant is normally so careful to preserve in his work. Viewed from a Kantian standpoint, Newton's *Principia* obviously cannot leap beyond the categories and pure intuitions that structure human experience and reach the thing-in-itself. Among other difficulties, Newton requires the concept of cause and effect to make his great treatise work, though Kant cannot permit this concept to be applied beyond the subjective sphere. More than this, Newton is one of the staunchest advocates of an absolute space and time existing as empty containers outside our minds, which is one of the least Kantian ideas that can be imagined. Kant leaves plenty of room in his work for science as a science of *a priori appearances*, but no room at all for a Schelling–Grant-type speculation on nature itself.

Third and finally, DGW make the surprising claim that Berkeley was never an idealist, but always a realist. Though they try to present this as a relatively straightforward and commonsensical claim, it amounts to a radical rereading both of Berkeley's significance and of the very meaning of realism. They try to argue that Berkeley was attempting to attack not reality *per se*, but only the atomistic or corpuscular view of nature. As they put it: "Berkeley was disputing the adequacy of mechanistic materialism not only as an explanatory model, but as an ontology. Now the claim is often made that this amounts to being anti-science, and yet it is clearly not so. Rather, Berkeley opposes a particular scientific account in explaining things" (5). Leaving this point aside for the moment, let's turn to the other centerpiece of DGW's revisionist reading of Berkeley: the claim that idealism is really just another form of realism. This theme is aired early in the Introduction, when DGW argue that "to call Berkeley an anti-realist is therefore to beg the question concerning the character of reality." In their Introduction alone, there are at least three other passing remarks in which the "idealism is just a different kind of realism" argument can be found. Number one: "the idealist, rather than being anti-realist, is in fact additionally a realist concerning elements more usually dismissed from reality . . . Idealism, that is, is not anti-realist, but realist precisely about the existence of Ideas" (4). Number two: "idealism is the sole philosophical means by which to arrive at an adequate theory of matter in so far as this must involve an explanation of the existence of all phenomena, including the Ideas about which idealists are realists" (6). And number three: "to be a realist concerning Ideas entails having a theory of what they are" (7). We will deal with this argument shortly as well.

Before proceeding to OOO's critique of each of these three points, let's consider one important matter on which we would surely agree. Namely, DGW proclaim that one of their motives (though not the only one, they insist) for embracing idealism is as a way of overcoming today's predominant naturalism; here I embrace their motive, if not their vehicle for carrying it out (2). Philosophers have become extremely timid in saying anything about nature to scientists and have tended voluntarily to confine themselves in the claustrophobia-inducing, non-natural, ethico-political zone carved out by Fichte and his successors. It is always refreshing when someone quotes the physicist Smolin's request that philosophers should challenge science more directly, and DGW do not fail to do so (255). They also claim that, thanks to the Pittsburgh Hegelians and others, philosophical idealism has been too restricted to "constructing a metaphysics on the basis of a normativity posed as an alternative to naturalism" (1). Here I share their suspicion of "normativity" as the purported key to every philosophical lock. Like them, I also salute the more speculative physical tone found in such scientific thinkers as Bernard d'Espagnat (1921–2015), Julian Barbour (b. 1937), Kauffman, and Roland Omnès (b. 1931).[18] It is also likely that Grant and I, despite our measured skepticism towards the philosophy of Badiou, would both agree with Badiou's complaint that contemporary philosophy (which he calls "democratic materialism") is devoted to a weak twofold ontology of "bodies" and "languages."[19] Shortly after the Goldsmiths workshop, Gwenaëlle Aubry and Quentin Meillassoux noted a close resemblance they had detected in London between Grant and OOO. This resemblance is perhaps best captured by saying that we both want to bring inanimate reality back into the philosophical sphere, though without the fetishistic worship of mathematics and science that is too often coupled with visceral aversion to the arts and humanities found among naturalists, Brassier included.

We now return to the three points by DGW covered above, responding to each in turn. The first point was that "idealism" is better used as a word for those philosophies that accept the reality of ideas than for those phenomenalist positions that deny reality outside the mind, a position that DGW say is not defended by any great number of thinkers. Idealism in this broadened DGW sense should be distinguished not only from the usual interpretation of Berkeley's philosophy but also from panpsychism: if DGW merely maintain that ideas are real too, and Berkeley claims that "to be is to be perceived," panpsychism asserts that to be is *to perceive*, so that nothing can exist without having some sort of mind, however primitive. Moreover, "vitalism" is a term often confused with panpsychism, though the former means simply that everything that exists is alive, while the latter requires that everything have actual mentality rather than a merely plant-like capacity for nourishment and reproduction. The question is why DGW would wish to eliminate the usual sense of "idealism" as entailing that reality means mind-dependence. We can salute their claim that ideas should count as realities too, but in that case the term "flat ontology" should suffice rather than "idealism." As we have seen, they also tell us that idealisms are motivated by the need for systematic completeness, not by skeptical concerns (4). Yet it is unclear why full-blown idealism needs to be linked with skepticism. The skeptic *doubts* whether anything exists independently of our encounter with it, and there is no such doubt to be found in Berkeley, whose trademark doctrine is that to be *simply is* to be perceived. Properly speaking, skeptical doubt should be ascribed not to idealists but to those philosophers Meillassoux terms "correlationists."

This brings us to the second point, which is DGW's view that it is hardly worth talking about idealism in the usual sense, given that no one really holds that nothing exists outside the mind. But in the first place, this is literally false. We will see that their attempt to evade the literal, mainstream reading of Berkeley fails, and that Berkeley can very well serve as the paradigmatic idealist philosopher in the usual sense of the term. DGW themselves come very close to conceding that the same is true of Fichte, who disposes of nature as anything other than a utensil for free human beings and who regards "the world" as at best a source of resistance to human actions. And all this is to say nothing of Žižek, whose supposed "materialism" has the paradoxical requirement that the world not exist independently of our encountering it; the same holds for his intellectual hero Jacques Lacan (1901–1981), for whom the Real cannot exist outside an entangled Borromean knot with the Imaginary and the Symbolic, neither of which could possibly be found in inanimate matter.[20] We will see that even DGW concede that Maturana and Varela tend towards solipsism on account of their over-emphasis on closure in their theory of autopoiesis. So in fact, there are plenty of examples of radical idealist thinkers in the mainstream sense of the term. Yet this is not even quite the point. For it is not a question of which *philosophers* are idealists but a question of which *philosophies* meet this description. That is to say, a philosophy is not always equivalent to what its author tells us about it. For example, Leibniz tells us that there is plenty of room for free will in his philosophy, though it is not easy to make such a case for a philosophy in which monads are subject to pre-established harmony, meaning that Leibniz can only rescue free will by means of terminological games. I have often argued that a philosophy such as Meillassoux's, which thinks it is able to capture the primary qualities of entities by mathematizing them, will have a very difficult time trying to explain the difference between, say, the mathematical model of a tree and the tree itself. The rejoinder has sometimes been made – not by Meillassoux but by his self-appointed deputies – that of course Meillassoux is not stupid enough to confuse a thing with a mathematical model of it. And indeed he is not; there is nothing stupid about the man. Yet the question is not what Quentin Meillassoux "realizes" as a sane and balanced human being but whether his *philosophy* accounts sufficiently for all that he sanely realizes. My point is as follows. Even if we were to follow DGW's lead and say that there has never actually been a consistent idealist on planet Earth, since no normal person is unhinged enough to walk off cliffs or swim through vats of acid to demonstrate their faith in idealism, there are plenty of *philosophies* that entail a consistent idealism, or which at least lead in that direction. Grant might even agree with my view that Hegel is such a case, given his low estimate of what Hegel does with nature. He might also agree with me that Husserl is a full-blown idealist (though Husserlians love to deny it), given that Husserl finds it absurd to think that anything could exist without being, at least in principle, the correlate of some act of thought.

Once we shift the discussion away from what philosophers think they know to what their philosophies actually entail, it is easy to see that idealism is a serious problem that goes well beyond whatever limited group of philosophers we agree to call idealists. Indeed, the risk is great enough – from both idealist and correlationist philosophies – that using the term "idealism" when we mean something more like "flat ontology" leaves us without a name for a rather important enemy. For these reasons, I disagree with DGW as to the meaning of idealism. *At a minimum*, realism ought to mean the view that "reality exists outside the mind," though even this is not enough. The reason it is not enough is because reality exists outside much more than the mind. There is a reality outside rocks, a reality that determines whether they be left in peace, sent down a mountainside in an avalanche, or liquefied by a stream of molten lava. There is a reality outside the solar system that determines how long that system will remain stable before being interfered with by passing rogue stars. Reality is not "outside the mind," a formulation that could arise only in the modern era in which the mind's ontological status was rated much too highly, but outside of *anything*.

But let's turn specifically to Berkeley, who is the poster child of idealism for most readers, though DGW treat him as a misunderstood realist. We recall one of their arguments from earlier, to the effect that Berkeley's apparent denial of the existence of anything outside the mind was really just a strategic attack on scientific atomism. To refresh the reader's memory: "Berkeley was disputing the adequacy of mechanistic materialism not only as an explanatory model, but as an ontology. Now the claim is often made that this amounts to being anti-science, and yet it is clearly not so. Rather, Berkeley opposes a particular scientific account in explaining things" (5). Much as I admire DGW's *Idealism* book on other grounds, it is not clear if this particular claim can pass the straight face test. Surely DGW are right that merely opposing mechanistic materialism is not enough to make one deserve to be called "anti-science." Nor is this a mere straw man: scientistically inclined philosophers are often rather dogmatic in limiting what they are willing to count as acceptable scientific discourse. And yet, such narrow devotion to mechanistic materialism is clearly *not* Berkeley's central target; he is hunting much bigger game. Let's take a moment to remind ourselves of who this man Berkeley was. Here is one of the clearest statements of his philosophical standpoint, taken from early in his most important book:

> It is indeed an opinion strangely prevailing amongst men, that houses, mountains, rivers, and in a word all sensible objects have an existence natural or real, distinct from their being perceived by the understanding. But with how great an assurance and acquiescence soever this principle may be entertained in the world; yet whoever shall find in his heart to call it in question, may, if I mistake not, perceive it to involve a manifest contradiction. For what are the forementioned objects but the things we perceive by sense, and what do we perceive besides our own ideas or sensations; and is it not plainly repugnant that any one of these or any combination of them should exist unperceived?[21]

This is no critique of atomism. Clearly, it is a critique of *realism* in the widely understood sense that reality exists independently of being perceived. It is not only meant to annihilate mechanistic materialism, but would hold good against any form of scientific realism at all: the pre-Cartesian medieval doctrine of substantial forms inhering in matter, Descartes' own view of matter as a unified plenum describable in mathematical terms, and even Schelling's model of nature as an unconditioned productive force. If neither houses, nor mountains, nor rivers are to be permitted existence "distinct from their being perceived by the understanding," then we obviously have idealism in its purest form.

DGW are certainly not the first to counter that Berkeley is a realist nonetheless, because he is a "realist about ideas." Yet it is unclear what is accomplished by this maneuver, except for devaluing the word "realism" by making it apply to absolutely every philosophical position. By the same stroke we might say of complete solipsists that they are realists nonetheless, since they are "realists about themselves." The usual motive for this cheapening of the word "realism" is that one views it as an enemy that needs to be defanged. One example of this is John D. Caputo's claim that Derrida is a philosopher of the "things themselves," despite the latter's clear denial in *Of Grammatology* – and elsewhere – of a reality free of all context.[22] The motivation driving Caputo is clearly to disempower the various "naïve realists" who dismiss his hero Derrida as a radical anti-realist. A similar motivation guides an author whom I like much better, Bruno Latour, who in *Pandora's Hope* deflates the value of the term "realism" as a strategic move in his conflict with those scientific realists who unfairly dismiss his work. Yet this is clearly not the motive of DGW, who not only have no especial animus against realism but are even concerned to demonstrate that idealism *is* a form of realism, after all! The strategic motivation in DGW's case is apparently to turn our attention towards what they regard as the *positive* side of idealism (namely, the causal reality of ideas), which they think is unfortunately suppressed by idealism's usual opposition to realism. An analogous thing happens with my own co-author DeLanda in our book-length dialogue *The Rise of Realism*, when he makes the same argument about realism as do DGW: "A devout Christian is surely a realist about heaven and hell, since he would not accept that my disbelief in those transcendent spaces in any way impinges on their actual existence. Yet, such a Christian realist would clearly not be a materialist."[23] Now, DeLanda is if anything even more ardently pro-realist in his views than DGW, but just like them, he is willing to devalue the term "realism" in order to promote a term that he values even more highly – in his case, *materialism*. For my part, I think realism is too important a term to be sacrificed, deflated, or downplayed. Contemporary philosophy is still not demanding enough in its standards of what ought to count as realism, and until we have a significant change of philosophical atmosphere, I would prefer that we keep the term realism polished, rigorous, and ready for use.

The points we have just discussed, all of them touched on already in DGW's Introduction, are the core ideas of the book as a whole. What follows is a series of consistently rich interpretations of major figures from the history of philosophy, viewed from the standpoint of a Grantian ontology of nature. From amidst these riches, we have time to discuss only a small number. I will limit myself to covering DGW's discussion of three historical turning points in idealism and three contemporary trends. Their historical turning points are (1) the way that Neo-Platonism established the three basic types of idealist philosophy encountered in all future idealisms; (2) Descartes' idealist innovation beyond the previous, Platonic kind; and (3) the difference between Berkeley and Kant, with DGW coming down in favor of Berkeley as a surprisingly realist figure and Kant as an idealist one, despite his insistence on the thing-in-itself beyond human cognition. The contemporary figures we will visit in the company of DGW are (1) Maturana and Varela; (2) Kauffman; and (3) Deleuze, who is the not-so-hidden key to Grant's philosophy as a whole.

Let's begin with what DGW say about the threefold interpretation of Plotinus as yielding three possible forms of idealism that persist to this day. This is closely connected with the various possible ways of interpreting the famous dictum of the pre-Socratic philosopher Parmenides, which runs roughly: "for being and thinking are the same." What exactly does this mean? One possible interpretation would be to say that there is no being outside thought, as in the readings of Plotinus put forth by the scholars William Ralph Inge and Maria Luisa Gatti (25). Since both scholars "make Plotinus's metaphysics into a precursor of the subjective idealisms found in Berkeley or in Fichte, for whom the only reality there is depends on mind for its being" (25), it should be obvious that this is not the version of Plotinus favored by DGW. A second option would be a "panlogicist" reading that interprets Plotinus in terms reminiscent of Hegel, yielding an idealism that looks like an "objective" idealism that purports to overcome the supposed subject/object distinction (25–6). Again, this is not the idealism that DGW are looking for. The third option, the one that is obviously embraced by our trio of authors from Bristol, is "a 'naturalistic' strand of idealism whose legatees are Leibniz, Schelling, and Bosanquet" (26). The authors conclude that "Neoplatonism's systematic ambitions encompass Idealism's three major subsequent variants: subjective, objective, and naturalistic" (26).

We have seen that DGW do not agree with the "subjective" reading of Parmenides and Plotinus, though they also do not agree with the scholar Myles Burnyeat's thesis that "it was not even *possible* to conceive of idealism prior to Descartes, as idealism requires the subjective epistemological shift that Descartes acquires through hyperbolic skepticism: a shift that used tools not available to even the ancient Greek sceptics" (34).[24] DGW seem more inclined to support the contrary thesis of Darren Hibbs, stated in an adventurous counterfactual spirit, that it was possible for subjective idealism to have appeared as early as Plotinus, though there was no good philosophical motivation at the time to have embraced such a dotrine.[25] DGW push Hibbs's thesis further by arguing that "what is important in Descartes' philosophy is not only the subjectivist move that made the phenomenalist position conceivable but also that he introduced the *motivation* for defending such a view by advancing a fully developed mechanistic theory of the extended world that attempted to explain every aspect of physical nature" (35). DGW go on to add that, because of Descartes' two finite substances, *res extensa* cannot explain the mind while *res cogitans* in principle *can* explain physical extension, the balance was shifted in favor of idealism and then developed further by Leibniz and Berkeley. But this is somewhat odd, since their argument implies that Descartes paved the way for a *phenomenalist* idealism, although DGW want to play down this element in Leibniz and even Berkeley. But what is interesting in the argument is DGW's willingness to explore other possible avenues of the history of philosophy in a way that is too seldom attempted.

We turn next to DGW's weighing of the respective merits of Kant and Berkeley. Here they reach a somewhat surprising conclusion: "If reality affects knowability, the common target of the [pro-realist] critiques of Moore, Bosanquet and Burnyeat should be Kant, not Berkeley" (207). This statement captures our notice, since it departs so markedly from the usual assessment of these thinkers. Whereas Berkeley is the prototypical idealist on account of his famous assertion that to be is to be perceived, Kant insists

on the existence of the thing-in-itself beyond all perception; in the opening pages of his *Prolegomena*, Kant even indignantly rejects the supposed
similarity between himself and Berkeley on this key ontological point.[26]
Nonetheless, DGW conclude that Kant would be the more proper target
of what they claim to be misguided attacks on Berkeley. On what basis
do they draw this conclusion? Their first step, we have seen, is to deny the
usual view that Berkeley is a phenomenalist idealist, a view shared not just
by most contemporary readers but by important philosophers of the past as
well: "[G. E.] Moore was not alone in considering Berkeley an illusionist:
Kant makes similar accusations in his first *Critique*. Nevertheless, both
philosophers are in error and miss the importance of Berkeley's sensory
realism" (202). As they see it, Moore views Berkeley as an idealist solely
because he thinks his philosophy is motivated by skepticism, and he even
ventures the argument that if Berkeley is skeptical about matter then he
needs to be equally skeptical about mind, which would lead in turn to "the
denial of all reality" (203). But DGW see this dismal result as being far from
where Berkeley stands, since "Berkeley is in fact a *common-sense realist* who
follows this common-sense realism as far as it will go. If we are to trust our
perceptions, why trust these senses only partially?" (203).

They state that their case for a realist Berkeley becomes clear if we compare him with his immediate predecessor John Locke (1632–1704), whose
distinction between primary and secondary qualities leads to a representa-
tional theory of knowledge as opposed to the direct appearance of the real
found in Berkeley, or at least the appearance of the most reality there is to
be had (203–4).[27] In other words, DGW convert the traditional realist/
anti-realist dispute over the existence of a mind-independent reality into a
purely epistemological conflict in which Berkeley ends up looking like the
realist, since he claims to grasp everything that can be grasped – a claim that
Locke obviously cannot make. Even less can Kant make such a claim, and
hence the passage from DGW quoted above: "If reality affects knowability,
the common target of the [pro-realist] critiques of Moore, Bosanquet and
Burnyeat should be Kant, not Berkeley" (207). Now, what is DGW's motive
in trivializing the established question of mind-independence? We have seen
that, in part, it is a result of their not quite accurate view that hardly anyone
denies a mind-independent reality in the first place. We countered by saying
that it is a question not so much of what people claim they know or believe
as of what their philosophies actually entail. But an even stronger motive for
DGW seems to be their wish to turn our attention to a different question
that they see as central, not to mention truly "ontological," unlike that of
mind-independence. The true difference between positions traditionally
regarded as realist and those seen as idealist is that, "whereas the realist

starts from atoms and builds up, the idealist starts from structure and builds down" (208). Naturally, DGW do not remain neutral on this question but choose the idealist side, just as we would expect. The advantage they see in this position is that, in idealism unlike realism, "mind is no longer conceived as an external spectator of a passive and inert nature" (208) but as an intrinsic element of nature.

Since we have already considered DGW's interpretation of philosophers from the pre-Socratics through Schelling and Hegel, let's turn now to their account of some more recent important figures. The first are the Chilean team of Maturana and Varela, who had a tremendous influence on the great German sociologist-philosopher Niklas Luhmann (1927–1998).[28] Working in the field of immunology, Maturana and his younger associate Varela were led to ask fundamental questions about how a living organism relates to the outside world. Among their conclusions is that the living cell aims primarily at *homeostasis*, or keeping itself in a stable internal state, rather than at accurately representing the surrounding environment. In Luhmann's hands, this became a markedly pessimistic theory according to which human beings do not interact directly with their societies: only *communications* communicate, not individuals. Readers familiar with OOO will notice some similarities.[29]

Yet it is not just OOO that is both very close to and very far from autopoiesis theory: the same holds true of Grant's philosophy as well. We recall his ambivalent relation to the thing-in-itself. In one sense Grant salutes Schelling's effort to leap beyond human finitude and give us reality as it truly is; in another, he is skeptical of naturalist claims to reach the in-itself directly, given that any thought about nature is itself a *product* of nature, and therefore different in kind from that which it hopes to know. This ambivalence serves DGW well, since the same double mixture of immanence and transcendence lies at the heart of autopoiesis theory from the start. For in one sense, Maurana and Varela are all about homeostasis and closure – about the living cell never really being able to reach beyond itself. In DGW's words: "it has long been a tenet of cybernetic theory that [autopoietic] machines reproduce themselves and maintain certain aspects of themselves constant through the mechanism of feedback. Such feedback produces homeostatic effects. Autopoietic living entities are a mass of such feedback loops" (233). As opposed to extreme relational philosophies like those of Whitehead or Latour, the emphasis of autopoiesis theory on homeostasis means that it limits the effects the environment can have on any given cell: "organisms do not normally vanish or disintegrate as a consequence of their cognitions" (238). Yet despite all this, it is impossible to read Maturana and Varela as straightforward Kantians, with their cells confined to their inner finitude while unable to reach the Great Beyond.

DGW see this clearly: "Like Hegel, and unlike Kant, Maturana and Varela are quite convinced of the capacity of the human intellect, in principle, to grasp the autopoietic reality of life" (227). More than this, Maturana and Varela "mock the suggestion that life is impervious to our intellect" (227–8). Beauty, for them, has nothing to do with inaccessibility (228). Sounding a bit like DGW's version of Berkeley, Maturana and Varela are read as saying that "there is no representation in cognition. Neither we, nor any other organism, extract information from a pre-given world and 'represent' it to ourselves . . . Cognition, then, is not *of* a world; rather (as for Berkeley, Kant, Hegel and Whitehead in slightly different ways) cognition '*brings forth a world*'" (234). From this it should be clear why Maturana and Varela count as "idealists" in the DGW sense of the term. And yet, DGW are somehow more alarmed about the consequences for autopoiesis theory than they were in the case of Berkeley. While Berkeley was celebrated in contrarian fashion as a commonsense realist who aims only at consistent trust in our senses, Maturana and Varela are presented as a cautionary tale. For on the one hand, it is good that they "provide, in the theory of autopoiesis and cognition, an excellent example of the power of idealism in science" (237). No question about it. Yet there is also no question that Maturana and Varela's "account of organizational closure, and the complete specification of structural modulation by the organization, [is] overplayed. This results in, at best, Kantian or phenomenological constructivism, and, at worst, complete nihilistic solipsism" (237). DGW close their explanation of autopoiesis with a powerful account of the philosophical problem at play: "the environment cannot simply be a 'trigger' to structural modulations. Some form must pass from the environment to the autopoietic entity" (238). Stated differently, though the thing-in-itself is not directly knowable, it must still *somehow* be knowable, and not just an external causal factor that fails to break through into the self-contained inner world of the cell.

DGW's discussion of Stuart Kauffman follows immediately after their section on Maturana and Varela. The transition is not a hard one to make: Kauffman, like the Chileans, is a biologist who cuts against the grain of Darwinian orthodoxy, and who is especially concerned with the independent capacities of the living organism. Rather than autopoiesis, Kauffman speaks of "autonomous agents" (241), by which he means "something that is self-reproducing and does a 'thermodynamic work cycle'" (241). A work cycle absorbs energy from the outside and uses it to drive the system towards a far-from-equilibrium state in which "overall the amount of entropy in the universe may have increased, but locally some new order has been produced" (241). This is true even of factory machines, though of course (so far in history) they lack the self-reproductive capacity that would make them true autonomous agents. For Kauffman, such agents are "part of the ontological furniture of the universe" (243) and thus cannot be further reduced to their components. Yet such agents are not the *whole* of the furniture of the universe. Above and beyond them are the "attractors" that govern the behavior of agents, a concept found not only in Grant and DeLanda but everywhere in complex systems theory. As DGW summarize Kauffman: "[Attractors] are real entities that are not substantial in themselves, but which give rise to the organization found in apparently substantial entities. This is a strong idealist theme throughout his works" (240). Now, DeLanda would counter that attractors are a strongly *realist* concept, given that they govern the real behavior of the natural world. But we have seen by now that Grant's unusual sense of "idealist" is not incompatible with the usual sense of "realist." For as DGW add: "[Attractors] are real entities with real determining force. They are clearly allied to the idealist concept of organization that we have already encountered. Indeed, it seems that organization can be conceived of as a multiplicity of such attractors: an organized hierarchy of Ideas" (245). Yet this formulation may be more holistic than what Kauffman has in mind; more generally, Grant's focus on nature as a general productive force and the relative downplaying of individual entities in his ontology seem to point to a major disagreement between Grant and the systems theorists, one that is never clearly identified in DGW's *Idealism* book. In any case, DGW summarize Kauffman as answering the Maturana–Varela "solipsism" problem by realizing that the *organizational* aspect of an autonomous agent should not be overly stressed. Disorder is also important if adaptation and change are to occur. The autopoietic agent needs to "[live] in the boundary region between order and chaos" (247). For "it is as 'sensitive' as it can be without falling apart" (247). The way this works is that "multiple perturbations tend to converge into the same structural effect on the agent. In other words, *many similar perturbations are registered as equivalent*" (247). Here there are obvious echoes of the celebrated ecological writings of Jakob Johann von Uexküll (1864–1944), for whom muscles respond to all stimuli by contracting, and for whom the environment (*Umwelt*) of each animal species is but a small portion of their true objective surroundings (*Umgebung*).[30]

Yet perhaps the most fascinating aspect of Kauffman's work for Grantian purposes is its opposition not only to reductionism but to an even more important pillar of science, namely: "Kauffman seems to be moving towards a denial of entropy in general" (253). He "shows that chemical diversity inevitably increases in any system unless there are mechanisms to limit it" (240). In other words, by now "the universe is far from equilibrium, but early on was relatively featureless" (249). In order to explain this, Kauffman goes so far as to propose a "possible fourth law of thermodynamics" (249–50) which states roughly that, on average, systems tend to produce diversity as fast as they can without destroying the inherited order that makes diversity possible. DGW plausibly link this to Whitehead's fascination with novelty and creativity. As for Kauffman, he is fairly specific about how this happens. If we consider any set of organic molecules and call them "the actual," we know that they will react to produce a number of other molecules just one reaction step away that are not currently actual but, rather, "adjacent possible" (250). Kauffman suggests that the inevitable flow into adjacent possibilities, rather than the more commonly cited second law of thermodynamics, is the true root of "time's arrow," or the fact that time seems to flow only in one direction rather than being reversible. With 100 trillion organic chemical species in existence, there are 10^{28} possible reactions between them – a vast number indeed (251). As Kauffman puts it: "other things being equal, *the total system 'wants' to flow into the adjacent possible*" (251). What is important here for Grant is that such a flow does not seem easy to describe in terms of efficient causation, since it can be interpreted as involving a backward or retroactive causation from the future (adjacent possibilities) onto the present (current actualities). Thus the long-discredited theme of final causation comes back into play for Grant no less than for DeLanda, with the notion of "attractors" being just one vivid example. It is also worth noting that, whereas DGW made one major objection to Maturana and Varela (their tendency towards solipsism), no especially flagrant complaints about Kauffman's views can be found in their account of his work.

We come at last to DGW's pages on Gilles Deleuze. When reading Grant's account of his most favored historical figures, such as Plato and Schelling, one often has the sense of a deeply Deleuzean background to his discussions. Although Brassier, like Grant, also came through the doctoral program at Warwick University, and though Brassier did his time with Deleuze like most of the students at Warwick during that period, it would be safe to say that Grant is the most Deleuzean of the original Speculative Realists. DGW's reading of Deleuze will not be surprising for anyone who knows Grant's solo-authored work. For despite the fact that "Deleuze has often been interpreted as some kind of materialist . . .," with DeLanda's interpretation being probably the finest example, "it is our contention that Deleuze is, in fact, a philosophical idealist" (284). DGW are crystal clear as to what they mean by this claim: "in *Difference and Repetition*, Deleuze is quite explicit and overt in his development of a philosophy of the Idea. There he offers an account in which the Idea is ontologically primary, and actual physical substance a very late abstraction from a world of actualities generated by the Idea" (284). Like Badiou, DGW interpret Deleuze as a monist.[31] If this is the case, then Deleuze faces the same predicament as every other monist in the history of philosophy, namely: "Deleuze faces the problem of accounting for the multiplicity of actual manifestations of a unified being. How can a multiplicity of forms arise in the world? He does not take the existence of these particular things as given, but asks how they are generated. It is this that is, perhaps, Deleuze's basic question, informing his entire philosophy" (284).

DGW now turn their attention to the most basic and familiar of Deleuzean terminology: "Using a vocabulary derived and modified from the work of Henri Bergson, Deleuze refers to these two aspects as the 'virtual' and 'actual' aspects of real existence . . . The virtual aspect generates the actual aspect, and is always immanent to it, so that the actual particular things that appear in the world are generated by some underlying virtual activity" (285). Here, as in Grant's Schelling book, we cannot speak of a "resemblance" between Ideas and actual forms but only of a genetic link between them: "[Deleuze's] theory of the Idea is that it plays the role of an omnipresent, inexhaustible and eternal potential for the genesis of actual forms" (285). If we join Deleuze in thinking of Ideas as "problems" that are never effectively "solved" by any of their specific incarnations, we can speak of "an unresolved, and unresolvable, tension between forces, powers, and 'intensities'" (287). Intensities are forces whose identities cannot be absolutely determined, since they are only differentiated in reciprocal interaction with each other. "Ideas can be conceived of . . . as mobile arrangements of such reciprocally determined intensities" (287), which drive towards a state of equilibrium without ever being able to reach it. What we learn from this constant flow of intensities is that, for Deleuze, "genesis is differentiation," and therefore "actual qualitative particular things are the outward manifestation of immanent intensive flows arising from . . . intensive differentia" (287) that are "pre-individual, pre-objective" (288). Given that "consciousness itself and all its mental contents are themselves products of the same 'cancellation' of difference that gives rise to all actual things," we are plagued by a "blindness to the underlying intensive genesis of things that leads us into the illusion of 'representation,' in which we conceive of mental contents as representations of given particular things in the world" (288). DGW compare this philosophy to that of Whitehead, but I have argued in print that this view of Whitehead is incorrect.[32] Although the apparent commitment of both Deleuze and Whitehead to "process" might mislead us, "actualities" for Deleuze are the end result of a pre-individual process, while for Whitehead individual actualities are the very *starting point* of philosophy, the element from which everything else builds up. My fear is that the hasty tendency to bunch together the Bergson–Simondon–Deleuze set of thinkers with the vastly different Whitehead–Tarde–Latour set can only obscure the vastly different fates of individual entities in both. More generally, despite Grant's evident commitment to Deleuzean differentiation, my one wish about his books is that they would contain more differentiation between the thinkers who are his greatest and most sympathetic influences. He does a fine job showing how Schelling fits with Plato, how both discuss themes that become central for Deleuze, how the complexity theory of Kauffman explores very similar themes, and how all of these contribute to Grant's own philosophical position. But the reader would profit even more if Grant were to present more points of *tension* between these various authors, given that intellectual tension rather than agreement is always more likely to contain the seeds of the future.

Study Questions for Section C

1 What is the usual definition of philosophical idealism, and how do Dunham, Grant, and Watson (DGW) conceive of it differently?
2 The philosopher George Berkeley is normally treated as the most extreme idealist in the entire Western philosophical tradition. Why do DGW disagree with this assessment? Do you think they are right in doing so?
3 Give at least one reason why DGW view the Neo-Platonists as so important.
4 DGW continue Grant's individual interest in nature as the primary topic of philosophy. Why do you think they place less emphasis on important *artificial* things such as cities, hand-tools, oil refineries, or hydroelectric dams?
5 Although DGW view Plato as a powerful influence on later idealist philosophers, they do credit Descartes with an important idealist innovation. Explain in what this innovation consists. What is the disagreement on this point between the scholars Burnyeat and Hibbs, and which scholar's view do DGW prefer?
6 According to DGW, what is the inherent philosophical danger of the autopoietic biological theory of Maturana and Varela?

3   Object-Oriented Ontology (OOO)

The term "object-oriented philosophy" apparently dates to some notes I made in 1997, though the prehistory of this approach stems from 1991–2, in the course of a graduate student's early efforts to make sense of Heidegger's famous tool-analysis.[1] It is worth noting that none of the other strands of Speculative Realism owe a significant intellectual debt to Heidegger or phenomenology. By contrast, my version of OOO treats Husserl and Heidegger – not Derrida, Deleuze, or Badiou – as the most recent great philosophers with whom we still must come to terms. From 1997 onwards, other key influences on OOO included Whitehead and Xavier Zubíri (1898–1983); beginning in 1998, Latourian actor-network theory became a key point of reference.[2] Nonetheless, the true roots of OOO can be found in Husserl and Heidegger, as will be discussed later in this chapter. But, first, let's consider how OOO was presented at the famous Goldsmiths workshop.

A OOO at Goldsmiths

My presentation at Goldsmiths takes up pages 367 to 388 of the transcript, followed by almost twenty pages of discussion. As for the presentation itself, it touches on three of the four points to be emphasized in later sections of this chapter: the role of Heidegger in OOO, the role of Husserl in OOO, and the need for a theory of vicarious causation. The fourth point, not addressed at length at Goldsmiths, concerns the great emphasis OOO places on aesthetic experience. If natural science is Brassier's exemplary mode of gaining access to reality, and mathematics is Meillassoux's, OOO sees aesthetic experience – not just in the arts, but in philosophy too – as the most important form of cognition.

The day before the Speculative Realism workshop on April 27, 2007, Goldsmiths hosted a one-day conference on the horror fiction of H. P. Lovecraft; if memory serves, it was organized by the late Mark Fisher (1968–2017), mourned by all who had the pleasure of knowing him. It is worthy of note that, although the four original Speculative Realists do not share a single philosophical hero in common, all of us turned out independently to have been admirers of Lovecraft. Though the reasons for this are different in each case, my own interest stems from my view that his weird fiction sets the stage for an entire philosophical genre.[3] As I put it in my April 27 talk: "as yesterday's Lovecraft conference title indicated, realism is always in some sense *weird*. Realism is about the strangeness in reality that is not projected onto reality by us. It is already there by dint of being real. And so it's a kind of realism without common sense."[4] While my references to "weirdness" have sometimes been met with chuckles from mainstream scientific realists, there is an important philosophical force to the term "weird realism." By and large, realism in philosophy has been employed in the service of either common sense or natural science; to be a realist is to shut down uncouth speculation by wild eccentrics and focus on the hard and fast data provided by the eyes or by scientific instruments. Sometimes philosophy begins with a promising weirdness and ends with a dull appeal to scientific orthodoxy. A good example is the theory of reference of Saul Kripke (b. 1940), which begins by "rigidly designating" things beyond any possible description of them (gold may not actually be a yellow metal) but ends by claiming that the essence of gold is to have exactly 79 protons. As I put it at Goldsmiths: "the reason I call [Kripke's philosophy] 'disappointing realism' is because it ends up being the physical structure of things . . . that is real about them. So what's real about gold is that it has 79 protons. I find that very disappointing" (380). The commonsensical presence to the eyes of that yellow metallic look of gold is subverted by Kripke's appeal to an unknown *je ne sais quoi*, only to be replaced by the scientific privilege of 79 protons.[5] While there is no good reason for continental philosophy to downplay scientific fact, as it has too often done, Kripke's proton trick is simply a case of what I later termed "undermining": replacing a thing with its causal, material, or compositional elements. When OOO speaks of *weirdness*, it is trying to capture the gap between reality and its explicit manifestations, one that is found not only in the writings of Lovecraft but in Shakespeare's *Macbeth*, Milton's *Paradise Lost*, Toni Morrison's *Beloved*, in nearly anything written by Edgar Allan Poe, and in a wide range of other literary classics. Given that any entity is more than its undermined components and also a surplus deeper than all of its "overmined" effects, OOO holds that any realism that is not weird is simply a capitulation, an agreement to become the handmaid of either common sense or natural science.[6]

As mentioned earlier, OOO began from an interpretation of Heidegger, whom I still regard as the leading philosopher of the twentieth century: "it occurred to me at a certain point fairly early [in 1991 or 1992] that all of Heidegger boils down to . . . just one fundamental opposition that keeps recurring, whether he's talking about being or tools or [human] Dasein or anything else: a constant, monotonous reversal between the hiddenness of things and their visible presence-at-hand" (369). The tool-analysis occupies an undeniably important place in Heidegger's philosophy, comprising the first concrete discussion in his major book *Being and Time*, and also making up the centerpiece of his first university lecture course eight years earlier: *Towards the Definition of Philosophy*. Whereas Edmund Husserl's phenomenology asks us to focus solely on how everything *appears* to us, the rebellious young Heidegger points out that appearance is a fairly rare case in human experience. For the most part, we simply rely on entities or take them for granted, usually noticing them only when they break or otherwise go wrong. This is why Heidegger presents us with his basic difference between ready-to-hand equipment (*Zuhandenheit*) and present-at-hand entities (*Vorhandeheit*). The distinction is well known even to beginners in Heidegger studies, and specialist scholars in the field always feel confident that they understand this opposition fully. Nonetheless, OOO holds that Heidegger's tool-analysis has almost always been badly misread, perhaps even by Heidegger himself.[7] Above all, the tool-analysis is usually taken to mean that all theory and perception are grounded in a previously unnoticed background of practical behavior: before we notice any individual things, we are already enmeshed in a total system of practical purposes in largely unconscious fashion. OOO regards all of this as a series of trite pragmatist mottoes that fail to grasp the real depth of what Heidegger has shown. As I put it in the April 27 talk: "it also occurred to me that praxis does not get at the reality of the object any more than theory does – that was the next step. Yes, by staring at this chair I don't exhaust its being, but by sitting in it I also don't exhaust it. There are so many deep layers to the reality of that chair that the human act of sitting is never going to exhaust" (371). In other words, theory and praxis both live on the same side of the fence: the side of the surface of things, which doesn't do justice to the depth of their reality. Over against theory *and* practice stand the objects themselves.

This brings us to a second widespread misreading that OOO wishes to correct, one that is unfortunately produced by Heidegger's misreading of his own great thought experiment. We mentioned the difference between ready-to-hand equipment and present-at-hand entities, and even for Heidegger an entity can shift its status from one to the other. At one moment we unconsciously use the hammer while absorbed in the purpose of building a new café; in the next moment the hammer has shattered in our hands, becoming the explicit object of our attention and annoyance. So far, so good. But Heidegger also claims that ready-to-hand equipment such as the functional hammer belongs to a total *system* of relations, while present-at-hand entities such as a broken hammer have become isolated and broken off from their previous relational being. On top of this, Heidegger pastes a rank-order onto his distinction, one in which relational reality is primary while non-relational reality is derivative or secondary. There are two serious problems with this way of looking at it. First, there is nothing the least bit non-relational about present-at-hand entities, since they exist only in relation to the Dasein (human being) for whom they are visible. There is no such thing as a surprising broken hammer in isolation, because it is always surprising for me or for someone else. For this reason, the supposed rift between ready-to-hand and present-at-hand is not very wide at all: both exist only in relation to human beings. And we have already seen that the real lesson of the tool-analysis is the existence of objects deeper than theory or praxis, deeper than the usual understanding of both *Zuhandenheit* and *Vorhandenheit*. But this means that objects are deeper than any of the relations they have to human beings. Heidegger should have known this, since, despite his claim that tools always exist only in relation to a total system of other tools, he also calls our attention to the fact that tools can *break*. And a tool could not break if it were nothing more than its functional relations to all other beings. In order for something to break, it must contain a stubborn surplus beneath its current effects and impacts, a surplus that one day erupts like a symptom and demands that we take it seriously.

Up to this point, the OOO reading of Heidegger has already established two counterintuitive points. First, theory and practice are not two terms of a grand philosophical opposition but are both ways of dealing with things that come up short of exhausting them; looking at a tree, developing theories about it, and using it for shade or lumber are all *translations* of the tree that never deploy its full reality. Second, the pair "ready-to-hand" and "present-at-hand" *is not* equivalent to the pair "relational reality" and "non-relational reality." Both of Heidegger's famous modes of intraworldly being (*Zuhandeheit, Vorhandenheit*) exist purely in relation to human beings, and, despite Heidegger's celebration of relational being as more primary than the non-relational sort, tools can relate only because they previously have a non-relational being. The hammer does not break *because* it is in relation to the entire construction site, but *because* it has an internal weakness or fracture that the construction site never took into account. But OOO adds yet another twist to the picture, one that takes us entirely outside the framework of post-Kantian philosophy. For Kant, human cognition is haunted by the thing-in-itself that lies beyond all possible human access. Yet for the OOO version of Heidegger, both theory and praxis only translate a deeper being of things that can never fully be deployed in its relations with us. In other words, the thing-in-itself escapes us not because we are humans who think, but because we are *entities that relate*, just like fire relating to cotton or raindrops to a tin roof. For this very reason, Kant's point about the finitude of human perception and cognition ought to have been broadened into a point about the finitude of fire when it burns a cotton ball without interacting with all of the cotton's properties, or the finitude of rain when it strikes the tin without relating to real features of the tin that happen to be irrelevant to rain. In short, the lead distinction in modern philosophy between thought and world must be replaced with one between objects and relations. It is this distinctly non-modern touch in OOO that leads many modernist (and "post"-modernist) observers to have a visceral dislike for what they wrongly regard as its bizarre personification of inanimate matter.

We now have the basic OOO model of the cosmos: it is packed full of objects that withdraw from each other, incapable of direct contact. Here we encounter another aspect of this philosophy that many critics find hard to swallow. For is it not obviously the case that objects influence each other all the time? Does science not calculate these interactions with extraordinary precision, using the results to make badly needed medical devices and launch probes deep into the solar system? OOO is aware of this, of course. Its point is not that objects do not make contact, but that they cannot do so *directly*. In an obvious-looking case such as two billiard balls colliding on a table, the collision obviously occurs; we do not dispute this point. But as seen from the OOO reading of Heidegger's tool-analysis, the collision of these balls is really a question of both balls interacting only with the most superficial features of each other. When the red ball strikes the blue ball, it is not striking the blue ball itself, but only a translated blue ball accessible to the red ball's fairly impoverished world. By way of these impoverished blue-ball-features, the red ball makes indirect contact with the blue ball itself, which also makes contact with its own blue-ball-features, though in a different way. It is a question of indirect causation or, as OOO calls it, *vicarious* causation.[8] Already in early Islamic speculation, the Ash'arite school of Basra held that God was not just the only Creator in the universe but also the only causal agent. As I put it at Goldsmiths: "[for such thinkers,] God is there to explain all actions, recreating everything constantly. And although the theology seems a bit outrageous to us now, it's a very profound metaphysical idea, the idea that things cannot relate, inherently, that things-in-themselves are totally sealed off from each other" (374). After centuries of delay, this idea finally entered European philosophy as what we call *occasionalism*. For Descartes, God must be invoked to explain the otherwise baffling interactions of mind and matter. In the works of his admirer and successor Nicolas Malebranche (1638–1715), it is not just mind–body interactions but also body–body interactions (as with the earlier occasionalists of Iraq) that need God's intervention to occur. God also plays an exclusive causal role in such pivotal modern philosophers as Baruch

Spinoza (1632–1677), for whom the whole of nature is a single divine substance; G. W. von Leibniz (1646–1716), who held that the ultimate substances or monads "have no windows" but are pre-coordinated by God to *seem* like they interact; and Berkeley, for whom there are only images rather than independent things, with the images being coordinated by God to give us the impression of reliable natural laws, spiced up from time to time by amazing miracles to dazzle the faithful and convert the skeptic.

While this might seem like nothing more than a quaint closed chapter from the history of early modern philosophy, a variant of such occasionalism is found in more contemporary-looking modern philosophies such as those of Hume and Kant. While neither of these thinkers claims that causation is a matter of divine intervention, both root all causation in a different privileged entity: human experience. In Hume's case, what we call cause and effect is merely our experience of a "customary conjunction" of food entering our mouths and abating our hunger or of placing our hands near a flame and feeling extreme heat. In Kant's case, causation is turned even more explicitly into a category of the human understanding rather than a feature of the world outside the mind. As I said at Goldsmiths: "for the occasionalists: 'No one else can [create relations between things]? Oh, God can do it.' For Hume [and Kant], my mind does it, my mind creates objects ('bundles') through customary conjunctions, creates links" (375). Yet it seems utterly arbitrary to choose one magical super-entity – whether it be God or the human mind – able to create causal links when no other object is able to do so. This leads OOO in search of a different kind of solution.

That solution, oddly enough, comes from the phenomenology of Heidegger's teacher Husserl. Although Husserl still has numerous allies who claim that he already knew what Heidegger teaches us about the withdrawal of things from immediate presence, this claim is untenable. For Husserl, it would be absurd to consider that something might exist that is not in principle the object of some conscious mind; in other words, Kant's thing-in-itself is a contradictory notion. This puts him on the same side as the German Idealists in their dispute with Kant. As for Heidegger, though he is certainly not a consistent realist, and while he perpetually overstates the role of human Dasein in his philosophy, he is also the one who wrote as follows in his famous book on Kant: "What is the significance of the struggle initiated in German Idealism against the 'thing in itself' except a growing forgetfulness of what Kant had won, namely, the knowledge that the intrinsic possibility and necessity of metaphysics . . . are, at bottom, sustained and maintained by the original development and searching study of the problem of finitude?"[9] In this respect, Heidegger remains much closer to OOO's realism of the things-in-themselves than Husserl. Yet Husserl also adds some pieces to the puzzle that are simply invisible to Heidegger, and these pieces must not be lost amidst the general triumphalism over Heidegger's advance beyond his teacher.

The first puzzle piece is Husserl's rejection of the entire empiricist tradition concerning what an object is. As I remarked at Goldsmiths: "If you read the whole first half of [Husserl's] *Logical Investigations*, after he's done refuting psychologism, his real enemy is British empiricism, and what he is up against is the notion that what we encounter are qualities, and that somehow the qualities are bundled together by us" (376). Empiricism tends to view "objects" as nothing but a set of qualities bundled together by our own minds; the objects of experience have no inherent unity, since they are merely assembled by us from pre-given qualities. There is no taxi cruising down the street, only an assemblage of colors and shapes that our mind somehow organizes into a "thing." In what is perhaps the core insight of phenomenology – much more so than its unconvincing denial of any reality beyond mental life – Husserl reverses this empiricist bias. What comes first is the object itself: even though the qualities of that object constantly shift as we experience it from different angles and distances, the object stands fast as an unvarying unit. Indeed, this is what phenomenology is all about: stripping away all the varying qualities and silhouettes of a thing, its "adumbrations" (*Abschattungen*), as Husserl calls them, in order to arrive eventually at what he calls the "essence" of the object.

As a reminder, the "object" Husserl speaks of here is still immanent in the sphere of consciousness and is therefore not the same as the real object that breaks or surprises us in Heidegger's tool-analysis. If Heidegger leads us to *real* objects, Husserl had spoken instead of "intentional" objects aimed at by the mind. But given the ugliness of the word "intentional," and the frequent confusions that surround this word in contemporary philosophy, OOO prefers to call them *sensual* objects. There is thus a duality of real and sensual objects, which turns out to be accompanied by a further duality of real and sensual qualities. And since there are no objects without qualities and no free-floating qualities without objects, the world ends up being describable in terms of four possible object–quality pairs: SO–SQ, RO–SQ, RO–RQ, and SO–RQ. In my book *The Quadruple Object* (2011), these terms are explained as the root of time, space, and what OOO calls essence and eidos.[10] More broadly, Husserl's sensual objects also provide an important clue as to how to solve the vicarious causation problem. Recall that this problem arises because two *real* objects proved unable to make contact, since both withdraw completely from each other. It is similar to working with magnets and asking how two north or two south poles can ever touch, given that they repel each other. In the case of magnets, the solution is simple: flip one of the magnets and let the north pole of one touch the south pole of the other; in this way, an endless chain of magnets can be constructed. Something similar holds with objects in general. While it is impossible for two real objects to touch, there is no difficulty at all for a real object to touch a sensual one: after all, touching sensual objects is exactly what real objects do. Fire burns by making contact with sensual cotton, even if it is forever barred from the real cotton just like everything else is barred from it, including human farmers. Against all expectations, Husserl's phenomenology provides resources to solve the deep ontological mystery of causation. But it does so in a rather strange way, and this leads to our next point.

The second puzzle piece offered by Husserl is even stranger than the first. Quoting again from the Goldsmiths transcript: "Husserl made another bizarre discovery that no one ever really talks about, which is that one object contains others: namely, consciousness" (377). In a strange but real sense, intentionality is both two and one. In a first sense, I the real object lean on the table as a sensual one; or vice versa, the table as the real object reacts to the pressure from me as a sensual object (not all relations are reciprocal, though this one is). But at the same time, the intentional relationship between me and the table is also numerically one. How so? "Because I can talk about this relation, I can retroactively think about it, I can have other people analyze it for me . . . and none of those analyses ever exhausts the relation, which is enough to make it an object" (377). Note that this new compound object is a real one, not a sensual one, because it is there whether anyone is paying attention or not. What this means is that a real and sensual object can meet only on the interior of a third object; causation occurs solely in the mental realm, as long as we take "mental" in the sense of sensual objects in general, not just in the sense of what pertains to animal brains. Continuing from Goldsmiths: "I know it sounds strange. But I generalize from there to say causal relations always occur on the inside of a third entity. It's not just something that's true of human consciousness and phenomenology. Containment is what a relationship *is*" (377).

So much for the basics of OOO. The remainder of my remarks at Goldsmiths were an attempt at a brief summary of disagreements with the other three Speculative Realists so as to spark discussion. With Brassier, two related divergences came to mind. It is very important to Brassier that realism be able to *eliminate* certain obvious non-beings, with hobbits and the Tooth Fairy apparently high on his priority list (378). OOO prefers to err on the side of inclusiveness and flatness, since surely even hobbits and the Tooth Fairy have *some* ontological status that philosophy must take into account; the same point is made against Brassier's nihilism by another contemporary realist, Markus Gabriel of Bonn.[11] A related disagreement has to do with Heidegger's term "ontological difference," or the difference between Being and beings. For Heidegger, always hostile to the claim to cognitive priority made by the natural sciences, even the most rigorous scientific result still tells us nothing about the *Being* of the entities described, except perhaps in cases of scientific revolution. Therefore, science remains "ontic" rather than truly ontological, with "ontic" ranking as one of Heidegger's most hostile pejorative terms. For Brassier, who is cognitively more enamored of the sciences than Heidegger is, there is no such thing as a question of Being that trumps scientific discoveries about beings. It is an issue that Brassier and I had often debated in private well before Goldsmiths, and my response to his question was that "for me the ontological difference is the difference between the thing itself and its relation to anything else" (379). In other words, the Being of any object is its non-relational reality. But for Brassier, there is no clear distinction between the thing in its non-relational and relational status. He adheres instead to Sellars's distinction between the manifest and scientific image of anything: for example, the manifest image of the moon might show us a specific color and inspire certain poetic moods, while the scientific image of the moon tells us what sort of rock it is made of, which is nothing poetic but was simply created by a terrible collision billions of years ago.[12] My objection to this argument at Goldsmiths, though Brassier was not yet speaking very much about Sellars in 2007, is that Brassier risks falling into the "disappointing realism" of Kripke, who simply gives us 79 protons as the ultimate answer to how gold is not identical with its description as a yellow metal. This sort of scientism has always been a danger for Brassier and his circle, though they usually respond by ridiculing the term "scientism" as a straw man – which it is certainly not, since Brassier *in fact* wishes to grant "maximal authority" to science on all questions about the world. "Scientism" is a perfectly accurate term for this sort of scientific authoritarianism. The broader point is this: the manifest image and scientific image *are both images*. To commit oneself solely to the project of eliminating manifest images with nothing better to offer than a new sort of image, or some background horizon of nullity speaking to the "being-nothing" of these images, will inevitably fail as a philosophical project. For it cannot adequately account for the difference between an entity itself and the scientific image of that very entity.

As for OOO and Grant, the obvious difference concerns whether individual beings are the primary stuff of philosophy or are derivative of some deeper force. "The big difference is that Iain is against what he calls 'somatism' and I'm totally in favour of it. For him, philosophy is not about the bodies, it's about a deeper force . . . from which the bodies emerge. For me it's nothing but objects, there is no pre-individual dynamic flux that surges up into various individuals" (383). I also expressed the opinion that this difference might have something to do with Grant's fondness for Deleuze, whose emphasis on surges, flows, trajectories, and lines of flight rather than individual entities prevents him from being one of OOO's intellectual heroes (though Levi R. Bryant is an exception). This same point leads OOO and Grant to a serious disagreement about Aristotle. As I put it at Goldsmiths, "[Grant] sees Aristotle as being on the same side as Kant. He sees Aristotelian substance as being on the same side as the Kantian phenomenon, which I wouldn't agree with" (383). By contrast, from a OOO standpoint: "Aristotle's one of the good guys if you're a realist. He traditionally has been seen that way, so Iain's making a radical move by saying Aristotle's actually on Kant's side, and [that] Plato's one of us – counterintuitive, but interesting" (383–4). These disagreements culminate in a final point of dispute: "I would also oppose Iain and defend product over productivity, which I know is very unfashionable. In recent decades the avant garde has always been about process and not product. [But] I would defend product over process, because I think much of [the] process is lost when the product is created, and you don't need to know the process. Much information is lost" (384).

When it comes to the differences between OOO and Meillassoux, the main one is fairly obvious: Meillassoux thinks that the primary qualities of things are those that can be mathematized, whereas for OOO there is no direct access to them through mathematics or anything else. But this was not the difference I stressed during my Goldsmiths talk. The difference on which I focused was the same one raised in my 2007 *Philosophy Today* article on Meillassoux.[13] This point was incorrect, as noted by Meillassoux on the spot and by Christopher Watkins in his book covering Meillassoux's theology.[14] But it was wrong for an interesting reason, as we will see. Early in my presentation I had said: "Quentin is the only one [of the Speculative Realists] opposed to causality *tout court* – there's no chance of any necessary relations between anything in his vision of the world" (369). Later in the transcript, I continue the theme: "causation is the key for me, and for Meillassoux causation disappears . . . He absolutely *knows* that there's no causal necessity between things" (385). And finally: "what [Meillassoux is] really doubting is that there's any relationality at all. Everything's absolutely cut off from everything else, because if one thing could be connected to another or could influence another thing, then we wouldn't have absolute contingency anymore . . . this is why I have called Meillassoux a hyper-occasionalist" (386). But this is not quite right. As Meillassoux responds in the question period: "I say that laws exist. There are laws. For example, if I'm a Newtonian, I can say there are gravitational laws. I don't deny the existence of laws. I don't deny the stability of laws. Maybe these laws will persist for eternity, I don't know. I just say that it is *possible*, really possible, that laws just stop working, that laws disappear" (393). In other words, Meillassoux does not put contingency *everywhere* in the cosmos but is a dualist about contingency and necessity. Laws of nature can change at any moment for no reason whatsoever: this is the famous Meillassouxian "hyper-chaos." But for as long as we occupy any given moment of time in which certain laws prevail, those laws *are* in fact laws and do govern the behavior of everything to which they apply. Here as always, everything for Meillassoux hinges on chaos *over time*; there is no chaos in the present moment, since the current laws of nature do in fact apply in a rigorous manner.

The entire question period following my presentation was interesting, including objections by Toscano concerning whether "reality" can be totalized, by Daniel Miller on the Kantian difference between real and imaginary coins, and by Peter Hallward on whether it's a good idea to remove relations from ontology as OOO aims to do. But with space running short, I will confine myself to recalling the objection by Robin Mackay of Urbanomic, who published several of my articles in his journal *Collapse*, though he has generally been negative towards OOO over the years. The reason for recounting it is that I think Mackay's claim lies at the root of why so many newcomers to OOO have reservations about placing objects at the basis of the world. In Mackay's own words: "I'm very sympathetic to the idea that we have to try to break reality out from its incarceration in our relation to it . . . but it seems to me that physics already does that, but it does it precisely at the expense of the commonsense idea of what an object is. And what puzzles me about your system is that you seem to carry over that commonsense idea of what objects are into this other realm" (404). Later in his remark Mackay turns to the writings of Lovecraft, while apparently also referring to natural science: "for me this is the profundity of Lovecraft, why he's a profound realist. Because when you go through the gates, when reality is revealed to you, it's just this complete chaos which you can't objectify. And obviously Lovecraft is Kantian in that respect, but I can't see how your system can get past that problem" (404–5).

There are at least two separate claims contained in Mackay's remarks as quoted here. The first amounts to saying that the commonsense notion of objects is – and ought to be – eliminated by physics, since it is clearly just a pre-philosophical artifact of our everyday experience. The second is the claim that, once we "go through the gates," whether of advanced horror fiction or of natural science, we encounter not objects but "just this complete chaos which you can't objectify." Let's begin with the second point.

Although quantum theory (the textbook example of a scientific theory at odds with common sense) proposes a quantum world that does not behave in the way that our everyday macro-world seems to behave, the quantum domain is by no means a "complete chaos." Far from it, since an unfettered chaos would not enable quantum theory to be the most accurate strain of science ever developed, essential to the creation of such important devices as lasers and fiber optics. On top of this, the very basis of quantum theory is the rather object-oriented-sounding claim that reality comes in discrete packets rather than in continua. On the whole, natural science is the last place to look if one seeks a world of "complete chaos." As for the horror of Lovecraft, his world too is populated by objects, and they are objects *precisely in the OOO sense*: impossible to perceive or even describe with the normal mechanisms of human intelligence.[15]

This leads us back to Mackay's first claim. When Lovecraft speaks bizarrely of that which "bubbles and blasphemes at the center of all creation" or of "a color that was really a color only by analogy," he is stripping away our comfortable sense of what it means to be an object.[16] But by no means is he *eliminating* objects: we recall that, for OOO, "object" means nothing more than a unified thing that cannot be exhaustively reduced either to its components or to its effects. It is simply untrue that OOO projects objects of commonsense onto the pre-perceptual world, since the entire point of OOO is to say that objects are irreducible to their relations to common sense or to anything else. Indeed, the case could be made that OOO has provided the most Lovecraftian sense of objects in the history of Western philosophy, since none of the commonsensical features of objects apply to OOO's *real* objects. Nonetheless, OOO's *sensual* objects are often rather commonsensical, but this is no reason not to preserve and discuss them in ontology, even if for Brassier the sensual realm is suitable only for destruction. After eliminating from the cosmos everything that one happens to dislike, one recalls that people *have* spoken of hobbits and the Tooth Fairy, and that philosophy needs to be able to account for such entities as much as for quarks and still undiscovered entities destined for scientific recognition. Mackay's appeal to Kant as holding that we cannot thingify what lies beyond consciousness might easily have been expanded to include Badiou, who holds that before anything is counted there is simply a formless "inconsistent multiple," which Brassier in turn reads as a nullity.[17] This amounts to the old philosophical claim that you cannot look at something without looking at it, and if you objectify it when looking at it you cannot be sure what it was like before you looked. The problem with this claim, now as ever, is its assumption that there are only two options: either we look at the world and therefore stamp it with the features of our own cognitive mechanism, or we do not look at it and therefore know nothing of it. But this outlook is deeply unphilosophical, since it reduces the alternatives to wisdom or nothing, leaving no room for the Socratic *love* of wisdom on which our profession is based. Philosophy is not science – and, indeed, is not a knowledge at all. It approaches reality not by discursive prose propositions but by hints, allusions, and innuendoes in the manner of the arts. We will discuss the point again below.

Let's try this once more. Mackay's objection – and I have often heard it from others since Goldsmiths – seems to boil down to this: "the everyday world might seem to consist of objects, but reality itself is object-less, so you are illegitimately projecting a false commonsensical world-view onto reality itself." But that is not what OOO is doing. What *is* it doing?

In the first place, unlike Brassier and Metzinger, OOO follows Husserl in acknowledging that the sensual sphere is made up of objects rather than free-floating bundles of qualities. The Brassier–Metzinger move is to say that we have no reason to trust phenomenological experience on this score and should instead trust a scientific account of what is really going on in everyday experience. OOO's response, as stated in chapter 1 above, is that Metzinger's proposed experiments to discover the "minimally sufficient neural correlates" of Husserl's so-called intentional objects cannot be conducted without presupposing the same distinction between objects and qualities that is central to phenomenology itself. Metzinger too must be able to identify his data as being the *same* data even as he views them from different angles and in different moods. There is no scientific access to reality that can leap beyond the basic rift between objects and their shifting qualities.

In the second place, the OOO argument that the *real* world is broken up into objects too is not that "lived experience seems to be made up of objects, so let us simply assume that the same is true even of the real world deeper than experience." No. The argument, instead, is that we soon reach an impasse if we adopt a dualistic theory in which the world itself is not articulated into objects, but then somehow human experience *is*. This predicament first appears in pre-Socratic *apeiron* theorists such as Anaximander, Pythagoras, Anaxagoras, and their intellectual cousin, the "being is one" theorist Parmenides, none of whom can convincingly explain how a single lump of reality could ever be carved up into pieces. The problem endures into the philosophy of the past century, whether in Levinas's theory of a unified *il y a* ("there is") that is broken into pieces only by the human mind, or in the claim of James Ladyman and Don Ross (who were once in great favor in Brassier's circle) that individual objects come into existence simultaneously with our human encounter with them.[18] The postmodern philosopher Karen Barad (b. 1956) does much the same when she argues, appealing to the great Niels Bohr, that relata do not precede their relations.[19] From the evident failure of such efforts we can deduce that the world is many prior to any encounter with it by everyday commonsense experience. As for Mackay's variant "world as chaos" theory, this chaos is either one or many (Badiou's "inconsistent multiplicity" simply tries to have it both ways at once). If it is one, then Mackay is just another pre-Socratic monist; if it is many, then the object-oriented position has already been conceded. Equally pointless is the solution of Deleuze, credited to Bergson, that the virtual is "both heterogeneous and continuous," which joins Badiou in the effort to have the many and the one simultaneously without paying the price.[20]

Study Questions for Section A

1 What does OOO think is the problem with the usual interpretation of Heidegger's tool-analysis?
2 According to OOO, what do Heideggerians miss in Husserl that is so important?
3 Why does OOO deny direct causation and go to such great lengths to argue instead for vicarious causation?
4 Whereas Brassier supports Sellars's distinction between the "manifest image" and the "scientific image," OOO thinks this distinction misses the point. Explain both sides of the argument.
5 Explain why OOO and Grant do not see eye to eye about Aristotle.
6 What is the nature of the disagreement between OOO and Meillassoux about causation?

B The Withdrawn

The first public appearance of the term "object-oriented philosophy" was as the title of a conference lecture given at Brunel University near London in 1999.[21] The first time the term appeared in print, however, was in my book *Tool-Being*. In view of the simultaneous publication of Manuel DeLanda's *Intensive Science and Virtual Philosophy*, a realist interpretation of Deleuze to go along with *Tool-Being*'s realist Heidegger, 2002 was a banner year for the emergence of realism in continental philosophy. *Tool-Being* consists of three lengthy chapters: the first giving an unconventional reading of Heidegger's famous tool-analysis, the second engaging in critical dialogue with some of the most prominent analytic and continental Heidegger scholars, and the third being an effort to push the book's reading of Heidegger in an original philosophical direction. While *Tool-Being* has now been in print for a generation, it has had little discernible impact in the petrified forest of mainstream Heidegger studies, though it has found a wide readership in other disciplines.

Before looking at the most important passages from *Tool-Being*, a few preliminary remarks are in order about the frequent hostility provoked by its key term "withdrawal." Many critics of OOO seem to think it sufficient to mock this term with sarcastic quotation marks, forgetting that the point is to mark an unrepayable debt to Heidegger's use of it. Another interesting twist came when an ambitious young Derrida scholar claimed to have invented the term himself, in the context of accusing one of my OOO colleagues (who had borrowed the term from me) of plagiarism from his book, though it had been published later than *Tool-Being*, and hence a good deal later than any of Heidegger's own works. But perhaps the most important critique of the term, however ill its intentions, came from a supercilious professor of design who archly questioned me in public as to why objects should "withdraw" in the first place, and who seemed to enjoy repeatedly calling it "just a simple question" even after it was answered successfully on the first try. Though the tone of the exchange was insufferable, the objection would have been useful if posed in a more honest spirit and is therefore worth a few lines here. If I grasp the gist of the question, it seems to assume that the natural state of objects is somehow to be directly present, whether to us or to each other. This supposedly being the case, it might be wondered why objects should then magically withdraw into some inaccessible place in the cosmos. But withdrawal is not a supplementary and gratuitous act imposed upon a default state in which things are present in the world. The point is that each thing has a form or structure of its own, and when one object makes contact with another it cannot perfectly replicate the form of the first. It is not as if a giraffe, for example, were simply a form inhering in matter, so that I could extract that form and bring it into my mind without also bringing the matter along – one of the least convincing features of Aristotle's philosophical tradition. Instead, the giraffe-form that I think does not coincide with the giraffe-form in the giraffe itself. If this were not the case, then perfect mathematical knowledge of a giraffe would itself be a giraffe, a clearly absurd position that is directly entailed by the views even of many who deny that they hold it. This is true even of as brilliant a philosopher as Meillassoux, who tries to keep his distance from Pythagoras by insisting on a "dead matter" to which mathematics refers, though no one – including Meillassoux himself – has any idea what such neutral and formless matter would be. In short, "withdrawal" does not refer to some needlessly mystical disappearance of things from the immanent earth but is simply another way of saying that a form can exist in only one place; it cannot be moved – into a mind or anywhere else – without being translated into something different from what it was. This misunderstanding is so frequent that I have recently begun to use the term "withhold" instead of withdraw; time will tell which is better.

Returning to the importance of this topic for OOO, it was first spelled out in "The Invisible Realm," section 1 of *Tool-Being*,[22] which can serve as our primary text here. Withdrawal is one possible equivalent for Heidegger's key term ready-to-hand (*Zuhandenheit*), as contrasted with its opposite, presence-at-hand (*Vorhandenheit*). There are several different examples of presence-at-hand in Heidegger, including the sheer presence of visible objects lying before us, the broken tool that no longer works but obtrusively demands our attention, or things as objectified by the natural sciences in terms of mass and spatio-temporal position. According to Heidegger, what all such examples have in common is not just their presence rather than their absence, but their purported existence as independent entities inherently unrelated to anything else. It is fair to say that Heidegger's entire career is based on the claim that presence-at-hand has dominated Western thought since Plato and that, despite the obvious theoretical triumphs of this standpoint (such as mathematical physics and advanced technology), it is leading us towards civilizational disaster. Heidegger's first argument against the reign of presence-at-hand is that, despite the phenomenological claims of his teacher Husserl, our primary contact with the world *is not* by way of the direct presence of things to the mind. For despite what phenomenology tells us, "all human action finds itself lodged amidst countless items of supporting equipment: the most nuanced debates in a laboratory stand at the mercy of a silent bedrock of floorboards, bolts, ventilators, gravity, and atmospheric oxygen" (18). Insofar as equipment functions smoothly, we tend to forget it until something goes wrong: "Instead of encountering 'pane of glass,' we tend to make use of this item indirectly, in the form of 'well-lit room.' We do not usually contend with sections of cement, but only with their outcome: an easily walkable surface area. As a rule, tools . . . work their magic upon reality without entering our awareness" (18). It is a masterful analysis by Heidegger, but one that includes at least three needless prejudices that must be addressed if his philosophy is ever to be overcome.

The first of these biases stems from the human-centered character of the tool-analysis. Since the story of the hammer and its breakdown is a tale easily interpreted as an anecdote about everyday human life, there is a widespread tendency to claim that the tool-analysis proves the "priority of practical activity over theoretical reason." And in all fairness, Heidegger himself might even agree with this interpretation. Nonetheless, it does not work very well. If I stare at a hammer rather than using it, then it is merely present-at-hand; the hammer I see is merely a caricature of its being. The same is true if the hammer startles me by breaking, and equally true if for some reason a scientist carefully weighs and measures it. Yet it *is not* the case that *using* the hammer suddenly frees us from caricature and gives us the hammer itself. True enough, in the cases of staring at, being startled by, or weighing and measuring the hammer, we are not explicitly conscious of it, while in using it we tend to be mostly unconscious of it. But it hardly follows from this that "conscious" vs. "unconscious" is a basic ontological rift that deserves to lie at the foundation of Heidegger's system. After all, to use a hammer is to distort, translate, or caricature it no less than when we stare at it directly. To use an object is just as indirect a relation as to look at it.

But the real point of OOO requires another step along this path. For it is not just that objects withdraw from being encountered both theoretically *and* practically (a point that causes the pragmatist reading of Heidegger to fail from the start), but that objects withdraw from each other as well. This is the anti-Kantian moment of OOO, which agrees with Kant concerning the existence of things-in-themselves beyond the phenomenal realm of presence-at-hand, but disagrees with Kant's assumption that the noumena haunt *human* relations to the world but not relations more generally. As *Tool-Being* puts it: "Heidegger seems to think that human *use* of objects is what gives them ontological depth, frees them from their servitude as mere slabs of present-at-hand physical matter" (16). But against this flawed self-interpretation, "*objects themselves* are already more than present-at-hand. The interplay of dust and cinder blocks and shafts of sunlight is haunted by the drama of presence and withdrawal no less than are language or lurid human moods" (16). This is why OOO is an object-oriented philosophy, not a human Dasein-oriented philosophy like Heidegger's own.

The second prejudice in Heidegger's self-understanding is his view that presence-at-hand refers to entities taken is isolation, whereas readiness-to-hand implies that tools are assigned to each other and to us in a grand holistic system. It is quite clear that he thinks so, given his view that there is no such thing as "an" equipment: "Bolts and wires taken alone enjoy a rather minimal reality. In combination with thousands of other minutely engineered pieces, they blend into the composite visible equipment known as a bridge" (22). Tools form a single empire, all of it organized by my own potentiality for being, since the meaning of all the equipment is ultimately determined by the uses I envision for it, whether implicitly or explicitly. Nonetheless, the sense of readiness-to-hand as being in holistic relation to all surrounding equipment is a derivative one, not primary, despite Heidegger's claims to the contrary. The reason is that tools are not just assigned to each other; we also know that they can *break*, which means that each tool-being is a surplus not fully inscribed in the current tool-system. Indeed, the mere fact that there are individual beings at all is enough to disprove the existence of equipmental holism, since otherwise we would have a monism in which all beings are one, much as with Parmenides, whom Heidegger resembles in several respects. Sounding more Deleuzean than usual, *Tool-Being* puts it as follows: "Drifting over the earth, we encounter a crystallization of parrot-event and glacier-event, each of them defining a fateful tear in the contexture of meaning, the birth of an individual power to be reckoned with" (47).

Third and finally, *Tool-Being* claims that the analysis of tools and broken tools already contains the entire philosophy of Heidegger. The reason this claim is usually resisted by scholars is that it seems to deal only with "intraworldly" entities, such as *vorhanden* and *zuhanden* beings. Even Heidegger seems to suggest that human Dasein and Being itself cannot be reduced to such terminology. Yet this reservation makes sense only if we misread the point of the tool-analysis as being limited taxonomically to specific *types* of beings. If we read it instead as being about the permanent Heideggerian interplay between the concealed and revealed, then clearly it pertains to everything, including both Dasein and Being. For in one sense, my deepest Dasein is hidden from me just like everything else (*zuhanden*), while in another I do have at least a partial self-understanding (*vorhanden*). And even for Heidegger the same is true of Being, which hides from all presence while nonetheless being partly revealed in each historical epoch. In light of these considerations, we have reached the first major axis of OOO: there is a dualism between the real (readiness-to-hand in the deeper, *non*-relational sense) and the sensual (presence-at-hand, as expressed most clearly in Husserl's phenomenology).

Study Questions for Section B

1 What is OOO's response to those who ask why objects should "withdraw" rather than just staying where they are?
2 Explain Heidegger's distinction between present-at-hand (*Vorhandenheit*) and ready-to-hand (*Zuhandenheit*). How does OOO's interpretation of this distinction differ from the mainstream one?
3 What is OOO's objection to reading the tool-analysis in pragmatist or Kantian terms?
4 Heidegger interprets his analysis as proving the *holistic* structure of tools. Why does OOO think he is wrong about this?

5 Explain OOO's case that the tool-analysis is not restricted to hand-tools and machines but already gives us the question of the meaning of being.

C Objects and Their Qualities

The interpretation of Heidegger offered in the preceding section – in which everything hinges on a constant reversal between *Zuhandenheit* and *Vorhandenheit*, concealed and revealed, earth and world, thrownness and projection, or any of the equivalent pairs he uses – might sound a bit monotonous even to those who are convinced by it. Yet there is always a built-in advantage to philosophical thoughts that seem overly restrictive: "Only by acknowledging the most extreme dominance of the tool–broken tool opposition in Heidegger do we gain a genuine thirst for anything that might escape it" (80–1). And we turn out to be in luck, since there proves to be a second axis in Heidegger's thinking, one that OOO pushes as far as possible.

This second axis appears astonishingly early in Heidegger's career, in his very first university lecture course in 1919, just short of his thirtieth birthday.[23] For along with the classic Heideggerian dualism between the withdrawn and the present, the young thinker has already caught the scent of another. Imagine that we encounter a brown object such as a hat and wish to perform a phenomenological analysis of it:

> after a certain amount of reflection, I become explicitly aware that the object is brown. Upon further abstraction, I realize that brown is a color, so that the category of "color" was already applicable to that blurry object that crawled into my view from out of the life-world. Color, in turn, can give way to the even deeper categories that encompass it: "perception," "experience," "reality," and so on. (84)

In this way the phenomenologist proceeds level by level, moving from one aspect of the phenomenon towards its ever-deeper grounds or conditions. The young Heidegger calls this the "specific bondedness to levels" of phenomenological description.

Yet there is something else going on, a different point that is subtle enough that a reader might miss it, despite the young Heidegger's explicit handling of it. For

> there is another kind of theorizing that has nothing to do with this step- by-step uncovering of levels. At any moment in the process, whether at the level of "blur" or "brown" or "color" or "perception," we can also stop and note that any of these things is at least something rather than nothing. We can say

"the blur is," "the brown is," "the color is," "the perception is." This possibility belongs to any part of the environment that we might be discussing at any moment. (84)

Thus, we reach a distinction that seems to resemble the traditional opposition between "existence" and "essence." But given that Heidegger draws it from an interpretation of Husserl, it is better to give it a more phenomenological spin and term it a difference between "object" and "quality," despite Heidegger's personal distaste for the word "object." This is familiar from our interpretation of Husserl, who rejects British Empiricism by denying that objects are just "bundles of qualities"; instead, the object comes first, shifting its qualities from moment to moment while remaining the same. But what is most interesting is that the young Heidegger does not just recognize this second axis as occurring on the level of phenomenological appearance, which in 1919 he calls the "de-lived" realm of "occurrence" rather than the "living" realm of "events" (*Ereignis*), an early version of the *Vorhandenheit/Zuhandenheit* distinction. Instead, the deep or hidden layer of reality *is also* torn asunder by this new distinction between objects and qualities. Later in *Tool-Being* I tried to show that this fourfold structure discovered by the young Heidegger returns from time to time: first in the hidden relation between those key works of 1929, "What is Metaphysics?" and "On the Essence of Ground."[24] Then, of course, there is the explicit but mystical-sounding fourfold (*Geviert*) introduced in the 1949 lecture "Insight into That Which Is" and dominating Heidegger's celebrated late works of the 1950s. However strangely poetic the quartet of earth, sky, gods, and mortals may seem, I argue in *Tool-Being* that it was there in germinal form in 1919, thirty years before it first appeared explicitly.[25]

The clearest restatement of this fourfold in terms of OOO so far can be found in my book *The Quadruple Object*, originally commissioned by Meillassoux for the French Métaphysiques series he co-edits at Presses universitaires de France.[26] The OOO terminology, so different from Heidegger's, refers to the two axes of differentiation as real (R) vs. sensual (S) and object (O) vs. quality (Q). This gives us the four permutations of real object (RO), real quality (RQ), sensual object (SO), and sensual quality (SQ). And given the phenomenological insight that there is no object without qualities and no qualities without an object, there are four possible combination of these permutations: RO–SQ is called "space" and is also the place where aesthetics unfolds for OOO; SO–SQ is described as "time," in the sense of lived time rather than objective scientific time; RO–RQ can be termed "essence," since it refers to the concealed inner life of the thing and its properties; and finally, SO–RQ is "eidos," since this is the diagonal line along which what we call *knowledge* occurs. OOO's confidence in this still widely unfamiliar model stems from its confidence in the underlying dualisms from which the model is built. Numerous fourfold models have recurred in the history of thought, but this time I think we have found the most important one. The research program of OOO can be described as a thorough exploration of what happens in RO–SQ, SO–SQ, RO–RQ, and SO–RQ tensions and of how these links are transformed into one another: not like lead into gold, but like gold into different shapes of gold.

Study Questions for Section C

1 Along with the "specific bondedness to levels" that the young Heidegger sees at work in phenomenology, what is the second axis he finds?
2 The fourfold of earth, sky, gods, and mortals is often regarded as Heidegger's most obscure and preposterous idea. Why does OOO argue for its profound importance?
3 Time and space are usually mentioned as a pair in philosophy and science, with no other terms ever added to the mix. Why does OOO add essence and eidos alongside time and space?
4 Of the OOO fourfold of time, space, essence, and eidos, which one is identified as the place where aesthetics occurs?

D Vicarious Causation

The conclusion of OOO that objects withdraw from direct contact with each other has one especially serious implication: namely, it seems to suggest that nothing is able to have an effect on anything else. This is obviously not the case, since objects affect each other constantly, even if not quite as thoroughly as holistic philosophers assume. OOO's point is not that causal relations do not occur, but that such relations are more difficult and paradoxical than is usually believed. In the end, how can one object affect another if they are forever mutually withdrawn? The first hope of a solution to this problem arises from the fact that OOO distinguishes between the real and the sensual. If we ask ourselves how two *sensual* objects are able to make contact, the answer is clear: they make contact indirectly, through whatever real object (a mind, for instance) experiences both simultaneously. Otherwise, the dog seen to my left and the chair seen to my right have nothing in common at all: as sensual objects, they are merely correlates of my experience of them, unlike the real dog and real chair that are independent of my experience. And just as two sensual objects make contact only through a real one, two real objects make contact only through a sensual one. Though the dog-in-itself remains permanently withdrawn from me and everything else, I nonetheless experience the sensual dog. In that way, I gain indirect contact with the real one.

We saw above that OOO adopts a different solution to the problem from that found among the so-called Occasionalists in early Islamic Iraq and, much later, in seventeenth-century France. Among the Arabs, it was a question of a particular passage in the Qur'an referring to divine intervention in a battle on behalf of the outnumbered Muslim forces. Though the usual reading of the passage treated this battle as a special one-time incident, others read it as meaning that God intervenes in *every* event: God is not just the only creator, but the sole causal agent in the universe. Everything disappears in every instant but is immediately re-created by God; no created being has an effect on anything else, since only God is capable of causing anything to happen. In Europe, occasionalism was spurred not by theological considerations (indeed, the need to preserve free will in Christian theology probably helped delay the entry of occasionalism into Europe by centuries) but by the problem of how the two finite Cartesian substances – thought and extension – are able to communicate. Some version of occasionalism was upheld by such important modern thinkers as Malebranche, Spinoza, Leibniz, and Berkeley. But we saw that even the abandonment of occasionalist theory by Hume and Kant owes a deep debt to this now quaint-sounding school. For whereas occasionalism solved the problem of cause and effect by calling upon God to enact every link, Hume and Kant simply replaced God with the human mind. For Hume, what we call cause and effect is really just a phenomenon of habit, of the "customary conjunction" of placing one's hand in the fire and always feeling pain as a result, or of eating food and feeling one's hunger disappear, even if we cannot "prove" that one event caused the other. Meanwhile, for Kant, cause and effect is treated even more explicitly as a category of the human understanding, not as something occurring independently in the noumenal world. Although the solutions of Hume and Kant are ostensibly more plausible, given that their replacement of God with the human mind is more in keeping with today's secular attitudes, they nonetheless repeat a more important occasionalist mistake. For whether God or the mind is chosen as the locus of all causation, one *specific* entity is granted the magical power of relating to other things, a power simultaneously forbidden to everything else. OOO's "vicarious causation" is designed to approach the occasionalist problem without arbitrary recourse to some magical super-entity made responsible for all cause and effect.

My article "On Vicarious Causation" was published in 2007, the same year as the Goldsmiths workshop. While Brassier wants to leave the study of causation in the hands of natural science, the OOO approach is to suggest that philosophy should never have abandoned the inanimate world to science in the first place: "The uniqueness of philosophy is preserved, not by walling off a zone of precious human reality that science cannot touch, but by dealing with the same world as the various sciences but in a different manner."[27] The article continues: "In classical terms, we must speculate once more on causation while forbidding its reduction to efficient causation. Vicarious causation, of which science knows nothing, is closer to what is called formal cause" (190). Here we see another key feature of OOO's vicarious causation, which sharply distinguishes it from Meillassoux's own treatment of cause and effect. For OOO, the meaning of causation is not just that one entity affects another. Instead, causation is primarily a matter of *composition*: gold's ultimate cause is its inherent form, but otherwise it is caused more by the atoms and molecules internal to it than by the far-off supernova in which it was forged. A corollary of this is that, whenever something seems to be caused by an "event," the event needs to be interpreted as having formed a new object – however briefly – that had retroactive effects on its pieces, with these pieces then detaching themselves from the new object and resuming an independent existence. In the 2010 article "Time, Space, Essence, and Eidos," I analyzed the collision of two airplanes in this way. If the planes are able to smash one another and have other mutual effects, it is because they coalesced for a time into a single object, which then retroactively molded both of its components. The airplanes then detached and became independent post-collision airplanes, following the rather brief collision-object that gave them their new and mournful properties.

Another point worth noting is that, while real objects struggle to make indirect contact, sensual objects have the opposite problem. Crowded together into the sensual experience of some other entity (such as a human observer), they might be expected to interact with all of their neighbors in a flash rather than remaining separate, individual sensual things. As "On Vicarious Causation" puts it: "why do all the phenomena not instantly fuse together into a single lump? There must be some unknown principle of blockage between them. If real objects require vicarious causation, sensual objects endure a buffered causation in which their interactions are partly dammed or stunted" (195).

Whereas most challenges to Kantian philosophy – such as Meillassoux's – follow the path of trying to eliminate Kantian finitude in favor of a new access to absolute truth, OOO takes the opposite approach. That is to say, for OOO the problem with Kant is not that he left us stranded in finite ignorance by positing a thing-in-itself beyond all access, but that he restricted this thing-in-itself to human experience. For OOO, the thing-in-itself is not a residue that uniquely eludes poor finite human beings, but is the object itself as distinct from *any* relation in which it becomes involved, including inanimate ones. When hailstones strike village roofs, they strike *phenomenal* roofs, not the roofs-in-themselves that are a permanent surplus beyond any relation anything might have to them. This entails that OOO broaden the usual sense of intentionality ("every mental act is aimed at some object"), which for Franz Brentano (1838–1917) and his student Husserl still refers solely to the mental life of conscious beings. Every relation can be considered an intentional act, even inanimate relations, since the relata necessarily relate to sensual objects rather than real ones.

With this in mind we turn to OOO's analysis of intentionality, which is so different from the mainstream phenomenological way of approaching the problem. As the article puts it: "It is not widely known that Husserl . . . stumbles across the paradox that intentionality is both one and two. For in a first sense, my encounter with a pine tree is a unified relation; we can speak of the encounter as a whole, and this whole resists exhaustive relation." But in a different sense, "I clearly do not fuse with the tree in a single massive lump; it remains distinct from me in perception. This gives the strange result that in my intention of the tree, we both inhabit the interior of the total intentional relation" (197). Experience, by which I mean the encounter of a real object with a sensual one, can unfold in one place only: the interior of another, larger object. In short, experience has nothing to do either with "transcendence," or with its currently more popular sister "immanence," but involves a burrowing downward through the joint entities that we ourselves always help to compose. The article continues: "This seemingly dry observation has not sparked much interest in [Husserl's] readers. Even so, if combined with Heidegger's insight into the withdrawal of real objects behind all relations, it provides all the pieces of a new philosophy" (197).

What are these pieces, which the essay likens to the elements of an intellectual jigsaw puzzle? They are itemized in a list on pages 199–200. First, there is the relation of *containment*. This refers to the way in which a pine tree and I are both contained on the interior of our encounter, a new object inside which we both find ourselves. Second, there is the *contiguity* between all the sensual objects in my experience at this very moment, which "lie side by side, not affecting one another" (199). Third, there is *sincerity*, a widely derided term that nonetheless effectively refers to the real object's being occupied with a sensual object: "At this very moment I am absorbed or fascinated by the sensual tree, even if my attitude toward it is utterly cynical and manipulative" (199). Clearly our relation is not one of containment, since the sensual tree is contained not *in me*, as idealism thinks, but in the joint object composed of myself and the tree that makes our sensual encounter possible in the first place. Nor is it a relation of contiguity, which refers only to the side-by-side existence of sensual objects rather than the confrontation between a real object (me) and a sensual one (tree). Fourth, and most importantly, there is *connection*, the relation by which two real objects form a new one. But we know that connection can happen only indirectly, through a sensual mediator. Fifth, and also crucially, there is the case of *no relation at all*, a permutation that is not taken seriously enough by holistic philosophies that overemphasize the prevalence of relations. As the essay puts it, "[no relation at all] is the usual state of things, as denied only by fanatical holists, those extremists who pass out mirrors like candy to every object that stumbles down the street" (200). We can conclude that "the objects populating the world always stand to each other in one of these five relations" (200).

Of the five, which is the most important, the root of all change in the world? It cannot be "connection," which is precisely what we are trying to explain; once entities are connected, the difficult work has already been done. It obviously cannot be "no relation at all," which points to the ongoing separation of objects until something happens to bring them into relation. "Containment" is the result of a link between objects rather than the cause of it, and "contiguity" merely gives us the side-by-side co-existence of sensual objects rather than a connection between real ones. That leaves just one possibility:

> The only remaining option is sincerity. This must be the site of change in the world. A real object resides in the core of an intention, pressed up against numerous sensual ones. Somehow, it pierces their colored mists and connects with a real object already in the vicinity but buffered from direct contact. If light can be shed on this mechanism, the nature of the other four types of relation may be clarified as well. (213)

In any event, we have seen that the relation between two real objects can only be a form of touching without touching, just as Socrates loves virtue or friendship without ever having them. The congenital vice of every philosophical rationalism is its assumption that we have either direct contact with the real or no contact at all. Discursive, conceptual language is the only acceptable sort of speech for the rationalist; everything else is either negative theology or mystical hand-waving. By contrast, OOO sees language and thought primarily as matters of *allusion*, and philosophy itself as the great art of allusion to a real that cannot manifest itself directly. Yet this is not true only of language and thought: "Relations between all real objects, including mindless chunks of dirt, occur only by means of some form of allusion. But insofar as we have identified allure with an aesthetic effect, this means that aesthetics becomes first philosophy" (221). On this note, we pass to the importance of aesthetics for OOO.

Study Questions for Section D

1 According to the article "On Vicarous Causation," causation between real objects is "vicarious" while causation between sensual objects is "buffered." What is the difference between these two kinds of causation, and why does real go with vicarious while sensual goes with buffered?
2 Why does the article argue that every case of thought confronting an object occurs on the interior of another object?
3 The article claims that there are five possible types of relations: containment, contiguity, sincerity, connection, and no relation at all. Explain each of the five and give an example of the conditions under which each of them occurs.
4 The term "intentionality" means that every mental act is directed towards some object. Usually it has been thought that only humans or other highly intelligent beings are capable of intentionality. On what grounds does "On Vicarious Causation" claim that it is found everywhere, including the inanimate realm?
5 Of the five types of relations mentioned in question 3 above, the article argues that *sincerity* is ultimately the most important of them all. What is the basis for this claim?

E The Crucial Place of Aesthetics

Given OOO's tendency to focus on the withdrawal of real objects from direct access, it has sometimes been accused of a "negative theology" that tells us only what objects *are not* rather than what they are. This accusation reveals a lack of philosophical imagination, and an equal lack of sense for the history of the discipline; it assumes that on one side there is knowledge and on the other there are nothing but vague gesticulations towards the unknowable. But in fact, there is a vast middle ground between these two extremes, and human cognition has always made use of this middle ground. For there are numerous ways of gaining *indirect* access to the real by way of allusion. If this were not the case, art would be pointless, since it clearly does not give us direct *knowledge* of the real. More than this, philosophy itself in the original Socratic sense of *philosophia* would be pointless. For there is no passage in any Platonic dialogue in which Socrates gives us a successful definition of justice, virtue, love, or anything else. Likewise, there is no artwork that can be translated into a literal prose exposition of what this artwork really means. Or rather, there may be cases in which this can be done, but this would show us only that the artwork in question is nothing but propaganda for some idea that might as well have been stated in clear prose terms rather than being tarted up as art. The most prominent OOO essay on the relation between philosophy and art is my booklet *The Third Table*, commissioned for the Documenta art festival in 2012. While this piece clearly differentiates philosophy and art on one side from scientific knowledge on the other, it does not go into the technical side of the discussion in terms of the interaction between real objects and sensual qualities (RO–SQ). For this reason, we will begin with a brief discussion of *The Third Table* before turning to the slightly more technical chapter on aesthetics in the recently published *Object-Oriented Ontology: A New Theory of Everything*.

The phrase "the third table" is a gently mocking reference to the famous metaphor of the two tables used by the physicist Arthur Stanley Eddington (1882–1944), a metaphor often commented upon by philosophers since its publication in the 1920s. As Eddington puts it: "I have settled down to the task of writing these lectures and have drawn up my chair to my two tables. Two tables! Yes; there are duplicates of every object about me – two tables, two chairs, two pens."[27] In a manner that foreshadows Sellars's later appeal to the duality of manifest and scientific image, Eddington speaks of the co-existence of a first table (practical, solid, colored, and hard) and a second one (scientific, made up of empty space swarming with electrons and other tiny particles and invisible fields). As a physicist loyal to his tribe, Eddington obviously prefers the second table to the first, though he admits that the first cannot be eliminated by any amount of scientific labor; ultimately, he agrees to permit both tables to be regarded as existing. From a OOO standpoint, however, both of Eddington's tables are equally non-existent: "When weighing the respective merits of the everyday and scientific tables, we shall find that both are *equally unreal,* since both amount simply to opposite forms of reductionism. The scientist reduces the table downward to tiny particles invisible to the eye; the humanist reduces it upward to a series of effects on people and other things."[28] Stated more candidly, "both of Eddington's tables are utter shams that confuse the table with its internal and external environment, respectively" (6).

Another way of looking at it is that Eddington's two tables are the tables produced by undermining and overmining, respectively; they are the two tables of *knowledge*. By reducing the table downward to the subatomic particles that compose it, as Eddington the good physicist prefers, we are replacing it with its components. The reason this does not work is because "the table as a whole has features that its various component particles do not have in isolation. These are often called emergent properties, and there need not be anything mystical about them" (7). But by reducing the table upward to its practical properties or relations to other things, we are replacing it with its effects. The problem here is that all the effects of the table, and even the sum total of its *possible* effects, are not enough to add up to a table: "even the table encountered in *practical use* does not exhaust the table's reality. In one moment it reliably supports paperweights and our midday meal; in the next it collapses to the ground, shattering everything. This shows that just as the table could not be identified with the one we *saw*, it was also not the same as the one we *used*" (9). Knowledge is the translation of any given thing into the terms of its components or its effects, thereby necessarily losing the thing itself. But the thing itself is the third table, and this means it is not a thing of knowledge. As stated in *The Third Table*: "Eddington's first table ruins tables by turning them into nothing but their everyday effects on us or on someone else. Eddington's second table ruins tables by disintegrating them into nothing but tiny electric charges or faint material flickerings. Yet the third table lies directly between these other two, neither of which is really a table" (10).

We now seem to be in an impossible position, since the two forms of knowledge that exist cannot give us the real table; thus, we seem to have reached the dead end of negative theology, of which rationalists so often warn. What we need is a way for things to be accessible without being *directly* accessible in the manner of knowledge: "Just as erotic speech works when composed of hint, allusion, and innuendo rather than of declarative statements and clearly articulated propositions, and just as jokes or magic tricks are easily ruined when each of their steps is explained, thinking is not thinking unless it realizes that each of its steps can only be oblique" (12). The usual tools of knowledge are of little assistance when we are hunting for objects, because knowledge is designed to replace the object with some set of verifiable properties that belong to it rather than to give us the object itself. And this can only be done indirectly: "The world is filled primarily not with electrons or human praxis, but with ghostly objects withdrawing from all human and inhuman access, accessible only by allusion and seducing us by means of *allure*" (12). Allure means alluding to the existence of an object without replacing it with a literal description of its qualities. And this is precisely the type of communication of which artists already make use: "For on the one hand art does not function by dissolving white whales, mansions, rafts, apples, guitars, and windmills into their subatomic underpinnings . . . But on the other hand [art] also [does] not seek the first table, as if the arts merely replicated the objects of everyday life or sought to create effects on us" (14).

The Third Table gives a good explanation of what OOO sees as the difference between scientific knowledge on one side and philosophy and art on the other. Yet it doesn't go at all into the technical side of the question, meaning the way in which aesthetics deploys the rift between real objects and sensual qualities – or RO–SQ, in the shorthand language of what *The Quadruple Object* calls "ontography." There is a more detailed recent discussion of this topic in the book *Object-Oriented Ontology* (2018), to which we now turn, though we will follow its discussion in the opposite order.[29] We should speak first of so-called aesthetic *formalism*, which for OOO has both a helpful and an unhelpful face. Formalism in aesthetics can mean several different things, but it is perhaps best defined as the view that works of art are self-contained units whose primary purpose *is not* to make protests against the socio-political wrongs of its age, or to provide information about the historical and biographical context from which it arose, or even the intention of the artist in producing the work. The artwork is independent and autonomous and ought to be approached in a spirit of disinterested contemplation. Twentieth-century formalism is often traced to Russian figures such as Viktor Shklovsky (1893–1984). In the United States, some of the major names are the New Critics such as Cleanth Brooks (1906–1994) in literature, and the formidable art critics Clement Greenberg (1909–1994) and Michael Fried (b. 1939). Given that OOO is itself a theory of autonomous objects, it naturally endorses the formalist view that an artwork be a self-contained unit – an idea that has been unfashionable in the arts since the late 1960s. Yet OOO rejects the additional, tacit formalist assumption that the autonomous art object must be devoid of human ingredients or participants. For OOO, art is essentially *theatrical*, a compound object made up of the (usually) physical work plus the spectator, just as water is a compound object made up of hydrogen and oxygen.

While Kant never literally called himself a "formalist" in aesthetics – though he did so in ethics, and for similar reasons – he is clearly the philosophical forerunner of the movement. His first point about art is that the artwork must be a self-contained experience of beauty, not one that serves the ulterior motives of cheering us up, flattering our political views, or teaching us something about how the world works. It is the same argument Kant made in his ethical philosophy: for an act to be ethical, it must be performed for its own sake, not in order to avoid hell after death, to gain public favor as an upstanding citizen, or even to sleep at night with a clean conscience. Ethical acts must be done solely from a sense of duty. Kant also holds that aesthetic pleasure is not really about the art object itself but about the subjective conditions of judgment shared universally by all humans that, among other things, ensure a general consensus of taste as to which artworks are the greatest of them all. Oddly, Kant's formalist adherents Greenberg and Fried reverse this priority, so that the art object itself is the site of aesthetics, with the human subject being subtracted as much as possible from consideration. But this difference is not so important, since the essential formalist move is the *separation* between thought and world specifically: supposedly it is fine for the artist to mix canvas and pigment, woodwinds and strings, heroes and villains, hobbits and orcs, but never must the human beholder of art mix with the physical elements of the work. The role of the beholder is to engage in calm and detached contemplation.

OOO's flat rejection of this assumption is best seen by considering its reading of Fried's "Art and Objecthood," a title that uses "object" in precisely the opposite sense from OOO. The occasion of the article is Fried's criticism of the minimalist sculptors of the 1960s, who would place a naked white cube or wooden rod or metallic beam in a room. Fried criticizes the minimalists for two separate vices that he treats as intimately united: *literalism* and *theatricality*. By "literalism," Fried means that there is no aesthetic elusiveness in these works; when you encounter a white cube, what you see is what you get. Surface literalism is precisely what Fried, like Heidegger, means by the term "object" (though OOO uses "object" to mean what *hides* beneath the literal surface). By "theatricality," Fried means that, given the intrinsic lack of drama in the minimalist work itself, it can only be designed to provoke a reaction from us. Theatricality, he holds, is the very death of art. Now, our concern here is not with whether Fried is being fair to the minimalists. Let's assume for the moment that his critique hits the mark. Even so, OOO's response to Fried is that he is wrong to identify literalism and theatricality, since these are two separate and unrelated things, the first one bad and the second one good. Art cannot be literal, reducing art objects to their visible surfaces, since in that case it would not be art. But it must be theatrical, for reasons that display the essential inadequacy of formalism. To explain this, it is easiest to consider the case of metaphor.

Let's begin by imagining a literal statement made by a simpleton: "dawn is like dusk." Although they occur at opposite times of day and each has a different role in our practical lives, there is indeed something similar about dawn and dusk. On both occasions the sun is not clearly visible, and the sky is mostly dark with some colorful patches near one horizon. We cannot deny the literal truth of what the simpleton has told us. Not only does it seem to be explicitly true, but the order of his sentence can be harmlessly reversed: "dusk is like dawn" means exactly the same thing, in ordinary language, as "dawn is like dusk." But let's turn now to a case of so-called figurative language. One of the most frequently recurring metaphors in Homer is this: "dawn, with her fingertips of rose." Here we immediately notice several differences from the case of the literalist simpleton. First, the dawn does not literally have fingertips; there are no fingers in the sky, which is how we know this is a metaphor. Second, the metaphor is not reversible in the manner of the literal statement. If a poet were to say instead "her rose-colored finger, with its tips of dawn," we have a metaphor as well, but not the same one as before. Homer spoke of the dawn and ascribed finger-qualities to it, whereas our imagined second poet speaks of fingers and ascribes dawn-qualities to them. Third, the collision between a familiar object and unfamiliar qualities causes us to lose our sense of the object and to approach it in a spirit of ignorance. We all know what the dawn is, but are never *entirely* sure – no matter how often we read Homer – what a finger-tipped dawn is like.

Here already, we are moving right down OOO's alley. The non-reversibility of metaphor shows that the two objects combined in it play vastly different roles. In the Homeric example, dawn plays the role of object (O) and the fingertips provide the qualities (Q); in the second example, the reverse holds true. But we saw earlier that OOO recognizes two types of object (RO, SO) and two types of quality (SO, SQ). Which types are we dealing with in Homer's metaphor – or in any other for that matter? The fingertip-qualities are clearly SQ, since if there were no discernible qualities in the metaphor to hold onto, we would be dealing with silence rather than language. But just as clearly, dawn in the metaphor is an RO, since we have seen that the finger-tipped dawn is a mysterious one in a way that an everyday dawn is not. This monstrous new dawn stands at a respectful distance from us, commanding our interest, withdrawing into shadow. In short, metaphor can be analyzed as an RO–SQ pair. But the same holds true for all aesthetics, which differs from normal experience in presenting a non-literal object rather than a literal one.

Yet we still have a problem. From phenomenology we learned that there are no objects without qualities and no free-floating qualities without objects. In this case, metaphor has turned out to be an object with the structure RO–SQ. Yet real objects (RO) are by definition *withdrawn*, inaccessible to any direct relation. How can Homer's dawn play any role at all in the metaphor, given that it retreats into shadow and hides from all contact? The answer is strange enough that it surprised me greatly the first time it appeared – always the sign of a strong new idea. Yes, the dawn is withdrawn, and therefore it cannot enter directly into the metaphor, and hence it must be replaced by another real object that *does not* withdraw from the situation. What is this substitute dawn that stands in for the hidden real one? It cannot be the sensual dawn, because then we would be back in the realm of literal language and no metaphor would occur. It must be another real object that replaces the real dawn, not a sensual object.

The answer is that *I myself*, the aesthetic beholder, am the only real object on the scene that is capable of replacing the dawn. In metaphor and all other aesthetic experience, it is I myself who am theatrically drawn in and become the aesthetic object. The idea may sound a bit odd, though it is not entirely foreign to the arts, since it is already the basis of the American "method acting" derived from the system of the great Russian thespian Konstantin Stanislavski (1863–1938).[30] In the case of the Homeric metaphor, *provided the metaphor works* (which it will not for bored, distracted, or mentally dull readers), I the reader am a method actor playing the dawn playing fingertips. Upon analysis it can be shown that this is true of all aesthetic experience, not just metaphor. It could also be shown, though this is a later OOO development not yet fully described in print, that knowledge works along a completely different axis from aesthetics: SO–RQ, the same one that is so crucial for phenomenology. Let this serve as a simple first introduction to the crucial role of aesthetics in OOO.

Study Questions for Section E

1 What are Eddington's two tables, and why does OOO reject both?
2 What does OOO see as the common link between philosophy and the arts?
3 Explain the meaning of "allure" as a technical term for OOO.
4 Why is Kant's *Critique of Judgment* widely considered to be an early theory of aesthetic formalism?
5 In what ways does OOO agree and disagree with such formalism?
6 Explain why OOO argues for the theatrical character of all aesthetics.

4   Speculative Materialism

At the time of the Goldsmiths workshop, Quentin Meillassoux (b. 1967) was employed at the École normale supérieure in Paris, where he had been a student some years earlier. In 2012 he was called to the faculty of the Université Paris 1 Panthéon-Sorbonne, where he remains to this day. His father was the eminent Africanist and economic anthropologist Claude Meillassoux (1925–2005). After a youthful fascination with the 1960s Situationist movement, the younger Meillassoux turned to philosophy full-time as a university student and was eventually captivated by Badiou's powerful work *Being and Event* (1988). Later, Badiou and the younger Meillassoux became intellectually very close, and Badiou wrote a glowing preface for his protégé's debut book *After Finitude* (2005). This work has been translated into numerous languages and already deserves to count as a classic of twenty-first-century philosophy.

In 2011, I published an entire book on his philosophy entitled *Quentin Meillassoux: Philosophy in the Making*, which was issued in an expanded second edition in 2015. Readers wishing to read a detailed account of Meillassoux's philosophy are referred to that work. Here, I will do things a bit differently. We will begin here, as in the previous chapters, with a brief account of Meillassoux's presentation at the Goldsmiths workshop (section A). From there we will turn to an unavoidable discussion of the major themes of *After Finitude* (section B). Regretfully skipping his brilliant interpretation of Stéphane Mallarmé's poetry in *The Number and the Siren*, we will turn directly to the excerpts of his doctoral work, *The Divine Inexistence*, which he kindly allowed to be translated as an appendix to my book on his philosophy (section C).

A   Meillassoux at Goldsmiths

Meillassoux's presentation at the Speculative Realism workshop runs from pages 407 to 435 of the transcript, followed by an additional thirteen pages of questions and responses. While the other three speakers took an informal approach to their talks, Meillassoux read a prepared text, lending his argument a more structured and deductive character. His lecture begins by addressing his most famous concept – "correlationism" – a term that Brassier, Grant, and I immediately recognized as referring to our own theoretical enemy as well. Meillassoux apparently coined the term in 2002 or 2003, just a few years before the publication of *After Finitude*, in an attempt to prevent various anti-realist philosophies from claiming not to be idealisms. One good example of this would be Husserlian phenomenologists who contend that Husserl is "beyond" the realism/idealism question, since we are always already outside ourselves in aiming our attention at various objects. Another would be Heideggerians who assert that, since we always already find ourselves thrown into a world, the old realism/idealism dispute misses the point. Nonetheless, what such philosophies inevitably entail is that thought and world exist only as *correlated* or paired with one another, so that there is no way to talk about either in isolation. In Meillassoux's own words: "Even though these positions claim not to be subjective idealism, they can't deny, without self-refutation, that the exteriority they elaborate is essentially relative: relative to a consciousness, a language, a *Dasein*, etc. No object, no being, no event, or law which is not always-already correlated to a point of view, to a subjective access– this is the thesis of any correlationism."[1] In this respect, correlationism was the original sworn enemy of all Speculative Realists.

Nonetheless, Meillassoux stands alone in the group in *admiring* correlationism, and in holding that we can escape its consequences only if we start by endorsing its premises. As he openly tells us, he means not only to criticize correlationism but also to praise it:

> I insist on this point – the exceptional *strength* of this argumentation, apparently and desperately implacable. Correlationism rests on an argument as simple as it is powerful, and which can be formulated in the following way: No X without givenness of X, and no theory about X without a positing of X. If you speak about something, you speak about something that is given to you, and posited by you. (409)

To repeat, Meillassoux takes correlationism to be a serious philosophical position, one that cannot simply be ignored, to such an extent that we cannot work our way out of the correlationist circle but must radicalize it from within. Confusingly enough, Meillassoux denied this during my interview with him in August 2010.[2] But the textual evidence is explicit on this point, and Meillassoux's philosophy would not make sense if he did not accept the fundamental truth of the correlationist axiom: we cannot attempt to think something outside thought without turning it into a thought, thereby committing a pragmatic contradiction. At Goldsmiths, Meillassoux even defines "naïve realism" as the sort of realism that is unable to refute the correlationist circle and therefore simply ignores it (430). Responding to Suhail Malik in the question period, Meillassoux also attests that his "strategy is to access the absolute *through* the correlationist argument" (436). And quite aside from these memorable one-liners, the whole of Meillassoux's Goldsmiths presentation is saturated with the assumption that there is no way to escape the correlationist circle by simply denying it, and that a more "creative" solution is needed.

In any case, Meillassoux's lecture can be divided into three basic parts. The first discusses what he sees as the power of the correlationist argument with especial reference to Fichte, whose 1794 version of his book "*Science of Knowledge* is to date the most rigorous expression of the correlationist challenge opposed to realism" (410). The second part challenges Brassier's claim that Laruelle's non-philosophy finds a way to escape the correlationist circle, which Meillassoux holds is broad enough that Laruelle remains subsumed within it. This leads Meillassoux into a broader critique of non-rational methods of discrediting philosophical arguments that one cannot refute. The third part gives us Meillassoux's own positive philosophical argument for escaping correlationism and establishing an alternative theory of speculative materialism. Since the latter argument will be covered below in our treatment of *After Finitude*, we will focus here on the first two meta-philosophical parts of his Goldsmiths talk.

The concept of pragmatic or performative contradiction, drawn from the Finnish analytic philosopher Jaakko Hintikka (1929–2015), refers to a statement whose content contradicts the very act of uttering it. This is to be distinguished from the more usual sort of contradiction that occurs within the *content* of a sentence. In Meillassoux's own words: "[The performative contradiction] is not a logical contradiction – such as: 'Peter thinks and Peter does not think' – but a contradiction between the content of a sentence and its performance, its effective formulation" (411). An example would be as follows: "'I don't think' does not contain a logical contradiction, but consists in a pragmatic contradiction between the content of the proposition and the fact that I think or pronounce it" (411). An even more famous example, not mentioned by Meillassoux, is the ancient Liar's Paradox that involves the difficulty of interpreting the sentence "I am lying": for if the sentence is true then it actually lies, and if it is untrue then it is actually telling the truth. Graham Priest (b. 1948) has made an ambitious effort to build an entire philosophy on paradoxes of this sort; interestingly, the analytic philosopher Jon Cogburn (b. 1970) has tried to interpret all of Speculative Realism as consisting of different strategies for attempting to come to terms with performative contradiction.[3]

In any case, we have seen that Meillassoux regards Fichte as having provided the most powerful defense to date of the correlationist standpoint. In reference to Fichte's total rejection of the Kantian thing-in-itself, Meillassoux asks:

> What is a philosopher really doing when he claims to have access to a reality independent of the I? He posits, says Fichte, an X supposed to be independent of any [positing]. In other words, he posits the X as non-posited. He pretends to think what is independent and exterior to any conceptualization, but in doing so he doesn't say what he effectively does. (412)

Up to this point, Meillassoux is a fellow traveler of the German Idealists in their relation to Kant; only a bit later will he part ways with them. Much like Priest, Meillassoux ends up endorsing what he calls Fichte's "double bind":

> [philosophy] has both to posit the secondariness of thinking relative to an independent real – otherwise we couldn't explain the passivity of sensation – and at the same time it can't posit such a reality without contradiction. This 'double bind' . . . is ultimately still what 'realism' means for contemporary philosophy – we need it, but we can't claim it, so we claim *and* deny it . . . (412–13)

Any realism that denies or evades this bind can only count, for Meillassoux, as "naïve." As he lucidly puts it: "To be a contemporary realist means, in my view, to efficiently challenge the Fichtean fatality of pragmatic contradiction . . . If you think *X*, then you *think* X . . . Can a realism pass the test of pragmatic contradiction?" (413).

Clearly, Meillassoux finds the correlationist circle to pose a devastating objection to any realism that cannot refute it directly. For this reason, as we will see in the next section, he devotes his considerable speculative talents to finding a clever way both to accept the correlationist circle and to show that, when followed consistently, it leads to a surprising new form of the absolute. But one can question whether the circle argument is really as solid as it seems, and, towards the end of the Goldsmiths question period, Brassier does just that. After a well-deserved compliment on Meillassoux's stimulating lecture, Brassier goes straight to the point: "I wonder if the argument from performative contradiction – the key correlationist argument – is as strong, as irrecusable, as you seem to be suggesting" (446–7). Brassier continues with what has always struck me as a powerful objection:

> the claim is that to posit something non-posited is a performative contradiction. But the correlationist must claim to know that the difference between the posited real and the non-posited real is already internal to this concept, to this act of positing. So, in other words, how does the correlationist know

that there's no difference between the *concept* of an indifferent real and the indifferent real [itself]? (447)

Let's take an example. Imagine that someone speaks about an apple as it is in itself, outside our thinking of it. Meillassoux (like the correlationists he will later abandon for other reasons) calls this a "pragmatic contradiction," since the person who posits the apple outside thought is thinking it, and therefore contradicting herself. But Brassier objects that, in order to make this move, the correlationist must *absolutely* know that we cannot refer to a thing outside thought: that "apple for me" and "apple in itself" actually mean the same thing, since I am the one speaking of the apple-in-itself, so that therefore it is really just another apple-for-me. In this way the so-called correlationist is really just another idealist, so that Meillassoux's effort to radicalize correlationism while avoiding idealism is impossible.

Meillassoux's response is to turn the tables on Brassier, claiming that the correlationist does not claim to "know" anything, and that in fact it is the defender of a reality-in-itself – Kant, for example – who makes a false claim to *know* that there is a difference between the appearance and the in-itself (448). Yet there is something wrong here, and it is important enough to pose a threat to the consistency of Meillassoux's entire system. For in step one, the correlationist knows *absolutely* that there is no difference between speaking of an apple for us and speaking of an apple-in-itself apart from us; the "for us" is automatically implied in the second statement as it is in all others and cannot be removed, just as the bandage cannot be removed from Captain Haddock's finger in the Tintin comic reprinted in the Goldsmiths transcript (422). But somehow, in step two, the correlationist is a skeptic who simply *cannot be sure* if there is anything beyond thought or not. This is no word trick on my part, nor is it a minor matter. For this is the path along which Meillassoux eventually leads us away from correlationism towards his own position. In the first place, he gets us to reject both realism and the "weak correlationism" of Kant by arguing that it does not even make any sense to ask about what lies beyond thought, since to do so involves placing a sort of "Haddock's bandage" on every pretender to the status of thing-outside-thought. Someone says "apple outside thought," but immediately we see that it is an apple with a bandage stuck to it; the same holds for anything at all that we might try to think about. This would place Meillassoux in danger of being an absolute idealist, if not for his second move (in my view impossible), which is to make the strange claim that just because we can't think of an apple outside thought doesn't mean that *there is* no such thing as an apple outside thought. That is to say, we cannot even think of what it means to have an apple without a bandage, but somewhere there still *might* be an apple without a bandage: after all, no human has ever managed to explore a bandage-free world. But this cannot work. A Kantian skeptical argument about things-in-themselves cannot be brought in on the heels of a Berkeleyan "to be is to be affixed with a bandage" argument. Meillassoux cannot exclude all talk of the in-itself as *meaningless* and then claim that the in-itself might exist anyway: for what would this even *mean?* And if Meillassoux cannot add the second, skeptical step to his absolutist first one, then his acceptance of the correlationist circle leads him into blatant idealism.[4]

But let's turn now to the second portion of Meillassoux's presentation, which begins with a discussion of François Laruelle before steering towards more general matters. Laruelle, an extraordinarily difficult philosopher to read, has been a prolific author of books since the 1970s, though he has only recently become a well-known figure in the anglophone world. Among his most ambitious works are *Philosophy and Non-Philosophy*, *Principles of Non-Philosophy*, and a provocative polemic against his better-known contemporary entitled *Anti-Badiou*. The question of Laruelle's relation to Speculative Realism is well worth posing. Anthony Paul Smith, a Laruelle specialist who first came to public notice as a nagging online and offline critic of Speculative Realism, argues that Laruelle showed himself to be "concerned with a kind of 'realist' philosophy at least as far back as 1981 . . . long before Harman's or Manuel DeLanda's work."[5] The scare quotes around "realist" are already a sign that Smith's case for Laruellian realism is a poor one. But it is more interesting that on the same page Smith also quotes Laruelle, from an unpublished interview with Drew S. Burk, as saying that he has "always felt estranged from [Speculative Realism,] which is for me, it seems, marked by a kind of metaphysical nostalgia." There is no space in this book for a full discussion of Laruelle's (or Badiou's, or Latour's) relation to Speculative Realism. It is simply worth noting that Laruelle has always been one of the most polarizing authors within the Speculative Realist group itself. By the time of the Goldsmiths workshop, Brassier had already been known internationally for years as an advocate of Laruelle's "non-philosophy." Meanwhile, Meillassoux has never had anything positive to say about this non-philosophical current, while I myself wrote a critical review in 2011 of Laruelle's *Philosophies of Difference* that clearly angers Smith and other fans to this day.[6]

In *Nihil Unbound*, Brassier lodged the claim that Laruelle's "transcendental realism" is a better way of escaping the correlationist circle than Meillassoux's own solution. At Goldsmiths, one of Meillassoux's aims was to push back against this claim. In his own words: "[Brassier] suggests that what Laruelle calls 'philosophy' can be identified with what I call 'correlationism.' Consequently, Brassier claims that Laruelle, with his non-philosophy, works out a non-correlationism more radical and sure than my own version, burdened as it is by intellectual intuition" (416). For reasons of space we cannot follow Meillassoux's argument against Laruelle step by step but must limit ourselves to his most basic points. Meillassoux's goal, he tells us, is "to reconstruct Laruelle's position in a correlational way, showing how what he calls 'the Real' is nothing but a posited Real, and how the concepts created by non-philosophy just shift this contradiction without being able to abolish it" (418). The results of this reconstruction will not be surprising, since we have already encountered Meillassoux's high degree of admiration for the correlationist circle that he nonetheless aims to dethrone. "The real, [Laruelle] says, is radically indifferent to and independent of the circle of objectivity [by which philosophy proceeds]" (418). Cue the pragmatic contradiction theme music: "[Laruelle] says, the Real precedes thought – in particular philosophical thought, and is indifferent to it,' but the order of what he does is the opposite of what he says: he begins by thinking . . . The Real is truly a notion of the Real which is dependent on thinking . . ." (419). Meillassoux goes on to cast shade on Laruelle's famous term "non-philosophy," and in my view rightly so: have we not had enough, from Wittgenstein through Heidegger to many lesser figures, of claims to have *ended* philosophy? Yet this is precisely what Laruelle claims to have done. We become non-philosophers by abandoning the circle of objectivity "to think under the axiom of the Real. Then thought knows itself as determined-in-the-last-instance by the Real, says Laruelle. That is: thought knows itself as relatively, but not radically, autonomous" (420). Meillassoux concludes that Laruelle has not thereby escaped correlationism, since he has merely reached a "posited" Real just like anyone else, and his claim to do otherwise is the result of a mere *coup de force* rather than an argument. But in fact, this holds only if one agrees with Meillassoux that the correlationist circle is the inescapable initial horizon of philosophical speculation. And on this point I side instead with Laruelle and Brassier. I would object only to the way Laruelle goes about doing it, including his claim that "philosophy" needs to be replaced by "non-philosophy," in spite of the fact that even Socrates was already determined by the Real rather than by any correlationist circle. Furthermore, Laruelle also tends to view the Real as an unarticulated and immediately discernible One, which OOO obviously cannot endorse.

In any case, Meillassoux also takes this occasion to complain about how Laruelle would react to his supposedly inevitable failure to reach a non-posited Real. Realizing that he cannot win against the correlationist's claim that the Real we talk about is nothing more than a Real *for us*, Laruelle will blame the "resistance" of readers for not accepting his non-philosophy.

Indeed, Meillassoux sees this as the likely reaction of pretty much anyone upon encountering the correlationist, whom Meillassoux regards as having a uniquely powerful argument. He concedes that "this circle is both monotonous and apparently implacable. It is just the same objection, tedious and irritating: if you posit *X*, then you *posit* X. Sometimes we [even] encounter this enraging situation: a brilliant, subtle, and interesting theory is easily refuted by a well-known and trivial argument, put forward by a stupid opponent" (421). In such situations, the post-Kantian realist will become tired and furious, behaving like Captain Haddock when he is unable to remove his bandage from first one finger and then another.

According to Meillassoux, the Captain Haddocks of philosophy are thus left with nothing but a "logic of secession," looking for some way to leave the correlationist argument behind without having refuted it. He says that this effort takes two major forms in modernity. The first is what he calls the doctrine of the "Rich Elsewhere." As a historical example, "Schopenhauer said that solipsism was a fortress impossible to penetrate, but also pointless to attack, since it is empty. Solipsism is a philosophy nobody can refute, but also one that nobody can believe. So let's leave the fortress as it is, and let's explore the world in all its vastness!" (423). In critical remarks that seem to be aimed indirectly at OOO, Meillassoux calls this strategy "a rhetoric of the fruitful concreteness of things, the revenge of descriptions and style on repetitive quibbles. Latour, sometimes, severs all links with correlationism in such a way, and does so with much talent and humor" (423). Do not be deceived by the sprinkles of compliments here and there: Meillassoux firmly believes that any appeal to the Rich Elsewhere is a sub-philosophical way of dealing with one's opponents. The second form of the "logic of secession" sounds even worse, and consists in denouncing the *motivations* of one's opponents. Meillassoux traces this strategy to figures as great as Marx and Freud when they ascribe the views of their opponents to class interests or malformed libido (424). Philosophy must focus solely on arguments and cannot be allowed to degenerate into impatient frustration or the suspicion of ulterior motives.

Now, I will say – with no trace of sarcasm – that this commitment to reasoned argument sounds so ethically noble of Meillassoux that we may be in danger of accepting its truth out of a mere sense of shame. This is especially the case for those who live in anglophone or other countries dominated by analytic philosophy, which has browbeaten us for decades with the notion that "arguments" are all that count in philosophy. For Meillassoux's part, his model for thinking this way is not analytic philosophy but mathematics. He reminds us of this on the next page: "The [correlationist] circle argument *is* an argument and must be treated as such. You don't refuse a mathematical demonstration because the mathematicians are supposed to be sickly or full of frustrated libido, you just refuse what you refute!" (426). But is mathematics really a good analogy for what philosophy does, as Meillassoux and his teacher Badiou are often so quick to assert? I do not think so, and one great philosopher who agrees with me is Whitehead, as discussed at length in my book *Prince of Networks*.[7] The first relevant principle worth quoting from Whitehead is this: "a system of philosophy is never *refuted*; it is only abandoned."[8] If Whitehead is right – and I think that he is – then the obsession of analytic philosophers with finding "knockdown arguments" against this or that position misses the point. Parmenides' philosophy, in which Being *is* and Non-Being *is not*, was left behind not because of some devastating argument made against it by a later Greek thinker, but because its sparse austerity leaves the vast majority of reality out of the picture. In other words, Parmenides is easily outflanked by appeals to the Rich Elsewhere that he failed to address. Philosophers do not just make logical errors; even more importantly, they also fail to take large portions of reality into account. Whitehead addressed this point directly: "logical contradictions are the most gratuitous of errors; and usually they are trivial. Thus, after criticism, systems do not exhibit mere illogicalities. They suffer from inadequacy and incoherence."[9] Two pages later, Whitehead is even more to the point: "the primary method of mathematics is deduction; the primary method of philosophy [by contrast] is descriptive generalization. Under the influence of mathematics, deduction has been foisted upon philosophy as its standard method, instead of taking its true place as an essential auxiliary mode of verification whereby to test the scope of generalities."[10] We could go on at length about the many things that are wrong with the notion that "argument" is all that counts. Yet we should also point out that one can make powerful philosophical statements without any argument at all. Consider what was once one of Nietzsche's most inspiring aphoristic statements, until it entered pop culture and there became a widespread cliché: "What doesn't kill me makes me stronger."[11] Though presumably an "argument" could be given for this statement, it could only amount to a ludicrous downgrade of Nietzsche's original, argument-free assertion. Perhaps it would be something along the following lines: "As long as you survive an injury, you are able to learn from it and become more resistant to future calamities. Consider it an opportunity for personal growth. So, when you think about it, what doesn't kill you actually makes you stronger." Phrased as an argument, the vigorous exclamation of the Superman has just been reduced to a vulgar banality. There are thousands of powerful and even "knockdown" arguments in the marketplace, but ultimately only a handful of them resonate with us enough to become the basis of our own philosophies.

There is also the fact that no one treats all arguments equally, and not just for reasons of corrupt and petty human nature. If you are an atheist, you will be extremely resistant to any reports of a miracle, no matter how apparently well founded; the opposite will be true if you are a Christian. The philosopher Daniel Dennett, who is ardent in his view that there is no real "hard problem" of explaining first-person conscious experience, never gives an inch to even the most powerful counter-arguments made by David Chalmers.[12] Meillassoux himself is always unnervingly quick in responding to any objection to the supposed strength of the correlationist circle. It is simply not the case that we examine all the arguments lying before us as if they were equal in principle, then choose the best one after a careful examination of them all; we are by no means committed to the patient examination of each and every thesis set forth in our presence. Instead, each of us is committed to a general way that we think things ought to look when they have the ring of truth about them. While this may not be as blatantly operative in mathematics, Meillassoux's favored model of intellectual life, it is a well-known fact in the philosophy of science: Imre Lakatos (1922–1974) has written fascinatingly about how we all tend to be committed not to piecemeal knockdown arguments but to *research programs*. We stick with these programs even amidst strong objections and anomalies and abandon our favored program only once it seems to be degenerating.[13]

We now come to Meillassoux's second example of the "logic of secession": questioning the motives of one's opponents. In one sense, it is certainly true that *ad hominem* attacks are best avoided in discussion. But it would be hypocritical to claim that motives should never be taken into account. Imagine that you witness two angry Catholic priests arguing about the *materia signata* of (the Dominican) St Thomas Aquinas and (the Jesuit) Francisco Suárez's rejection of this theory. Later, someone tells you that the first priest was a Dominican and the second was a Jesuit. This is useful information, since you now realize that what seemed like a purely intellectual dispute probably had much to do with each priest predictably defending a philosophical hero of his own order. Or imagine that someone argues, very angrily though apparently rationally, that there is no moral law and that "might makes right," and you happen to know that they have a checkered background of violent gang activity and have been questioned in at least one murder case. In Meillassoux's case, too, it is helpful to know some of his motives for claiming that everything in philosophy is a matter of proof and refutation. For one thing, he is a rationalist and thus assumes that whenever philosophy is not rationalism it runs off the rails and into a ditch. For another, Meillassoux, unlike Whitehead, thinks that philosophy *is* essentially a matter of deduction from unshakeable first principles, and for him the correlationist circle serves as the first principle of them all: the one that must be overcome under penalty of living one's life as a "naïve realist." There may be moments when claims as to motivation would be distracting or even offensive, and in such cases they ought to be tactfully suppressed. But the idea that motives should never be addressed essentially amounts to the claim that there is no place for *rhetoric* in philosophy – a rationalist prejudice in its own right.

As concerns the Cartesian dualism at work in Meillassoux's philosophy, there is a quick sleight of hand that should be noted before we move on. The passage in question is the following: "But there are two main forms of the absolute: the realist one, which is *a non-thinking reality* independent of our access to it, and the idealist one, which is the absolutization of the correlate itself" (427; emphasis added). Meillassoux has no wish to reach the *idealist* absolute, which would essentially just turn him into Hegel – in whose philosophy the thought–world correlate is not finite as Kant holds, but an infinite relation into which the two opposing poles are sublated in the higher unity of the concept. Instead, Meillassoux aims to achieve the *realist* absolute, which he calls here a "non-thinking" reality independent of our access. But notice that he has quietly shifted the terms of the debate. The realist absolute was supposed to be a non-*thought* reality outside of our access to it, a reality that exists whether someone is thinking about it or not. But suddenly Meillassoux is also concerned that it be a non-*thinking* absolute as well, even though many of the things we hope exist outside our minds are our fellow humans, and we also hope that they turn out to be thinking things. What Meillassoux does here is to smuggle a gratuitous taxonomy into the discussion, a taxonomy in which there is one kind of thing that thinks (minds) and another that does not (dead matter). This taxonomy will have consequences for Speculative Realism, since just a few years later Meillassoux would employ this principle in his fascinating 2012 Berlin lecture to argue that both Grant's philosophy and OOO are vitalist "subjectalisms," and therefore not legitimate ways of overcoming correlationism.[14] For Meillassoux, the overcoming of correlationism must lead to a Cartesian mind–matter dualism on the basis of rationalist deduction, or it is no solution at all.

Study Questions for Section A

1 What does Meillassoux mean by "correlationism," and why is it such an important term for Speculative Realism?
2 Why does Meillassoux find the "correlationist circle" to be such a strong argument, despite ultimately wishing to escape it?

3 Why is Brassier inclined to reject Meillassoux's reliance on "pragmatic contradiction" as an argument in favor of the correlationist circle?
4 For what reason does Meillassoux discount Brassier's argument that Laruelle manages to escape correlationism?
5 Meillassoux is adamant that, in philosophy as in mathematics, arguments must only be met with counter-arguments, not with a "secession" from discussion. What are the two forms of sub-intellectual attack that he worries will result from the failure to observe this principle?

B Meillassoux's *After Finitude*

Meillassoux's wonderful debut book is no doubt the most famous individual work to have emerged from Speculative Realism. It earned rapid international acclaim, as seen from its translation into a dozen or more languages in the first decade of its existence. Though my own book on Meillassoux already includes a thorough treatment of *After Finitude*, it is too central to the origins of Speculative Realism to gloss over lightly here.[15] For this reason, I will cover all five chapters of this lucidly argued work, along with some critical remarks that I hope will spur fresh discussion.

The opening of the book proposes to revive one of the classic distinctions of modern philosophy: "The theory of primary and secondary qualities seems to belong to an irremediably obsolete philosophical past. It is time it was rehabilitated."[16] Locke generally gets the credit for the distinction, though it can already be found in germ in Descartes. The idea behind it is that certain properties of things – taste, color, odor, texture – do not exist in the things themselves, only in our *relation* to those things. These are the so-called secondary qualities. The primary qualities, which are said to exist whether we are aware of them or not, include such features of things as "length, width, movement, depth, figure, size" (3). These are purely physical and non-subjective properties and therefore do not need an observer to exist. It was Berkeley who first challenged this theory decisively, by claiming that the so-called primary qualities are actually secondary as well, since they exist only when witnessed by some human or divine mind. The final death of the theory was apparently sounded by Kant, who treated "length, width, movement, depth, figure, size" not as directly knowable real external properties of things but only as products of our pure spatio-temporal intuition and categories of the understanding. Since then it has been rare for any philosopher, at least in the continental tradition, to proclaim the existence and accessibility of primary qualities as distinct from secondary/relational ones. Meillassoux's attitude towards this situation is paradoxical, and the paradox is what gives his philosophy its unique cast. For on the one hand, Meillassoux thinks it is possible to gain direct access to the primary qualities of things as they really are; on the other, he is nonetheless *in agreement* with the correlationist objection that killed off the primary vs. secondary distinction in the first place. Let's take these points one by one.

It is fair to say that Meillassoux is more sympathetic to Descartes than to Kant, who can safely be described as the villain of *After Finitude*. Meillassoux wishes to resuscitate the Cartesian theory of primary qualities, even if he does not agree with Descartes' verdict as to which qualities can be described as primary. As he puts it: "In order to reactivate the Cartesian thesis in contemporary terms . . . we shall therefore maintain the following: *all those aspects of the object that can be formulated in mathematical terms can be meaningfully conceived as properties of the object in itself*" (3). Like his mentor Badiou, who holds that ontology is inherently mathematical, Meillassoux faces the problem of how mathematics (which is ideal) could ever accurately correspond to the things it describes (which are real). He tries to forestall objections on this score by placing a limit on his mathematism. Speaking later in chapter 1 about how a physicist would describe the accretion of the Earth more than 4 billion years ago (an "ancestral" time before the existence of all thought), he remarks that

> our physicist is defending a Cartesian thesis about matter, but not, it is important to note, a Pythagorean one: the claim is not that the being of accretion [of the Earth] is inherently mathematical – that the numbers or equations deployed in the ancestral statements exist in themselves. For it would then be necessary to say that accretion is a reality every bit as ideal as that of number or of an equation. (12)

What, then, is the difference between the actual accretion of the Earth and the mathematics that adequately describes the primary qualities of this process? For Descartes, the difference is that the actual accretion happens in *res extensa*, dead physical matter, while the mathematical description of it unfolds in *res cogitans*, the thinking substance known as human thought. In his 2012 Berlin lecture "Iteration, Reiteration, Repetition," Meillassoux himself draws on the same solution as Descartes. What mathematics primarily describes is the reality of "dead matter" as opposed to thought, which merely points to the forms that inhere in such matter by way of "meaningless signs." By contrast, Meillassoux contends, Grant and OOO are guilty of a "subjectal" vitalism that projects anthropomorphic properties onto dead matter. We cannot overstate the importance of this claim. Since Meillassoux wants to be both a mathematicist and a realist (or at least a "materialist"), he needs the concept of dead matter in order to separate reality from our mathematical descriptions of it. Thus he has to portray Grant and OOO as out-of-control vitalists, so that his basically Cartesian dualism of thought and dead matter can prevail. Mathematics must allow Meillassoux to gain access to the primary qualities of things as they are in themselves; this is the purported "intellectual intuition" that bothers Brassier (and OOO) so deeply.

We turn now to the second branch of the paradox. For if Meillassoux presents himself as a mathematically oriented realist, he still has nothing but scorn for what is usually called "naïve" realism. As we saw when discussing his Goldsmiths lecture, Meillassoux thinks that the argument against primary qualities is so strong that it requires some intellectual finesse to overcome. We cannot think of the thing outside thought without turning it immediately into a thought, an argument Meillassoux borrows from the great figures of German Idealism: "We cannot represent the 'in itself' without it becoming 'for us,' or as Hegel amusingly puts it, we cannot 'creep up on' the object 'from behind' so as to find out what it is in itself" (4). We have seen that Meillassoux's already famous term for this predicament is the "correlationist circle." As he puts it when first introducing the term: "the central notion of modern philosophy since Kant seems to be that of *correlation* . . . the idea according to which we only ever have access to the correlation between thinking and being, and never to either term considered apart from the other. We will henceforth call *correlationism* any current of thought which maintains the unsurpassable character of the correlation so defined" (5). Unless you want to be a naïve realist, Meillassoux holds, you have no choice but to run the gauntlet of the correlationist circle and come out alive on the other side. This gives a rather different cast to his claim that the primary qualities of a thing are those that can be mathematized, for we no longer have any direct access to the thing outside the correlationist circle en route to mathematizing it. Historically speaking, "up until Kant, one of the principal problems of philosophy was to think substance, while ever since Kant, it has consisted in trying to think the correlation" (6). In view of this situation, how can we mathematize things as they really are, and not just as they are "for us"? This is the central paradox that drives the development of Meillassoux's philosophy in an unprecedented direction, with such surprising results.

Now, what usually happens when mainstream continental philosophers first read Meillassoux is that they dismiss the term "correlationism" with a wave of the hand. After all, we have supposedly known for decades that the question of realism and idealism is a "pseudo-problem." More than this, correlationism is the very position that continental critics of Meillassoux claim is already stationed "beyond" realism and idealism. Unfortunately, it is my favorite recent school – phenomenology – that deserves most of the blame for this predicament. For Husserl, we are always already outside our minds in intending objects: blackbirds, mailboxes, imagined battles of centaurs. Yet this supposed access to the world outside thought is really (and I agree with Meillassoux) just an imprisonment among *correlational* objects, not real ones. In a case such as phenomenology, "[the] space of exteriority is merely the space of what faces us, of what exists only as a correlate of our own existence" (7). The juicy watermelon before me is not known in its own right but is only the essential kernel of a series of appearances that unfold before our minds; if all minds are subtracted from the picture, the melon has no existence, for there is no melon-in-itself outside a possible correlation with some observer. In the *Logical Investigations*, Husserl famously states that it would be absurd to imagine anything existing that is not, at least in principle, the object of some act by the mind. The same holds for Heidegger, since his famous term *Ereignis* (event) requires a "co-propriation" in which "neither being nor man can be posited as subsisting 'in themselves'" (8). Nor do we even need to sift through Heidegger's cryptic passages on *Ereignis* to prove the point, since even in *Being and Time* the world is already just a correlate of human Dasein. Instead of these mere correlate-objects of the phenomenological tradition, would we not rather venture back into "the *great outdoors*, the *absolute* outside of pre-critical thinkers"? (7).

Meillassoux's first step in this direction comes when he coins his terms "ancestrality" and "the arche-fossil" (10). He invites us to consider a simple scientific timeline: 13.5 billion years since the creation of the universe, 4.56 billion since the accretion of the Earth, 3.5 billion since the first appearance of life on Earth, and a mere 2 million since the physical origin of creatures that resemble modern human beings. The first three of these dates, at least, refer to a time pre-existing any consciousness at all, and therefore Meillassoux calls them "ancestral." As a related term, he speaks of "arche-fossil" to refer to "materials indicating the existence of an ancestral reality or event; one that is anterior to terrestrial life" (10). Now, what do ancestrality and the arche-fossil do to the position of the correlationist? Here Meillassoux is often misread as claiming that science somehow "disproves" the correlate. That is simply not the case; Meillassoux respects the correlationist argument too much for this to be true. After all, the correlationist can always convert these statements of pre-human dates into pre-human dates *for us*, so that the literal claims of science are subsumed by a wider correlationist ontology. If we imagine a statement of the form "Event Y occurred X number of years before the emergence of humans" (13), the correlationist would simply add the qualification "for us" to it. For example, it might be said that the Big Bang occurred 13.5 billion years before humans *for humans*. For the correlationist, "being *is not* anterior to givenness, it *gives itself* as anterior to givenness" (14). There is no way to jar correlationists out of this position simply by asserting scientifically determined facts about the ancestral past, since they can always reinterpret the ancestral past in correlational terms. Thus, as Meillassoux will clarify when asked, the appeal to ancestrality and the arche-fossil is not an "argument" but simply an interesting *aporia*. His point *is not* that the scientist is obviously right and the correlationist obviously wrong – at least not yet. His point, rather, is that a flagrant contradiction exists between these two standpoints. Given that Meillassoux has some sympathy for both sides of this contradiction, it is incumbent upon him to find a way to do justice to both.

Chapter 2 begins with Meillassoux repeating the formula that "to think ancestrality is to think a world without thought – a world without the givenness of the world" (28). In the same paragraph he restates the point in a way that he presents as synonymous, though it contains a subtle but crucial difference from the sentence just quoted, namely: "we must grasp how thought is able to grasp an absolute . . . capable of existing *whether we exist or not*" (28; emphasis modified). The difference between the two sentences is as follows: while the first asks us to think a world without the givenness of the world, the second shifts our focus to a world that exists "whether we exist or not." The two points are not quite the same. Notice that the demand to "think a world without the givenness of world" is a test passed perfectly well by Kant's thing-in-itself. For while Kant insists that we cannot *know* what the thing-in-itself is like, he also holds that we can *think* it. In Kant's philosophy, it is by no means nonsensical to ask what the walnut tree in front of me is like in-itself, outside my pure intuitions of space and time and the twelve categories of understanding; I simply can't know directly what the tree would be like. But for Meillassoux, who admires the correlationist argument, there is no thing-in-itself *in the current moment* lying beyond my thought of it. To think the walnut tree-in-itself is to *think* it, and therefore it ends up being a walnut tree for thought, not outside of thought. In short, Meillassoux subtly attempts to shift our standards of what "thing-in-itself" means. It is no longer something active here and now but still lying beyond our finite human capacity to grasp it; his book is called *After Finitude* for a reason. Instead, the thing-in-itself for Meillassoux turns out to be simply something that can exist *prior* to the existence of all thought (ancestrality) or both *prior* and *posterior* to the existence of all thought (dia-chronicity). Whereas for Kant the star called Betelgeuse is inevitably different right now from what we think Betelgeuse is, for Meillassoux this star *is not* different from what we think it is, provided we are thinking correctly and obtaining its primary qualities in the proper mathematical way. The only reason Betelgeuse is not a correlate of our thinking is because it is capable of existing both before and after thought *in time*. Stated differently, "thing-in-itself" for Meillassoux has nothing to do with our finitude; it has to do only with our belatedness and mortality as a thinking species. There is no inaccessible Betelgeuse-in-itself as long as the human species still exists; the in-itself really comes into play only as long as humans – and other thinking species – have not yet appeared or no longer exist.

Some critics of Meillassoux have accused him of "fetishizing mathematics," meaning that he relies too heavily upon mathematical procedures as a privileged route for gaining access to truth. Though the objection make sense, it is not entirely clear that this is so; at Goldsmiths he dropped a few hints as to why not. The bigger problem, in my view, is that he tends to fetishize *time*, with the example just given being one such case. Later in the book we find other indications of his almost exclusive preoccupation with time. For example, although Meillassoux makes the radical claim that the laws of nature could change at any moment for no reason whatsoever, he makes no claim that different laws of nature could be active in different parts of the universe at the *same* time. The shock of contingency is something that might await us *someday*, when we see the laws of nature change before our eyes for no reason at all, but this is not something we might also notice in spatial travel to a distant solar system. Another example is that Meillassoux holds there is no particular reason why billiard balls, rather than deflecting off each other in opposite directions, might not explode or turn into flowers or any number of other things – *in the future*. But once again, he treats causal necessity as something that unfolds solely over the course of time, forgetting that such "diachronic" causation is also paralleled by a "synchronic" kind that exists in any given moment rather than across time. For instance, gold atoms always seem to produce a gold molecule with specific gold properties. Although Meillassoux leaves room in his system for this chemical law to change for no reason in the future, he does not address why it should have necessity in this very moment. Why should it not be the case *right now* that an assembly of gold atoms might sometimes give us a molecule of gold, sometimes of platinum, and sometimes of carbon or uranium *in this very moment*? In short, our current instant of time or our possible spatial travel through the universe seem to be fairly dull affairs for Meillassoux, governed by iron-clad natural necessity. Only *time* holds stunning surprises in store for the speculative philosopher.

So far, at least, there is no sign that Meillassoux takes this objection seriously. Quite the contrary. In his 2012 Berlin lecture he makes a passing dismissive remark about those who would accuse him of privileging time over space, as if the objection were obviously groundless and trivial, worthy of nothing more than a sneer. Elsewhere, in some new pages added to *After Finitude* for the English translation (separated by asterisks and running from pages 18 to 26) he also dismisses the idea that a vase falling unseen in a country house could challenge correlationism just as well as an ancestral event from a time before consciousness existed. The falling vase, Meillassoux says, is simply a "lacuna" in consciousness, just as when Husserl says that I do not currently see the back of my house but could easily walk there and do it whenever I wish. As Meillassoux concludes: "The reason why the traditional objection from the unwitnessed occurrence . . . poses no danger to correlationism is because this objection bears upon an event when *there is already* givenness . . . For when I speak of an event that is distant in space, this event cannot but be contemporaneous with the consciousness presently envisaging it" (20). Yet this merely dodges the question at hand and assumes one side of the point under dispute – namely, whether something that temporally precedes all thought is inherently more dangerous for the correlationist than something that exists right now but is unwitnessed by that correlate. What makes this important is that it is just one of several instances in which Meillassoux seems obsessed with the chaotic powers of time, while assuming that the simultaneous events in all parts of the universe and in all part–whole relations must robotically follow the same ironclad laws of nature. His apparently horrifying hyper-chaos pertains only to future moments, not to what is going on right now.

We return to the argument of Meillassoux's intriguing second chapter. As already seen, though he finds it urgent that we overcome the correlationist circle, he finds it equally urgent that we not ignore the genuine strength of this circle: "we cannot go back to being dogmatists. On this point we cannot but be heirs of Kantianism" (29). As Meillassoux acknowledges, this poses an obvious challenge to his attempt to restore the Cartesian distinction between the primary and secondary qualities of things. Descartes is effectively a dogmatist or "naïve realist" when it comes to the existence of God and the world, assuming in pre-Kantian fashion that these can be established by direct rational argument. Unfortunately for Descartes (or so Meillassoux holds), the correlationist can always trump the Cartesian argument by saying "you have merely proven that God and the world exist *for us*; for there is no way to leap outside the thought–world correlate and see how things really are in their own right, apart from their being for us." Our starting point in trying to escape correlationism, Meillassoux holds, cannot therefore be Cartesian but must be Kantian. One relevant example comes when we consider Descartes' version of the famous "ontological proof" for the existence of God: since God is infinitely perfect, and existing is more perfect than not existing, God must therefore exist. Kant is the most famous critic of such proofs, as Meillassoux reminds the reader (32). For Kant, *if* a triangle exists then it must have three angles, but nothing is to say that the triangle must exist. The case of God is no different: *if* God exists, then He will be infinitely perfect, but His existence is not entailed just because "perfection" is taken to be one of His qualities. As Meillassoux memorably puts it: "there is no 'prodigious predicate,' we might say, capable of conferring *a priori* existence upon its recipient" (32). More generally, Meillassoux notes that this difference between Descartes and Kant on the ontological proof for the existence of God points to a wider difference between them on the question of whether there must be some *necessary being*. Meillassoux links this with Leibniz's famous principle of sufficient reason: the principle that for everything that exists, there is a reason why it exists rather than not existing. Although technically one could endorse the principle of sufficient reason without assuming that there is some ultimate necessary ground at the bottom of everything else (this is OOO's position), Meillassoux seems to exclude this possibility out of hand on account of the infinite regress it would entail: "If thought is to avoid an infinite regress while submitting to the principle of reason, it is incumbent upon it to uncover a reason that would prove capable of accounting for everything, including itself . . ." (33). But Kant does not simply *reject* the existence of a necessary being. Rather, the question of whether or not there is a necessary being is handled in one of Kant's four antinomies in the *Critique of Pure Reason*, meaning that he sees the question as unanswerable. By contrast, Meillassoux thinks the question is not unanswerable, but that it must be answered in the negative: a necessary being *cannot* exist, or we would be trapped in dogmatic metaphysics. Interestingly enough, Meillassoux also has a *political* reason for opposing necessity: "The critique of ideologies, which ultimately always consists in demonstrating that a social situation which is presented as inevitable is actually contingent, is essentially indissociable from the critique of metaphysics, the latter being understood as the illusory manufacturing of necessary entities" (34). Yet it is not clear, to this reader at least, that a total abolition of sufficient reason is a price that needs to be paid in order to view social situations as contingent. In any case, Meillassoux's opposition to sufficient reasons is why he, like Heidegger and the postmodernists, uses "metaphysics" as a pejorative term. His preferred term for his own systematic philosophy is "speculation." As he puts it: "Let us call 'speculative' every type of thinking that claims to be able to access some form of absolute, and let us call 'metaphysics' every type of thinking that claims to be able to access some form of absolute being, or access the absolute through the principle of sufficient reason" (34).

We have seen that, even if correlationism is his primary enemy,

Meillassoux does not simply dismiss it but tries to make an argument capable of countering what he takes to be a serious correlationist objection. And here, for the first time in the book, he makes a distinction between *two* kinds of correlationism, one that will prove decisive for his argument. The first kind is as follows: "Kantian transcendentalism could be identified with a 'weak' correlationism. Why? The reason is that [Kant] does not prohibit all relation between thought and the in-itself." The second kind has the expected opposite name: "the strong model of correlationism [by contrast] maintains not only that it is illegitimate to claim that we can *know* the in-itself, but *also* that it is illegitimate to claim that we can at least *think* it" (35). Note that, while Kant's weak correlationism and its alternative strong correlationism are both called "correlationism," what Meillassoux calls the "correlationist circle" holds only for the strong version and not for Kant's weak one. The circle tells us that we cannot think something outside thought without turning it into a thought, and this is a most un-Kantian argument, since Kant adheres to the opposite principle that we *can* think a thing-in-itself outside thought. Indeed, his German Idealist successors attacked him on precisely this point. Insofar as Meillassoux appreciates the argumentative merit of the correlationist circle (as seen with especial clarity in his Goldsmiths discussion of Captain Haddock's bandage), he favors strong correlationism over Kant's weak variety of the doctrine.

This is the right moment to introduce what I have elsewhere called "Meillassoux's Spectrum," a term he never uses, given how absurd it would be to name something after himself.[17] Imagine a spectrum of possible positions on whether or not a world exists outside thought. At the far left of the spectrum (we are not speaking of politics) there is the position that Meillassoux calls "naïve realism," which holds that a world exists outside the mind and we can know it. At the far right is the opposite position, which Meillassoux calls "speculative idealism": nothing exists outside the mind, and we can know this. This puts correlationism in the middle of the spectrum, and we have just seen that Meillassoux splits it into two types: a "weak" version, which holds that we can think of things outside thought without knowing them, and a "strong" version, which holds that weak correlationism contradicts itself by *thinking* the thing-in-itself that is said to be located *outside thought*. Weak correlationism is therefore disqualified as self-contradictory, and we are left with the trio of naïve realism, strong correlationism, and speculative idealism. Forced to choose among these three as the launching pad for his own philosophical position, Meillassoux chooses strong correlationism, though he will soon depart from it in a fascinating way. He rejects naïve realism because he thinks the correlationist circle has a good point: we cannot think the real directly, because to do so we must think it, and therefore it would be nothing but a real-for-us. He also rejects speculative idealism, because there is no reason to assume that there might not *be* something outside the supposedly absolute correlation of thought and world. Even if Berkeley is right that I cannot prove that rivers and mountains exist outside my or God's thoughts about them, this does not prove the opposite claim that they do not. This is why Meillassoux identifies more with the strong correlationist than with either the naïve realist or the speculative idealist.

Now, it should be obvious that the strong correlationist is different from the naïve realist. The latter thinks it is possible to access the real world directly and know things about it, while the strong correlationist flatly denies this. It is more difficult to distinguish the strong correlationist from the absolute idealist. In fact, it is my view that Meillassoux fails to do so and, given that his own speculative materialism – we will see – arises from a dashing reversal of strong correlationism, it seems to me that his speculative materialism is an impossible position. For what is the supposed difference between the strong correlationist and the speculative idealist? Both agree that we cannot think a thing outside thought without thinking it, thereby ensuring that the supposed thing-in-itself is merely a correlate of our thinking after all. The difference, Meillassoux claims, is that the speculative idealist *assumes* that because we cannot think a thing outside thought it cannot exist, while the strong correlationist holds that just because we cannot think it is no reason to conclude that it cannot exist. As I see it, this distinction fails, and the strong correlationist cannot escape idealism; only weak correlationism can do so, and this is precisely why OOO attempts to radicalize what Meillassoux would call weak correlationism rather than the strong brand he himself prefers. Seen from a OOO standpoint, Meillassoux tries to have it both ways, calling the thing-in-itself *meaningless* in order to defeat Kant but making it *meaningful* again in order to defeat the subjective idealist's boast that there is certainly nothing outside thought. Yet there is no real middle ground on this point. Either it is meaningful to speak of an ungraspable thing-in-itself, in which case we are weak correlationists, or else it is meaningless to speak of such a thing, in which case we are idealists. Ergo, strong correlationism is an impossible philosophical position. Seemingly aware of what a delicate philosophical maneuver he is making, Meillassoux asserts at least four times that *it is* a possible position despite the objection he clearly anticipates will be made. Here are the four instances I have found:

1. "For there is no way for thought to reject the possibility that what is meaningless for us might be veridical in itself. Why should the meaningless be impossible?" (36)

2. "Consequently, there is no sense in claiming to know that contradiction is absolutely impossible, for the only thing that is given to us is the fact that we cannot *think* anything that is impossible." (39; emphasis added)
3. "[N]othing can be said to be impossible, not even the unthinkable." (40)
4. "Thus the strong model of correlationism can be summed up in the following thesis: *it is unthinkable that the unthinkable should be impossible.*" (41)

The difficulty Meillassoux faces is that it is a question not just of the meaningless being impossible, but of treating the meaningless simultaneously as meaningful. That is to say, if we join Meillassoux in provisionally accepting the correlationist circle, then if we consider the statements "there is an apple on the table" and "there is an apple on the table for me," it is not just that the first is false and the second is true. Rather, both statements have exactly the same meaning, for according to Meillassoux the first converts instantly into the second. Since for correlationism "there is an apple on the table" automatically implies that it is there for thought, it means nothing different from "there is an apple on the table for me." Strictly speaking, this is *idealism*, since the strong correlationist forbids us from making any statement about something existing outside the thought–apple correlate that does not immediately collapse into a statement *about that very correlate*. But Meillassoux does not want to be an idealist, since he wants to be able to make meaningful mathematical statements about the primary qualities of things independent of humans. For this reason, in a second step he attempts to treat the phrase "outside of thought" as *meaningful* again – for if it were not meaningful, then we would not even be able to entertain any philosophical position other than idealism. In short, Meillassoux uses an idealist move against the weak correlationist and a weak correlationist move against the idealist. We cannot challenge idealism if it is not even *meaningful* to speak of a thing-in-itself outside thought. Yet the moment we concede it to be meaningful, we are suddenly weak correlationists again. Therefore, the strong correlationist position does not exist. We will soon see why this poses a dreadful problem that Meillassoux cannot overcome.

But first, we must consider his important argument about the essential *fideism* of contemporary thought. The end of metaphysics has meant the end of rationally provable absolutes. This makes every belief defensible, as long as no rational reason is given for it: "The end of metaphysics, understood as the 'de-absolutization of thought,' is thereby seen to consist in the rational legitimation of any and every variety of religious (or 'poetico-religious') belief in the absolute, so long [as] the latter invokes no authority by itself" (45). Stated differently, "the end of ideologies has taken the form of the unqualified victory of religiosity" (45). In other words, the end of metaphysics proves to be an unqualified victory for fideism, for the rule of faith over any responsibility to give reasons for one's beliefs. Among other negative features of fideism, it legitimizes blind fanaticism, which makes no pretense of defending itself with any reasons at all. Meillassoux closes chapter 2 with typically eloquent words on the topic: "Against dogmatism, it is important that we uphold the refusal of every metaphysical absolute, but against the reasoned violence of various fanaticisms, it is important that we re-discover in thought a modicum of absoluteness – enough of it, in any case, to counter the pretensions of those who would present themselves as its privileged trustees, solely by virtue of some revelation" (49).

Chapter 3 contains the philosophical core of *After Finitude*. Before Meillassoux proceeds to his innovative solution to the conflict between the correlationist circle and scientific realism, he helpfully resummarizes the terms of the problem (51). First, to think ancestral reality means to think a reality that is not merely for us, but absolute. Second, we cannot permit the existence of any necessary entity, since otherwise we would fall prey not only to dogmatism (which Kant effectively debunked) but to political ideology as well. Third and finally, we cannot go back to being naïve realists, because the correlationist circle is a powerful argument that must be faced head-on rather than ignored. For this very reason, when choosing between the weak and strong correlationist models, we must recognize the greater power of the strong model. In short, what we need is "a non-metaphysical absolute, capable of slipping through the mesh of the strong model" (51). Meillassoux adds the corollary that we cannot accept either a realist absolute or a correlationist one. For as just recalled, a realist absolute is excluded by the power of the correlationist circle, while a correlationist absolute "cannot pass through the meshes of facticity" (51). We should note in passing that, as examples of correlationist absolutes, Meillassoux gives the joint example of "idealist or vitalist" philosophies. This lumping together of idealism and vitalism is in fact ill-advised, though important enough to Meillassoux that it becomes the polemical centerpiece of his Berlin lecture. For in what sense do idealism and vitalism both "absolutize the correlate" of world and thought, as he claims in Berlin? Surely only in an equivocal sense. For what idealism does is exclude anything outside the thought–world correlate from existing at all, as in the philosophy of Berkeley (in the mainstream reading of Berkeley rather than Grant's). But "vitalism" – here Meillassoux really seems to mean "panyschism": the notion that everything thinks, not that everything is alive – vitalism, I contend, does no such thing. When a panpsychist philosopher tells us that this rock is thinking, and so is this grain of dust, and so is this tree and that star in the western sky, all she is saying is that everything thinks. She is not – repeat, *not* – saying that nothing exists outside thought. Stated differently, to say that something exists outside thought is called *realism* (in the mainstream meaning of the term, not Grant's) while to say that there is something in the world that does not think is called *Cartesian dualism*. These are two very different doctrines that Meillassoux is too quick to identify.

That objection aside, there are real sparks of brilliance in Meillassoux's strategy for addressing his predicament, caught as he is midway between correlationism and ancestrality, seemingly so opposed to each other. He sees more intellectual merit in the idealist response to Kantian correlationism than in the naïve realist one: "we must take as our exemplar the first metaphysical counter-offensive [i.e. German Idealism] against Kantian transcendentalism" (51). The greatness of these thinkers is that "they acknowledged correlationism's discovery . . . that we only have access to the for-us, not to the in-itself – but instead of concluding from this that the in-itself is unknowable, they concluded that the correlation is the only veritable in-itself" (52). Since Meillassoux finds this to be such a great breakthrough, why does he not simply become a Fichtean or a Hegelian and flatly endorse the idealist responses of these thinkers to Kant? The reason is that he thinks idealism fails to account for the *facticity* of the correlation: the fact that no reason can be given for why thought and world exist rather than not existing, and hence that the thought–world correlate is not a necessary being any more than are God or fate. For this reason, "we must try to understand why it is not the correlation but the facticity of the correlation that constitutes the absolute" (52; emphasis removed). At first, facticity seems to mark nothing but an epistemological limitation on human *knowledge* of the absolute; facticity has an air of something purely negative, even melancholic. But Meillassoux views this apparently dismal situation as a positive opportunity, much as Brassier did with nihilism: "facticity will be revealed to be a knowledge of the absolute because we are going to put back into the thing itself what we mistakenly took to be an incapacity in thought" (53; emphasis removed). The absence of reason that characterizes facticity, usually interpreted as a mark of human finitude, will instead be projected by Meillassoux into the things themselves: "absence of reason *is*, and can *only* be the *ultimate* property of the entity" (53). And again: "the ultimate absence of reason, which we will refer to as 'unreason,' is an absolute ontological property, and not the mark of the finitude of our knowledge" (53).

Naturally, the correlationist will claim that this is a misunderstanding, that facticity represents our fundamental ignorance as to how things really are, not our actual knowledge that existing things are contingent (53–4).

In order to answer the correlationist on this point, Meillassoux presents a marvelous imaginary dialogue between five philosophical characters, who need only fake Italian names to sound like characters drawn from the pages of Bruno. Instead, Meillassoux gives them simple descriptive names: the Christian dogmatist, the atheist dogmatist, the correlationist, the speculative idealist, and the speculative materialist (this last being Meillassoux himself). The argument begins with the two dogmatists quarrelling over the afterlife, with the Christian saying it is possible to know for sure that there is life after death, and the atheist countering that exactly the opposite can be proven. Along comes a correlationist: though it is not specified whether he is a "strong" or a "weak" one, he seems to be a strong correlationist. While both the Christian and the atheist are defending dogmatic realist views, the correlationist smugly counters that it is not possible to know anything about the afterlife itself. But now a fourth character arrives to trump them all: the subjective idealist. This triumphalistic personage notes that the two dogmatists and one correlationist are a lot more alike than they realize: "for all three believe that there could be an in-itself radically different from our present state, whether it is a God who is inaccessible to reason, or a sheer nothingness" (55). Stated differently: "because an in-itself that differs from the *for-us* is unthinkable, the idealist declares it to be impossible" (56). But it is not only the speculative idealist who feels theoretically unique in comparison with the other three interlocutors. The correlationist makes the same claim to supremacy for himself: for whereas the two dogmatists and one idealist all think they know the exact truth about what lies outside thought (heaven/hell for the Christian, nothingness for the atheist, and no outside at all for the idealist), the correlationist feels himself alone in remaining open to the possibility of some absolute otherness, alone in frankly acknowledging his ignorance while the three others make pompous claims to have the truth.

This debate having reached a deadlock, the Meillassouxian speculative materialist arrives: "She maintains that neither the two dogmatists, nor the idealist have managed to identify the absolute, because *the latter is simply the capacity-to-be-other as such, as theorized by the [correlationist] agnostic*" (56). Meillassoux's added twist, of course, is that the capacity-to-be-other refers no longer to our own ignorance, as the correlationist thinks, but to the *knowledge* that *any* of the options raised so far (heaven/hell, nothingness, and no change at all) are possible, along with many others. Why should we be persuaded of this, rather than simply of the correlationist's claim to ignorance? Here Meillassoux offers a clever argument: it is the correlationist himself who is forced to mutate into a speculative materialist, since other-wise he would become just another idealist. The argument runs as follows

(56–7). Unlike the idealist, the correlationist holds it to be possible that something exists outside the correlate. And this possibility cannot be merely *for us*, since in that case we remain absolutely trapped inside the circle of thought and are really just idealists in spite of ourselves. No. If correlationists claim to be something other than idealists, then the possibility of something existing outside the thought–world correlate must be an *absolute* possibility. Or, in Meillassoux's own words: "the correlationist's refutation of idealism proceeds by way of an absolutization (which is to say, a de-correlation) of the capacity-to-be-other presupposed in the thought of facticity . . ." (57). Though the correlationist continues to dispute the point a bit longer, his argument is already lost, and the speculative materialist spends the final two pages of the dispute tying up loose ends and celebrating her victory.

What should we make of this argument? Though spirited and novel, it seems to me to fail for the reason cited earlier. This form of the argument merely shows that the correlationist, *if he wants to claim to be different from the idealist*, must think of the capacity-to-be-other as absolute. And it is in fact true that, if the correlationist wants to avoid idealism, the only way to do it is to treat otherness as a real possibility in things rather than a simple limitation on our ability to know them; this is enough to turn the correlationist into a speculative materialist. But what Meillassoux does not prove in his four-page debate is that the correlationist *really is* different from the idealist. I stated earlier why I think the strong correlationist – the one Meillassoux honors most – *cannot* distinguish himself from the idealist. For the strong correlationist escapes weak correlationism (of which Kant is the most familiar example) only by saying that we cannot even *think* the thing-in-itself outside thought. To think something is to think it, plain and simple; if something is given to me, then it is *given* to me, as Meillassoux puts it at Goldsmiths. But in taking this line, the strong correlationist is effectively saying that the two phrases "a tree in-itself" and "a tree for-us" have the same meaning, since the former automatically converts into the latter. And that is an idealist position plain and simple, the very position adopted by German Idealism against Kant. To repeat, strong correlationism is just another name for idealism, not for a position distinct from idealism. Thus strong correlationism, and the speculative materialism that aspires to emerge from its absolutization, cannot get off the ground. It is simply another form of idealism.

In a clever wrap-up of the debate, Meillassoux claims to have "identi-fied the faultline that lies right at the heart of correlationism" (59). For if we accept that the strong correlationist and the idealist are different (as I do not, but let's play along for a moment), then the correlationist has two contradictory options, both of them requiring that the correlationist cave in and absolutize *something*. One option is simply to give up facticity and become an idealist, treating the thought–world correlate as the root of all reality, in the manner of the mainstream (non-Grantian) version of Berkeley. The other option is to give up the absoluteness of the correlate, though this requires absolutizing its *facticity*, which entails that something could always be other than it is, not just that we might be ignorant about it. This brings us to one of the most wonderful formulations in Meillassoux's book: "We are no longer upholding a variant of the principle of sufficient reason, according to which there is a necessary reason why everything is the way it is rather than otherwise, but rather the absolute truth of a *principle of unreason*" (60). The implications are profound, and now as always, *time* is at the center of the action for Meillassoux – just as it is, ironically, for the Meillassoux critic Peter Gratton.[18] For Meillassoux, it is "a *time* that would be capable of bringing forth or abolishing everything" (61). This time can be described as a "hyper-Chaos" (64), though not the sort of Heraclitean or Bergsonian flux one might imagine, since "both the destruction and the perpetual preservation of an entity must equally be able to occur for no reason. Contingency is such that anything might happen, even nothing at all" (63). Since Meillassoux declares that we have now passed successfully through the correlationist circle (63), we find ourselves face to face with a new absolute, though hardly a comforting one:

> what we see . . . is a rather menacing power – something insensible, and capable of destroying both things and worlds, of bringing forth monstrous absurdities, yet also of never doing anything, of realizing every dream, but also every nightmare, of engendering random and frenetic transformations, or conversely, of producing a universe that remains motionless down to its ultimate recesses, like a cloud bearing the fiercest storms, then the eeriest bright spells, if only for an interval of disquieting calm. (64)

It is this chaos that Meillassoux counts as the *primary* absolute of his philosophy, in comparison with which mathematics is only a *derived* absolute (65).

As disquieting as this hyper-chaos may be, Meillassoux holds that there is still an intellectual path leading beyond it. It consists in finding what he will call "figures" (80), his name for the necessary features of those contingent and non-necessary beings that he holds are all that is left to philosophy. Foremost among these figures are "non-contradiction and the 'there is' (i.e. that there is something rather than nothing) . . ." (80). Meillassoux gives us fascinating if unconventional proofs for both of these figures. Though non-contradiction might sound at first like a poor choice for a philosophy of sheer contingency and chaos, Meillassoux rejects the usual link made by philosophers between contradiction and sheer becoming. As he puts it: "it seems to us profoundly inaccurate to associate the thesis of real contradiction with the thesis of sovereign flux" (69). The surprising reason is that a contradictory entity would not be able to change at all: "such an entity could never become other than it is *because there would be no alterity for it in which to become*" (69). He continues the theme: "Let us suppose that a contradictory entity existed – what could possibly happen to it? Could it lapse into non-being? But *it is* contradictory, so that even if it happened not to be, it would still continue to be even in not-being, since this would be in conformity with its paradoxical 'essence'" (69). Stated more colorfully, "such an entity would be tantamount to a 'black hole of differences,' into which all alterity would be irremediably swallowed up" (70). As for the second figure, we can state Meillassoux's argument in more concise form: "it is necessary that there be something rather than nothing because it is necessarily contingent that there is something rather than something else" (76; emphasis removed). That is to say, for contingency to be real there must always be both existent things capable of not existing and inexistent things capable of existing. For now, let's simply note an interesting tension between this claim that something must exist rather than nothing, and the rather different claim, in at least one passage of *The Divine Inexistence*, that even dead matter (the lowest point in Meillassoux's cosmology as in Plotinus') can originate *ex nihilo* for no reason at all.

There is still a very large elephant in the room, and chapter 4 tackles it head-on with refreshing new resources. Meillassoux has now reversed the correlationist stance by taking its uncertainty of knowledge and transferring it directly into the things, which are now absolutely contingent rather than merely unknowable by us. In a famous passage that Brassier in particular dislikes, Meillassoux contends that we will "discover in our grasp of facticity the veritable *intellectual intuition* of the absolute" (82). We know that this absolute is hyper-chaos, in which the laws of nature might change at any moment for no reason at all. But if this is the case, then why does the world *seem* to be so stable? For even the most shocking natural disasters and historical collapses still seem to follow the same laws of spatio-temporal experience that appear to have governed all known periods of history and all measurable portions of the universe. In other words, why is the supposed hyper-chaos apparently so unchaotic? As a critic might say, "if physical laws were actually contingent, *we would already have noticed it* – moreover, it is quite likely that we would not be here to notice it, since the disorder resulting from such contingency would no doubt have atomized all consciousness" (84). Meillassoux addresses this objection by way of what he calls a speculative solution to Hume's problem, which can be defined as follows: "is it possible to demonstrate that the same effects will always follow from the same causes *ceteris paribus*, i.e. all other things being equal?" (85). By offering a "speculative solution," Meillassoux means one that is different from the metaphysical solution (Leibniz), the skeptical solution (Hume), and the transcendental one (Kant). Stated briefly, the Leibnizian metaphysical solution would prove the necessary existence of God and the best of all possible worlds; the Humean skeptical solution says that cause and effect are simply grounded in our habits of seeing things apparently happen the same way frequently; and the Kantian transcendental solution argues that no coherent experience would be possible if cause and effect were not imposed on reality by the structure of the human understanding itself. Meillassoux notes a common link between all of these different strategies: "What they all have in common is the fact that none of them ever calls into question the truth of the causal necessity" (90; emphasis removed). This is precisely what Meillassoux aims to do. Though it may seem strange to say that we cannot prove causal necessity *because there is none*, he asks us to consider the analogous case of non-Euclidean geometry. When the Russian geometer Nikolai Lobachevsky (1792–1856) tried to prove the absurdity of building a geometry that denied the Euclidean postulate that only one parallel to a given line can be drawn through any given point, he found that it was not absurd at all: instead, "[he] discovered a new geometry, which is just as consistent as that of Euclid, but differs from it" (92). Likewise, Meillassoux suspects that if we begin in a state of shock at his elimination of causal necessity, "little by little, we will discover that the acausal universe is just as consistent and just as capable of accounting for our actual experience as the causal universe. But we will also discover that the former is a universe devoid of all those enigmas that are part and parcel of the belief in physical necessity" (92). The road to this non-Euclidean philosophy will pass, unsurprisingly, through mathematics.

First, Meillassoux detours through a useful discussion of Jean-René Vernes (1914–2012), an old friend of the Meillassoux family who is most famous as a champion bridge-player and as the inventor of the popular board game Risk, but who is also the author of a number of philosophical books. Meillassoux thinks highly of Vernes's *Critique of Aleatory Reason* (still available only in French), which in his estimation is "written with a concision worthy of the philosophers of the seventeenth century" (95). Vernes provides the argument, missing from the classical philosophers, as to how we infer the necessity of the laws of nature from the apparent stability of the world. Though Meillassoux will quickly reject Vernes's argument, he respects it for its exemplary lucidity. Whereas Kant links the *a priori* realm with necessity, Vernes ties it to contingency. For example, if we have a pair of

151

normal six-sided dice, there are thirty-six possible results on any given roll. If we are simply adding up the numbers on the two dice, as in the game of craps, we will find that 7 is the most common total, while 2 and 12 are the least common. Knowing that each of the six numbers is equally possible for each die, we can proceed to calculate the probability for the result of each roll. But let's imagine that, at some point, the rolls no longer seem to be random. We have now been rolling the dice for an hour, and the same numbers have come up every time. It would hardly take us a full hour to conclude that there must be a hidden cause, such as a piece of lead hidden inside each die, that skews the results away from the purely random. Meillassoux now follows Vernes in imagining an even more extreme situation: "let us now suppose that the dice we are playing with have been landing with the same [faces] up not just for an hour, but throughout our entire lives, and even as far back as human memory stretches. And let us also suppose that these dice are not just six-sided, but possess millions and millions of sides" (96–7). If even the million-sided dice rolled for the entirety of human history were to yield the same results on every throw, then there would obviously be a very high probability that some hidden cause is guiding the results. Here, the bridge-player and game-designer Vernes does an admirable job of applying the gambler's logic of probabilities to the question of how we can be sure that the laws of nature apply.

Yet this probabilistic logic is precisely what Meillassoux rejects. The problem, as he sees it, is that Vernes "proceeds by extending the probabilistic reasoning which the gambler applied to an event that is internal to our universe (the throw of the dice and its result), to the universe as such" (97; emphasis removed). He imagines that the universe might be constructed not in such a way that the billiard balls rebound from each other in impact, but in a way that "results rather in both balls flying into the air, or fusing together, or turning into two immaculate but rather grumpy mares, or into two maroon but rather affable lilies, etc." (97). In other words, Vernes imagines the million- or trillion-sided die as representing many possible universes, and, "every time it is thrown, this dice-universe inevitably results in the same physical universe – mine, the one I have always been able to observe on a daily basis" (97). Vernes, more explicitly than Hume and Kant before him, thinks of the entire universe as resulting from the throw of a loaded die that is loaded not by a hidden piece of lead, but by hidden laws. Verne calls this hidden factor "matter," though Meillassoux complains that it might just as well be called "providence" (98).

On what basis does Meillassoux object to such probabilistic reasoning, which we all use every day to guide our intellectual and personal lives? The crux of his argument is that probabilities cannot be calculated unless we know the *totality* of possible results, the *totality* of faces of the die. The faces might even be infinite, mind you, as long as they can be totalized as such: "Take for example a homogeneous rope of determinate length, both of whose extremities are being subjected to equal tension. I can calculate the positive probability that it will break at one of its points, even though these 'breaking points' are theoretically infinite along the length of the rope, since they are 'dimensionless'" (102). But although probabilities can be calculated in this way even when it is a matter of infinite possible results, the situation changes if we speak of the *transfinite* realm discovered by Cantor, whose work is one of the linchpins of Badiou's philosophy no less than Meillassoux's own. One way of expressing Cantor's great discovery is to look at the standard Zermelo–Fraenkel (or "ZF") axiomatization of Cantorian set theory, which results in an "unencompassable pluralization of infinite quantities" (104). Stated more simply, there is not one greatest infinity that contains them all but many different sizes of infinity. Though initially rejected by most of Cantor's contemporaries (leading ultimately to his mental illness), the great German mathematician David Hilbert (1862–1943) famously stated in 1926 that "no one will be able to expel us from the paradise that Cantor created for us."[19] If, for example, we take an infinite set which has A elements and then define B as the total number of possible relations between all the parts inside A, then obviously B will always be greater than A. In this manner, we can construct a countless number of infinite sets, each of them larger than the one that precedes it. As Meillassoux puts it:

> It is possible to construct an unlimited succession of infinite sets, each of which is of a quantity superior to that of the sets whose parts it collects together. This succession is known as the series of alephs, or the series of transfinite cardinals. But this series itself *cannot be totalized*, in other words, it cannot be collected together into some "ultimate" quantity. (104)

By now, the observant reader may have discerned Meillassoux's strategy against Vernes. Whereas possible events internal to the world can be totalized and therefore calculated as to their probability, the number of possible worlds cannot be totalized, and therefore Vernes' reasoning is illegitimate when he calls it "extremely improbable" that the laws of nature would seem so stable if there were not some hidden cause lying behind them. In Meillassoux's view, it is neither probable nor improbable that the laws of nature should change at any given moment for no reason whatsoever, or conversely, that they should remain the same for millions of years or perhaps forever. As astonishing as this reasoning may seem, it will provide the major intellectual instrument for *The Divine Inexistence*, which we will soon see is completely devoted to a specific possible future event (the sudden birth of

God and resurrection of the dead) that sounds incredibly unlikely if calculated in terms of probability. Once people begin to feel more comfortable with this application of Cantor to the probability of events – though it will always be controversial and shunned by many – I suspect that we may begin to see other, younger philosophers start to make use of the argument.

The heavy argumentation of *After Finitude* now being complete, it is left to Meillassoux's brief chapter 5 to draw some more general conclusions and tie up some loose ends. His first order of business is to expand the concept of "ancestrality" into that of "dia-chronicity," a term that pertains to the future as well as the past. For it is a question not just of entities that existed *prior* to the emergence of thought but also of entities that might exist *after* the eventual extermination of thought. One important aspect of dia-chronicity is that, even if we imagine a scenario under which humans existed simultaneously with the birth of the universe itself (so that no arche-fossil ever existed), the possible *future* situation of a world without thought would still pose a valid objection to correlationism. For this reason, Meillassoux holds that "the Galilean–Copernican revolution has no other meaning than that of the paradoxical unveiling of thought's capacity to think what there is whether thought exists or not" (116). And hand in hand with this goes the discovery that "what is mathematizable cannot be reduced to a correlate of thought" (117).

While mathematics was in the midst of gaining access to that which is independent of thought, Meillassoux holds, philosophy was blowing a golden opportunity and doing exactly the opposite. For while Kant credits himself with making a Copernican revolution in philosophy, he actually gives us a "Ptolemaic counter-revolution" (110). For even as modern mathematical physics gave us, for the first time, a means of obtaining non-correlational absolute knowledge of the world, "[Kant's] transcendental philosophy insisted that the condition for the conceivability of physical science consisted in revoking all non-correlational knowledge of this same world" (118). Meillassoux is certainly right when he says that natural science has gone ever further afield, discovering new and more stunning landscapes in both the macro- and the microcosmic realms. To a large extent he is also right that the philosopher has become cramped into "an ever narrower 'zone,' terrain, or habitat, but one of which the philosopher remains lord and master" (121). His remarkable book closes with a stirring analogy that has already inspired numerous readers: "If Hume's problem woke Kant from his dogmatic slumber, we can only hope that the problem of ancestrality succeeds in waking us from our correlationist slumber, by enjoining us to reconcile thought and absolute" (128).

Study Questions for Section B

1 According to Meillassoux, how would the correlationist respond to a realist argument based on the "arche-fossil"?
2 What is the difference between "strong" and "weak" correlationism, and which does Meillassoux think has a more powerful argument? Give one or more examples of philosophers of each type.
3 What does Meillassoux mean by the "principle of unreason"?
4 Why does Meillassoux disagree with the attempted proof of the stability of laws of nature given by Jean-René Vernes? (Please refer to the mathematician Georg Cantor in your answer.)
5 Explain why Meillassoux thinks Kant is guilty of a "Ptolemaic counter-revolution." Do you agree with this claim?

C Glimpses of the Divine Inexistence

In most periods of recent continental philosophy, there have been one or more famous unpublished works eagerly awaited by a large audience. For some decades, Heidegger's *Contributions to Philosophy* was rumored as a hidden masterpiece that might be even greater than *Being and Time*, though in my view that proved not to be the case. Later, it was various unpublished essays by Derrida, circulated among only an elect few insiders. Badiou's *Logics of Worlds* was intensely awaited for seventeen years after the publication of its predecessor *Being and Event*, and, though some devotees of the earlier work were disappointed by the sequel, I tend to prefer the latter. The publication of Latour's important *An Enquiry into Modes of Existence* in 2012 came after nearly two decades of rumors and circulated drafts. In general, we can see that one of the cultural quirks of continental philosophy seems to be a built-in fondness for reportedly major works not yet revealed to the public. Today, the best candidate for such a highly anticipated unpublished book is probably Meillassoux's *The Divine Inexistence*. Though the original doctoral thesis version of the work (1997) is no longer difficult to obtain online, it has not been translated. Nor does Meillassoux wish to share prematurely from the reportedly multi-volume revision of the book now in preparation. But as a sort of compromise, he ultimately proved willing to let me comment on excerpts from a rewritten 2003 version of the original. The sole condition was that Meillassoux insisted that my commentary not appear alone, and that anything I might discuss from the book should also appear in its original form. This is why, as an appendix to my book on Meillassoux, I undertook to translate roughly one-sixth of *The Divine Inexistence* (the 2003 version) from French into English.[20]

Although the final look of *The Divine Inexistence* is anyone's guess, the major themes discussed in the 2003 draft are so quintessentially Meillassouxian that it is hard to imagine their disappearance from the eventual published book. The primary argument of the project can almost be guessed from the title: God does not exist but might exist in the future. The meaning of both phrases is easy enough to explain. Although it is common to hear philosophers say that "God does not exist" or "God is dead," this is not the spin that Meillassoux puts on the theme. Among other things, Meillassoux's notion of the divine inexistence is meant as a response to the famous problem of evil: if God is all-good, all-knowing, and all-powerful, then why does He permit evil things to happen, such as "allowing a child to be devoured by dogs"? (284). The twentieth century in particular was filled with numerous horrifically unjust deaths, and any God who allowed the Holocaust and the Killing Fields of Cambodia could count in Meillassoux's eyes only as a loathsome deity.[21] His fresh and surprising solution to the problem of evil is that God *does not yet exist*: He did not "allow" the atrocities of the twentieth century and all other ages to occur, because He was not yet here to stop them. An obvious alternative solution would be the atheist one: there is no God, and never will be, and we are all thrown together into an unjust world where there is no redemption in the afterlife for those who endured misery here below. For Meillassoux, this is nothing more than a cynical approach that gives up any hope of justice for the dead. As for the second part of the phrase, "God might exist in the future," the claim is shocking enough that, since being publicized, it has cost Meillassoux some of his erstwhile followers on the materialist-atheist Left. And yet, one can make a supportive case for Meillassoux here. The only real argument one can muster against him is that the odds of God suddenly springing into existence at some indefinite point in the future are so ridiculously small that we can hardly take the idea seriously. Yet with his daring use of Cantor near the end of *After Finitude to* destroy probabilistic reasoning, Meillassoux tries to eliminate probability as a criterion in ultimate ontological matters. With probability erased from the picture, we can focus instead on the *most significant* possibilities in our world. In fact, two or three of these astonishing events have already occurred, depending on how one reads a certain ambiguity in Meillassoux's presentation. It is not entirely clear from the textual evidence whether matter emerged at some point *ex nihilo* or whether it was always there; one can find passages in Meillassoux's work supporting both readings. But he is clear that life emerged from matter, and that thought emerged from life, for no reason at all. This leaves just one possible final emergence: that of justice and the virtual God from the existing World of human thought. Ominously enough, Meillassoux adds that there is no guarantee this will ever occur.

But let's go back to the beginning of the excerpts of *The Divine Inexistence* included in my book on Meillassoux.[22] There, he begins by clarifying what he means by advent *ex nihilo*, which sounds so much like a traditional religious notion of the sort he normally shuns. The Meillassouxian *ex nihilo* does not literally mean what it sounds like: "By advent *ex nihilo* we do not mean that being arose entirely from originary nothingness. What we mean, stated in classical terms, is that there is more in the effect than in the cause: that this 'more' therefore has no reason at all for its advent, and hence nothing (no law) can limit it" (226). This is clear already from Meillassoux's repeated discussions of the currently existing three orders of matter, life, and thought. No particular configuration of matter automatically gives rise to thought, just as no state of life automatically entails thought; at best, there is some sort of relation between the new order and its "underpinning" in the previous one, but no immediate causal relationship between them. At least one possible objection can already be raised: by claiming that the three main orders are matter, life, and thought, Meillassoux is adopting a rather traditional classification without ever arguing for it explicitly. We know that he has no patience for the sort of "vitalism" that blurs the lines between the mineral and vegetable kingdoms, and perhaps in this case the burden of proof really is on the vitalists. But why is the next gap located between life and thought in particular? Why are there not additional gaps within the animal kingdom? Is the gap between bacteria and dolphins really so negligible compared to the one between dolphins and humans? Here we find another point of lingering Cartesianism in Meillassoux's position, despite the latter's introduction of "life" somewhere between matter and thought, the only two zones of reality that Descartes accepts other than God. The reader searches in vain for any argument on this point in *The Divine Inexistence*, and even for any scientific anecdotes to this end, such as Heidegger was able to scrape up for his ultimately disappointing 1929/30 lecture course on animal life.[23]

We return to the theme of the effect containing more than is in the cause. This is an important notion for Meillassoux, and he presses the point in interesting ways. Not only is there more in the effect than in the cause, but possible effects do not precede actual ones. Rather than citing Deleuze on this point, as do so many contemporary thinkers, Meillassoux makes use of the language of Cantor: "The essence of the Universe is disclosed in the advent of a Universe of possible cases that cannot be recorded in a list (in fact or in principle) in the form of a Universe of Universes of cases, because the Whole of these Universes cannot exist" (227–8). And, in keeping with his opposition to the principle of sufficient reason (the only place I know of where he addresses part–whole relations no less than temporal causes), Meillassoux rejects any definite link between qualities and their underlying reasons: "A red is without why because no material counterpart can ever tell us how this red is red . . . For matter is not haunted by any potentiality of red, any pale pink specter, before the advent of red among the sensitive powers of the living" (230). This beautiful language is soon followed by even more: "If quality suddenly arises, it does so *from nothing*, not from the potentiality of a Universe-Whole where it would have lain in ambush for all eternity" (230). This way of looking at things allows Meillassoux to downplay the view of some philosophers that whatever emerges must have been present already in some early germinal form. In particular, he dislikes the argument of Denis Diderot (1713–1784) for hylozoism, the view that life is somehow cryptically present even in the lowest inanimate matter. We are already familiar with Meillassoux's negative view on this topic: "we can certainly go ahead and affirm that there is only a difference of 'degree' between matter and organic life . . . [Yet] no one has ever grasped what the continuity of mineral 'life' . . . would be with life carried to the point of maximum intensity" (231). In short, "*nothing* was alive before the advent of the living" (234).

Meillassoux now proposes what he calls an "immanent ethics." This phrase refers to "an ethics that posits this life as the only desirable life . . . an ethics that manifests . . . such a desire for this life that it wishes this life to be immortal" (236–7; emphasis removed). But what he has in mind is nothing like Nietzsche's eternal return, in which every detail of our lives will repeat itself an infinite number of times in the future. Instead, Meillassoux is thinking of the rebirth of the dead in *this* world, though with an open future in front of them rather than just the doomed Nietzschean repetition of what has come before. Though the rebirth of the dead may sound to mainstream enlightened secularists like a sad religious myth, we already know Meillassoux's low opinion of applying probabilistic arguments to important events in the universe: "[rebirth] is an event that would be no more astonishing than [the advent of life from matter, or thought from life] that *have* in fact *taken place*" (238). He introduces an unexpected piece of terminology when he counterintuitively uses the capital W "World" for specific worlds and the lower-case w "world" for the (non-totalizable) universe as a whole. His reason for doing so has philosophical importance: "Worlds arise suddenly from the world, and if these have a right to a majestic capital letter for the first time, it is because there is more in a World than in the world, since there is more in what ensues than there is in the origin . . ."

(238). For this reason it is actually a *good* sign that we human beings are relative latecomers to the world. Whereas Brassier speaks of the "pathetic" character of human self-esteem, Meillassoux ventures a dramatic *increase* in the self-esteem of our species: "humans have access to the eternal truth of the world. Thus nothing more can appear beyond humans considered as thinking beings" (239). There is no use awaiting hyper-genius artificial intelligence or the arrival of superior beings from other planets, since these would only be more efficient processors of the eternal truths that humans are already capable of reaching. This capacity for grasping eternal truths is not just some aloof intellectual exercise, for it also includes a sense of justice, defined as "the strict *equality* between all humans qua human. The eternal truths to which our condition grants access are in fact *indifferent to differences*, to the innumerable and necessary differences between thinkers" (240). And of all injustice, "the most extreme is still death: absurd death, early death, death inflicted by those unconcerned with equality" (240). Yet despite this unique capacity of humans for justice, a capacity not found in any lower order of the cosmos, Meillassoux still holds that we are dependent on matter, life, and thought (240). Justice could not exist if these three prior orders had not already come into being for no reason at all.

We should not fail to mention Meillassoux's particular use of the term "symbolization," which in his view "is one of the basic and original features" of his philosophy (243). He defines this term as meaning "an immanent rational link between being and the universal" (243; emphasis removed). Above all, Meillassoux's use of symbolization is opposed to ethical doctrines such as those of Nietzsche, for whom the creator simply *legislates* new values as a way of moving history along. For Meillassoux, values are supposed to help us *discover* something about the world, even if we cannot be sure at first if they are rational achievements and not simply the result of personal prejudice: "Every philosophical enterprise starts from a postulate that may well be impossible to demonstrate, and which may even be false or ideological . . . Philosophy begins with a wager on the still unjustified certainty that value is not a mere socially useful artifice, but rests on an ontological truth" (244). The symbol is meant to be a bridge between these two realms, and though we might imagine there are as many symbols as there are philosophers, Meillassoux acknowledges just *four* basic symbols that he sees as governing eras of history of vastly different length: the cosmological, the naturalist/ romantic, the historical, and the factial symbols (246).

The *cosmological* symbol, arising in Ancient Greece, is associated with the dawn of philosophy, "born from the initial separation of the discourses of value and being" (246), a separation Meillassoux terms a *scission*. For on the one hand, astronomy and pre-Socratic nature philosophy give up on mythical explanations of the sky, replacing them with rational ones. Yet nonetheless, ethics lingers for some time in the traditional way of thinking: "thus it is possible for a cultivated Greek to explain courage by narrating the exploits of Achilles even after ceasing to believe in such discourses as concerns the movement of the planets" (247). What Socrates and later figures attempted that the pre-Socratics did not yet try was to *repair* the broken link between the different discourses on nature and ethics. Ultimately, the cosmological Symbol pointed to the rationality guiding the heavens and asked humans to adopt such rationality in guiding their own affairs as well.

We now turn to "the collapse of the cosmological Symbol," which "can be linked to the Newtonian decomposition of planetary orbits into linear movements which by [nature] are identical to terrestrial movements" (249). The Aristotelian distinction between natural and violent motion is gone, and with it any hope of our being inspired by a cosmic rational justice in which no one can any longer believe. Meillassoux sees in this collapse the cause of "the voluptuous and libertine skepticism that runs like a thread through the figures of the Enlightenment" (249). The new Symbol, the naturalist or romantic one, is due to Jean-Jacques Rousseau (1712–1778), who tried "to replace the opposition between sublunary and superlunary found in the cosmological Symbol with one between natural and social" (250). The good is no longer found in the sky, which has become just another site of violent motions, but is now revealed in pity, in our sympathy for innocent children, and in living nature, animality, or the body. Yet this Symbol collapses in a matter of decades under the weight of its obvious flaws, such as the evident fact that "pity is no more common in the living than are war, violence, or cruelty" (250). What replaces this brief era is what Meillassoux calls "the true successor of the Greek Symbol," namely, the *historic* Symbol. No longer able to trust the Cosmos or Nature as guarantors of our values, we now take comfort in History as the source of what we value. Meillassoux holds that the Historic symbol is now fading before our eyes, following a good long run. It is easy to see why history seemed like such a good candidate to guide us properly: "The movement of history is not properly human, since it is not the result of any individual will. But like the laws of nature it is not absurd, since it knows a finality whose culmination is Justice" (251). This becomes especially visible in the two opposed teleological theories of economics. For the liberal, all the selfish acts of individuals combine to lead to the greater good, as in the famous fable of the bees of Bernard Mandeville (1670–1733). At the same time, "for the Marxist, the principle of social becoming occurs through the necessary auto-collapse of whatever alienates humans, and in this way their emancipation is attained" (251).

What all three of these Symbols have in common is a belief in real necessity – most recently, the belief that history and the economy will lead us in the right direction with inexorable logic. By contrast, "the factial proposes a new symbolization, the first *non*-metaphysical one" (255). The world is "no longer identified with a determinate and perennial substance, but rather with the possibility of lawless change" (255). As a result, we can no longer think of this world as inherently the best or worst of all possible worlds, since it could conceivably become either of these. If we embrace the factial Symbol, our enthusiasm for a possible World of justice will become invigorating. But what will happen if that World somehow becomes real? Would there not be something boring or depressing about such a perfect World? The difference between the present ethics that hopes for a World of justice and the ethics of that World once it has arrived is what Meillassoux calls "the ethical scission" (256–7). And he thinks it is possible "to determine the exact nature of the contradiction between an ethics ruled by the enthusiasm of the Symbol and an ethics ruled by a truer principle" (257).

Ethics cannot be grounded in God or in some tautological Kantian notion of duty. Nor can it simply be founded on "the pre-eminence of the human species" (258) over others, which would merely be the factual result of a power struggle. Instead, "it is a question of demonstrating the *necessary superiority* (*de jure* and not *de facto*) of the thinking being over all other beings, while refusing the idea of the necessary existence of such a being, which runs counter to our ontology" (258). There is a sense in which Meillassoux has already been pointing towards such a demonstration all along. He thinks that causes are always inferior to their effects, and he also holds that human thought is the final order at the end of the chain of causes. The value of the human "is drawn from the *thought* of the eternal of which it is the mortal stakeholder – not from the eternal itself, which only amounts to the neutrality of becoming" (259). While some critics might see this primacy of the human as just another case of the prevalent anthropocentric philosophy, Meillassoux insists that human superiority is an idea that has never been seriously maintained. After all, any previous claims in this direction tried to establish human superiority in derivative fashion, by giving humans value only through their contemplation of God or the good rather than (as Meillassoux recommends) through the *thinking* of these (259). Stated more concisely: "Value belongs to the act of knowing *itself*; humans have value not because of *what* they know but *because* they know" (260).

We now encounter another important difference between Brassier and Meillassoux, despite their shared commitment (foreign to Grant and OOO) to the exemplary role of science and/or mathematics in coming to grips with reality. I refer to Meillassoux's absolute rejection of any form of

Prometheanism, a doctrine he associates with power rather than justice: "Promethean humanism is nothing but a religious version of the human as self-fabricated. It is an idolization of power by humans: not power in God, but in humans become God" (262). Unfortunately, it is not even the best part of ourselves that we humans transpose into God. For "what humans transpose into the religious God is not their own essence, as [Ludwig] Feuerbach and the young Marx claimed, but rather the degradation of their own essence" (262). Religions normally reserve the most horrible actions and collective punishments for a vengeful and wrathful God. But if we accept the Promethean outlook, "if humans become God, then why should they deprive themselves of the same sorts of actions? All the crimes of God become accessible to humans and the deified human can always justify them with the same subtlety as that of the theologian deciphering the superior goodness of the Lord in natural catastrophes" (262–3).

Yet we face another ethical problem aside from the evil temptations of Prometheanism, namely: given the non-causal dependence of the World of justice on any present action – since if it arises this would be for no reason at all – what is to prevent us from falling into a "lazy fatalism"? (263). Rather than simply being lazy, I might even choose to go further and select the lifestyle of a Sadean libertine, knowing that whomever I exploit, torture, or murder at the peak of my pleasures may eventually be reborn in the World of justice anyway. If I have no afterlife to fear, and if all of my victims are to be reborn, then why not enjoy myself at the expense of anyone within reach? Meillassoux does not address the case of the Sadean criminal directly, though he does lay down the law for the lazy fatalist, who "really just manifests the arbitrary desire of his own vital perpetuation: an individual and capricious desire for rebirth that envisages this rebirth as an end and not as a condition of the end" (264). Ultimately, Meillassoux holds that a World of justice that is not actively awaited through acts of justice here and now would not really be a World of justice. For, "if rebirth occurred in such a way that no act of justice had awaited it, it would contain nothing of the universal; we would be dealing only with a blind recommencement imposed anonymously on our humanity" (264). Life in the fourth World should be conceived "as the hidden resumption of the course of our existence, charged with the memory of its past" (265). This has the strange implication that the possible World of justice would be so only for those who had actively engaged in acts of justice beforehand. What would be the experience in the World of justice of narcissistic and psychopathic killers, given that they did nothing to await it with just acts? This issue is left unaddressed, and at this point we can only speculate what Meillassoux might say about it.

We now reach the point of resolving the ethical scission "between the ethics of the present (an ethics of hope for the advent to come) and the ethics of the future that follows this hope and which thus appears to be, literally, an ethics of despair" (270). Once the World of justice arrives, our previous desire for justice is no longer relevant, and we now have an ethics "of a benevolence inherent in a condition emancipated from early death" (270). Yet this will not work for everyone, since there are those for whom justice is not an end in itself but only "the trace of something beyond thought" (271). Meillassoux obviously wants nothing to do with this fundamentally religious hunger for transcendence, since the recommencement of our current lives is for him a sufficient object of hope: "all 'morality' that does not support the perspective of the realization of its object is a religious morality" (271).

Ultimately, the link between being and humans will be provided not by yet another Symbol but by a Christ-like mediator who has at least one unique feature not found in the Christian version of Christ. Along with the expected goodness, omniscience, and omnipotence to be expected from this Messianic figure, there is also the original twist that this mediator *can* and *should* abolish their own superiority once rebirth occurs. "With this unique gesture, the contingency of the mediator's own power is subordinated to a will to become the equal of everyone else. In this way the mediator accedes to the sovereign human possibility of not being the chosen one of its own power, even in this case of omnipotence" (273). Strange as it may sound, this omniscient and omnipotent mediator will end up living among us, as just another average neighbor, once the rebirth of all humans has occurred. All of this obviously cuts against the grain of the always fashionable atheism of the philosopher class. But Meillassoux is no more a fan of atheism than he is of religion itself. The major problem with atheism is that amounts to "a ratification of the religious partition of existence" (274; emphasis removed). That is to say, "atheism consists in being satisfied with the unsatisfying territory that religion cedes to it . . . One begins by admitting that the territory of immanence is just as [bad as] religion describes it, then one declares that this territory is the only one that exists, and finally one invents every possible way of rendering it livable *despite* that fact" (275; emphasis removed). The atheist is left with little more than "the 'gallant' and 'ironic' joy of our finitude, a superior amusement procured by incessant struggles" (275), and the like.

The conclusion of the book begins with a question that is very familiar in recent French philosophy: "how can we think the unity of Jewish religion and Greek reason?" (277). Meillassoux certainly does not want such a unification to take place either on religion's watch or on that of the atheist: "for the atheist, God is a matter for the priest; for the philosopher, God is too serious a matter for the priests" (279). We are not the creatures of God but, rather, His possible ancestor, and many of our pains are perhaps just the birth-pangs of a God to come. And, further, though with an unfortunate echo of Descartes' inadequate theory of animals: "we suffer because, unlike the animal, which does not know the possible humanity of its becoming, we know the possible divinity of our own" (280). The book ends with a helpful discussion of the four possible relations of God with humans, of which three have already been tried. *First*, we can decide not to believe in God because He *does not* exist. This is of course the atheist position, which leads to "sadness, tepidity, cynicism" (286) and is therefore to be rejected. *Second*, we can believe in God because He *does* exist, which leads among other things to "the confusion . . . of God as love and God as power" and a theodicy that even justifies such atrocities as children being devoured by dogs (286). *Third*, there is the rarer option of not believing in God because He *does* exist, which Meillassoux identifies with the position of Lucifer, "of rebellion against the Creator which expresses a reactive need to hold someone responsible for the evils of this world" (287). Only the *fourth* option has not yet been tried: believing in God because he *does not* exist. This new alternative having finally been proposed, "one must choose" (287).

The great originality of *The Divine Inexistence* also poses the greatest future challenge for the project. As mentioned earlier, Meillassoux's natural readership had previously seemed to be rationalist, materialist, atheist, political Leftists of the same sort who have also flocked to the books of Badiou and to Brassier's *Nihil Unbound*. Although Meillassoux himself is beyond all doubt a rationalist, a materialist, and a political Leftist, the apparent non-atheist direction of his work is bound to alienate many readers who are otherwise sympathetic to his views. Part of this is because some readers of philosophy are simply unwilling to take seriously any theory that speaks of God at all, no matter how brilliantly argued it may be. Throw in the need for a Messianic mediator, as Meillassoux does, and the soup becomes even harder for many readers to swallow. Based on all these considerations, the most likely outcome for *The Divine Inexistence* would be that it finds a large number of admiring but incredulous readers, in awe of the dialectical originality of the book but not the least bit inclined to follow its religious-sounding conclusions.

Nonetheless, I am inclined to think that another of the book's most counterintuitive claims promises an important future for it. Quite apart from the fact that God is the subject of the book, the sheer improbability of the resurrection of the dead is enough to spark laughing disbelief among readers in a way that even the most surprising conclusions of *After Finitude* did not. But is there not something of lasting interest in Meillassoux's argument that, given the transfinite number of possible worlds, there is no way to call the laws of these worlds either probable or improbable? When judging the possible future fortunes of a philosophy, we are too often focused on which arguments will be plausible enough to convince the most people. But in fact, philosophies usually spread their influence by being overthrown – usually by being either *radicalized* or *reversed* – and thus they most often survive by being used for purposes the opposite of those for which they were designed.[24] Though stranger things have happened, I suspect that Meillassoux *will not* convince a significant number of younger philosophers to await the advent of a virtual God and the rebirth of the dead. Perhaps the most useful device in his strange toolbox, the one that will prove most fruitful for others of a vastly different mindset, is his critique of probability and the shifting of focus to the most *important* possible permutations of a situation rather than the most "likely" ones. One indication of this is that perhaps the most significant application of Meillassoux's work to another field so far has been in Elie Ayache's *The Blank Swan*, which applies Speculative Materialism to a new understanding of the stock market. I have a sense that other such applications of this wonderfully strange and perhaps not impractical philosophy will eventually arise.

Questions for Section C

1 What is the meaning of the phrase "the divine inexistence"?
2 How would Meillassoux respond to a critic who claimed that God suddenly existing in the future is absurdly improbable?
3 We saw earlier that Brassier views human self-esteem as "pathetic." We now see that Meillassoux views humans as the highest possible entity, not to be superseded by any alien race, no matter how intelligent. What are their respective reasons for these opposite views, and which do you find more convincing?
4 What does it mean when Meillassoux says that we must believe in God precisely because He *does not* exist?
5 Although many contemporary philosophers are atheists, Meillassoux does not consider atheism a valid philosophical position. Why not?

Conclusion:
The Two Axes of Speculative Realism

As is often true of new intellectual currents, Speculative Realism's initial audience consisted primarily of younger readers. One of the first of the established generation of thinkers to respond in print was Slavoj Žižek, with his typical alertness to new trends. In *Less Than Nothing* (2012), his colossal book on Hegel, Žižek took a brief detour to discuss the four Goldsmiths authors. He refers there to

> the limitation of speculative realism, a limitation signaled in the fact that it immediately split into four orientations which form a kind of Greimasian semiotic square: Meillassoux's "speculative materialism," Harman's "object-oriented philosophy," Grant's neovitalism, and Brassier's radical nihilism. The two axes along which these four positions are placed are divine/secular and scientific/metaphysical.[1]

Though attention from Žižek ought to be a welcome event for any author, there are already three problems with this opening passage. First, it is hard to see why the split of a group into four separate positions should count as a "limitation," especially given that the differences between us were already present well before the Goldsmiths workshop took place. As I see it, the diversity of positions was always the greatest *strength* of Speculative Realism, and it is the principal reason that I miss the days when the group still existed as a forum for friendly discussion. Second, the four orientations do not form a "Greimasian semiotic square." The fourfold structure analyzed by Algirdas Greimas is just one of a great many found in the history of human thought, and the markedly anti-realist field of semiotics is certainly not the right framework within which to understand four explicitly realist philosophies.

This brings us to the third and biggest problem with the cited passage. Žižek is right to imply that fourfold structures in philosophy generally result from the crossing of two separate axes or dualisms. Unfortunately, he gets only one of the axes right: "The two axes along which these four [Speculative Realist] positions are placed are divine/secular and scientific/metaphysical." The second of these is not just true, but also immediately clear to anyone who takes a quick dip into Speculative Realist writings. As Žižek accurately puts it: "Although both Meillassoux and Brassier advocate a scientific view of reality as radically contingent and apprehensible through formalized science . . . both Harman and Grant advocate a non-scientific metaphysical approach . . ."[2] Meillassoux actually emphasizes mathematics over the natural sciences, and I would not say that Brassier is particularly devoted to contingency in the full-fledged way that Meillassoux is. But leaving that aside, it is clear that Brassier and Meillassoux are the two Speculative Realists who see mathematics and/or natural science as privileged discourses about the nature of reality. Grant has plenty to say about science as well, though with a bit of a Schellingian "mad scientist" feel to his discussions; when it comes to contemporary science, Grant gravitates towards such currents as Maturana–Varela autopoiesis theory, the sort of thing that the ardently scientistic Brassier tends to dismiss out of hand. Though some devotees of Grant object that the latter's philosophy is compatible with "naturalism," we have seen that it is a naturalism rooted in a speculative metaphysics of the idea, rather than in the sort of eliminativist death-squad science that Brassier temperamentally prefers.

Where Žižek goes wrong is in his diagnosis of the second axis of Speculative Realism, which he calls divine/secular. It fails because it is needlessly forced: Meillassoux is the only one of the four SR authors who speaks of the divine at all. In order to find a second member of the utterly imaginary "divine" axis, Žižek has to misread OOO as follows: "Harman [opts] for a directly religious (or spiritualist, at least) panpsychism . . ."[3] There is nothing religious to be found in the writings of OOO so far, and certainly nothing that could be called "directly" religious, whatever that phrase might mean. Furthermore, OOO is no more compatible with panpsychism than Grant's philosophy is. We have already seen that OOO is not panpsychist, but offers a unified theory of objects at a level that *precedes* any distinction into mental and non-mental zones.

But at least Žižek takes an honest stab at identifying the second axis dividing the four Goldsmiths authors, which is no easy task. Even I, as an original member of the group who has spent much time over the years trying to understand the disagreements among the four positions, was not sure of the other principle of division until beginning to write this book. Yet it now seems clear to me that the second axis is one that puts OOO and Brassier on one side against Grant and Meillassoux on the other. For despite the recent glowering hostility of Brassier and his circle to OOO, there is one crucial point on which these two circles fundamentally agree: the special incommensurability between what Brassier calls thought and world or what OOO calls the sensual and the real (though without confining "sensual" to humans as Brassier does with "thought"). This is obviously not the case with Meillassoux, who sees no especial difficulty in grasping the in-itself through mathematization, a process that Brassier critiques for its appeal to an "intellectual intuition" that he finds (and I find) impossible. As for Grant, though there is a sense in which he too restores the noumenal, he is ultimately a monist who appeals to a single productive nature that becomes individualized only through various "retardations" or "contractions" of the unified nature-energy. There is thus no perilous leap for Grant between reality and its images in way that there is for both Brassier and OOO.

There is, of course, another significant difference between Brassier and OOO. Whereas both agree that we have direct access only to *images*, OOO sees both the manifest and the scientific image as being immeasurably distant from the real. Brassier condemns this approach as fruitlessly devoted to an "irrecuperable alterity," and insists that the scientific image "more closely tracks" the thing-in-itself than the relatively impoverished manifest image does. He holds that science can and must "measure" the distance between the scientific image and reality, though in all candor this seems more like a theoretical desire on his part than like anything he ever demonstrates. Coming from a continental philosophy background in which science is often held in absurdly low esteem, Brassier is no doubt right to oppose the imprecise Heideggerian dictum that "science does not think." His appreciation for the cognitive achievements of the hard sciences is admirable. Yet he flips too far in the other direction when he calls for a "maximal authority" to be granted to science, as if it were a question of law enforcement, and he generally speaks in derisive tones about other areas of human cognition. It is very important to Brassier that philosophy be equipped to silence any irrational nonsense it might encounter. OOO simply does not agree that nonsense is the biggest threat to philosophy, for it does not tend to last for very long, and hardly needs active theoretical persecution to be cleared from the field. As OOO sees it, the bigger threats to philosophy are narrowness and familiarity. Narrowness is found whenever too much of reality is excluded from a philosophy in order to restrict the scope of the world to what can be mastered with established intellectual methods. Familiarity is found always and everywhere, and is the hereditary enemy of the strangeness from which all philosophy is born.

It is my hope that the reader of this book now has a good sense of the various conflicting ideas that have made Speculative Realism such a fresh and surprising event in continental philosophy from 2007 onward. To cite Meillassoux's closing words at Goldsmiths, "I think that the title of our day – speculative realism – was perfectly chosen, and is in itself a sort of event."[4] As I see it, the four positions aired at the Goldsmiths workshop are still four of the most interesting orientations found on the philosophical landscape today. But no philosophy is really understood until it is refuted or superseded by something else. I would like to challenge the younger readers of this book, in particular, eventually to supersede the various Speculative Realist currents after first digesting what has made them important.

Notes

Introduction

1 Peter Gratton, *Speculative Realism*; Steven Shaviro, *The Universe of Things*; Tom Sparrow, *The End of Phenomenology*.

2 The first such case resulted in my writing *Bruno Latour: Reassembling the Political* for Pluto Press.

3 Ian Bogost, *Unit Operations*; Levi R. Bryant, *The Democracy of Objects*; Timothy Morton, *Realist Magic*.

4 For a more comprehensive picture of OOO itself, see Graham Harman, *Object-Oriented Ontology*.

5 Peter Wolfendale, *Object-Oriented Philosophy*.

6 See Graham Harman, "The Current State of Speculative Realism," and pp. 77–80 of Harman, *Quentin Meillassoux: Philosophy in the Making*.

7 Ray Brassier et al., "Speculative Realism."

8 Graham Harman, "Dwelling with the Fourfold."

9 Quentin Meillassoux, *After Finitude*.

10 Graham Harman, *Tool-Being*.

11 Meillassoux once told me that he came up with the term in 2002 or 2003.

12 Slavoj Žižek, *Less Than Nothing*, p. 640.

13 Alex Williams and Nick Srnicek, "#ACCELERATE MANIFESTO for an Accelerationist Politics."

Chapter 1 Prometheanism

1 Thomas Ligotti, *The Conspiracy Against the Human Race*.

2 Ray Brassier et al., "Speculative Realism," p. 308. Subsequent page numbers in the text refer to this transcript.

3 Alain Badiou, Robin Mackay, and Ray Brassier, "Philosophy, Sciences, Mathematics (Interview)."

4 Ray Brassier, *Nihil Unbound*, p. x. Subsequent page numbers in the text refer to this volume.

5 Knox Peden, "Ray Brassier, *Nihil Unbound: Enlightenment and Extinction*."

6 Martin Heidegger, *What is Called Thinking?*, p. 8.

7 Thomas Metzinger, *Being No One*; Graham Harman, "The Problem with Metzinger."

8 Carlo Rovelli, "Halfway Through the Woods," p. 182.

9 Alain Badiou, *Deleuze: The Clamor of Being*.

10 Søren Kierkegaard, *The Essential Kierkegaard*.

11 Plotinus, *The Six Enneads.*

12 Manuel DeLanda, *Intensive Science and Virtual Philosophy.*

13 Ray Brassier, "Prometheanism and its Critics," p. 469. Subsequent page numbers in the text refer to this article.

14 Ray Brassier, "Concepts and Objects," p. 47. Subsequent page numbers in the text refer to this article.

15 Graham Harman, "Undermining, Overmining, and Duomining."

16 Aristotle, *Metaphysics*, Book Theta, chapter 3.

17 Brassier, *Nihil Unbound*, p. 119.

18 Bruno Latour, "On the Partial Existence of Existing and Nonexisting Objects."

19 See my discussion of Latour's failure to incorporate metaphor sufficiently in Graham Harman, *Immaterialism*, pp. 101–4.

20 See Jamie Peck, *Constructions of Neoliberal Reason.*

21 Bruno Latour, *An Inquiry into Modes of Existence.*

22 David Stove, *The Plato Cult and Other Philosophical Follies.*

23 See James Ladyman and Don Ross, *Every Thing Must Go*; see also my response to them, Graham Harman, "I Am Also of the Opinion that Materialism Must Be Destroyed."

Chapter 2 Vitalist Idealism

1 Immanuel Kant, *Critique of Pure Reason, Critique of Practical Reason,* and *Critique of Judgment.*

2 Martin Heidegger, *Der deutsche Idealismus (Fichte, Hegel, Schelling) und die philosophische Problemlage der Gegenwart.*

3 Andrew Bowie, "Friedrich Wilhelm Joseph von Schelling."

4 Ray Brassier et al., "Speculative Realism," p. 334. Subsequent page numbers in the text refer to this transcript.

5 Roy Bhaskar, *A Realist Theory of Science*; Manuel DeLanda, *Intensive Science and Virtual Philosophy.*

6 Bruno Latour, "Irreductions"; Latour, *Pandora's Hope.*

7 Latour, *Pandora's Hope*, p. 137.

8 Timothy Morton, *Ecology without Nature, The Ecological Thought,* and *Hyperobjects.*

9 Ray Brassier, "Concepts and Objects."

10 Iain Hamilton Grant, *Philosophies of Nature After Schelling*, p. 8. Subsequent page numbers in the text refer to this volume.

11 Manuel DeLanda and Graham Harman, *The Rise of Realism*, p. 116.

12 Gilbert Simondon, *L'Individuation à la lumière des notions de forme et d'information.*

13 The classic discussion of these themes in contemporary philosophy is DeLanda, *Intensive Science and Virtual Philosophy.*

14 Martin Heidegger, *History of the Concept of Time*, pp. 72ff.

15 Aristotle, *Metaphysics*, p. 148. For a discussion of this issue from a OOO point of view, see Graham Harman, "Aristotle with a Twist."

16 Levi R. Bryant, Nick Srnicek, and Graham Harman, "Towards a Speculative Philosophy."

17 Jeremy Dunham, Iain Hamilton Grant, and Sean Watson, *Idealism: The History of a Philosophy*, p. 1. Subsequent page numbers in the text refer to this volume.

18 Bernard d'Espagnat, *On Physics and Philosophy*; Julian Barbour, *The End of Time*; Stuart Kauffman, *The Origins of Order*; Roland Omnès, *Quantum Philosophy*.

19 Alain Badiou, *Logics of Worlds*.

20 Slavoj Žižek and Glyn Daly, *Conversations with Žižek*, p. 97; Jacques Lacan, *The Sinthome*.

21 George Berkeley, *A Treatise Concerning the Principles of Human Knowledge*, p. 24.

22 John D. Caputo, "For Love of the Things Themselves"; Jacques Derrida, *Of Grammatology*.

23 DeLanda in DeLanda and Harman, *The Rise of Realism*, p. 116.

24 Myles Burnyeat, "Idealism and Greek Philosophy."

25 Darren Hibbs, "On the Possibility of Pre-Cartesian Idealism."

26 Immanuel Kant, *Prolegomena to Any Future Metaphysics*.

27 John Locke, *An Essay Concerning Human Understanding*.

28 Niklas Luhmann, *Social Systems*.

29 For a direct account of the resonance between OOO on one side and Maturana and Varela plus Luhmann on the other, see Levi R. Bryant's outstanding overview in *The Democracy of Objects*, pp. 137–74.

30 Jakob von Uexküll, *A Foray into the World of Animals and Humans*.

31 Alain Badiou, *Deleuze: The Clamor of Being*.

32 Graham Harman, "Whitehead and Schools X, Y, and Z."

Chapter 3 Object-Oriented Ontology

1 For the earliest extant examples of this approach, see the early chapters of Graham Harman, *Towards Speculative Realism*.

2 Alfred North Whitehead, *Process and Reality*; Xavier Zubíri, *On Essence*.

3 Graham Harman, "On the Horror of Phenomenology" and *Weird Realism*.

4 Ray Brassier et al., "Speculative Realism," p. 367. Subsequent page numbers in the text refer to this transcript.

5 Saul Kripke, *Naming and Necessity*.

6 Graham Harman, "Undermining, Overmining, and Duomining."

7 Graham Harman, *Tool-Being*.

8 Graham Harman, "On Vicarious Causation."

9 Martin Heidegger, *Kant and the Problem of Metaphysics*, pp. 252–3.

10 Graham Harman, *The Quadruple Object*; Harman, "Time, Space, Essence, and Eidos."

11 Markus Gabriel, *Fields of Sense*.

12 Wilfrid Sellars, "Philosophy and the Scientific Image of Man."

13 Graham Harman, "Quentin Meillassoux: A New French Philosopher."

14 Christopher Watkins, *Difficult Atheism*, p. 144.

15 Harman, *Weird Realism*; Harman, "On the Horror of Phenomenology," H. P. Lovecraft, *Tales*.

16 Lovecraft, *Tales*.

17 Alain Badiou, *Being and Event*.

18 Emmanuel Levinas, *Existence and Existents*; James Ladyman and Don Ross, *Every Thing Must Go*.

19 Karen Barad, *Meeting the Universe Halfway*. For a partly sympathetic critique of Barad, see Graham Harman, "Agential and Speculative Realism."

20 Gilles Deleuze, *Bergsonism*.

21 This lecture has since been published as "Object-Oriented Philosophy," chapter 6 in Graham Harman, *Towards Speculative Realism*, pp. 93–104.

22 Graham Harman, "The Invisible Realm," section 1 of *Tool-Being*, pp. 15–24. Subsequent page numbers refer to this volume.

23 Martin Heidegger, *Towards the Definition of Philosophy*.

24 These two brilliant essays can be found back to back in Martin Heidegger, *Pathmarks*, pp. 82–96 ("What is Metaphysics?") and pp. 97–135 ("On the Essence of Ground").

25 Martin Heidegger, "Insight into That Which Is," in *Bremen and Freiburg Lectures*.

26 Graham Harman, *L'objet quadruple*.

27 Graham Harman, "On Vicarious Causation," p. 190. Subsequent page numbers refer to this article.

27 A. S. Eddington, *The Nature of the Physical World*, p. ix.

28 Graham Harman, *The Third Table*, p. 6. Subsequent page numbers refer to this volume.

29 Graham Harman, *Object-Oriented Ontology*, chapter 2, "Aesthetics is the Root of All Philosophy."

30 Konstantin Stanislavski, *An Actor's Work*.

Chapter 4 Speculative Materialism

1 Ray Brassier et al., "Speculative Realism," p. 409. Subsequent page numbers in the text refer to this transcript.

2 Graham Harman, "Interview with Quentin Meillassoux," trans. Harman, in *Quentin Meillassoux: Philosophy in the* Making, p. 213.

3 Graham Priest, *Beyond the Limits of Thought*; Jon Cogburn, *Garcian Meditations*.

4 For further discussion of this issue, see pp. 137–41 of Harman, *Quentin Meillassoux: Philosophy in the Making*.

5 Anthony Paul Smith, *François Laruelle's Principles of Non-Philosophy*, p. 116.

6 Graham Harman, "François Laruelle, *Philosophies of Difference: A Critical Introduction to Non-Philosophy*."

7 Graham Harman, *Prince of Networks*, pp. 167ff.

8 Alfred North Whitehead, *Process and Reality*, p. 6.

9 Ibid.

10 Ibid., p. 8.

11 Friedrich Nietzsche, *Twilight of the Idols*, p. 6.

12 David Chalmers, *The Conscious Mind*.

13 Imre Lakatos, *The Methodology of Scientific Research Programmes*.

14 Quentin Meillassoux, "Iteration, Reiteration, Repetition."

15 Harman, *Quentin Meillassoux*, pp. 6–53.

16 Quentin Meillassoux, *After Finitude*, p. 1. Subsequent page numbers in the text refer to this volume.

17 Harman, *Quentin Meillassoux*, pp. 14ff.

18 Peter Gratton, *Speculative Realism*.

19 David Hilbert, "Über das Unendliche," p. 170.

20 Quentin Meillassoux, "Appendix: Excerpts from *L'Inexistence divine*."

21 For a compact version of the same argument, see Quentin Meillassoux, "Spectral Dilemma."

22 Harman, *Quentin Meillassoux*, pp. 224–87. Subsequent page numbers in the text refer to this volume.

23 Martin Heidegger, *Fundamental Concepts of Metaphysics*. In fairness to Heidegger, the sections of this lecture course on boredom are much more successful.

24 This idea was first developed in Graham Harman, "Meillassoux's Virtual Future."

Conclusion: The Two Acres of Speculative Realism

1 Slavoj Žižek, *Less Than Nothing*, p. 640.

2 Ibid.

3 Ibid.

4 Quentin Meillassoux, in Ray Brassier et al., "Speculative Realism," p. 435.

References

Works Authored or Co-Authored by the Original Speculative Realists

Badiou, Alain, Robin Mackay, and Ray Brassier, "Philosophy, Sciences, Mathematics (Interview)," *Collapse* I, reissued edn (2012).

Brassier, Ray, "Concepts and Objects," pp. 47–65 in *The Speculative Turn: Continental Realism and Materialism*, ed. L. Bryant et al. (Melbourne: re.press, 2011).

Brassier, Ray, *Nihil Unbound: Enlightenment and Extinction* (London: Palgrave Macmillan, 2007).

Brassier, Ray, "Prometheanism and its Critics," pp. 467–87 in *#Accelerate: The Accelerationist Reader*, ed. R. Mackay and A. Avanessian (Falmouth: Urbanomic, 2014).

Brassier, Ray, Iain Hamilton Grant, Graham Harman, and Quentin Meillassoux, "Speculative Realism," *Collapse* III (2007): 306–449.

Bryant, Levi R., Nick Srnicek, and Graham Harman (eds), *The Speculative Turn: Continental Realism and Materialism* (Melbourne: re.press, 2011).

Bryant, Levi R., Nick Srnicek, and Graham Harman, "Towards a Speculative Philosophy," pp. 1–18 in *The Speculative Turn: Continental Realism and Materialism*, ed. Levi R. Bryant et al. (Melbourne: re.press, 2011).

DeLanda, Manuel, and Graham Harman, *The Rise of Realism* (Cambridge: Polity, 2017).

Dunham, Jeremy, Iain Hamilton Grant, and Sean Watson, *Idealism: The History of a Philosophy* (Montreal: McGill–Queen's University Press, 2011).

Grant, Iain Hamilton, *Philosophies of Nature After Schelling* (London: Continuum, 2006).

Harman, Graham, "Agential and Speculative Realism: Remarks on Barad's Ontology," *rhizomes* 30 (2017), www.rhizomes.net/issue30/harman.html.

Harman, Graham, "Aristotle with a Twist," pp. 227–53 in *Speculative Medievalisms: Discography*, ed. E. Joy et al. (Brooklyn, NY: Punctum Books, 2013).

Harman, Graham, *Bruno Latour: Reassembling the Political* (London: Pluto Press, 2014).

Harman, Graham, "The Current State of Speculative Realism," *Speculations* IV (2013): 22–8.

Harman, Graham, "Dwelling with the Fourfold," *Space and Culture* 12/3 (2009): 292–302.

Harman, Graham, "François Laruelle, *Philosophies of Difference: A Critical*

Introduction to Non-Philosophy," *Notre Dame Philosophical Reviews*, August 11, 2011, http://ndpr.nd.edu/news/25437-philosophies-of-difference-a-critical-intr oduction-to-non-philosophy/.

Harman, Graham, "I Am Also of the Opinion that Materialism Must Be Destroyed," *Environment and Planning D: Society and Space* 28/5 (2010): 772–90.

Harman, Graham, *Immaterialism: Objects and Social Theory* (Cambridge: Polity, 2016).

Harman, Graham, "Meillassoux's Virtual Future," *continent* 1/2 (2011): 78–91.

Harman, Graham, *Object-Oriented Ontology: A New Theory of Everything* (London: Pelican, 2018).

Harman, Graham, *L'objet quadruple: une métaphysqiue des choses après Heidegger* (Paris: PUF, 2010).

Harman, Graham, "On the Horror of Phenomenology: Lovecraft and Husserl," *Collapse* IV (2008): 333–64.

Harman, Graham, "On Vicarious Causation," *Collapse* II (2007): 171–205.

Harman, Graham, *Prince of Networks: Bruno Latour and Metaphysics* (Melbourne: re.press, 2009).

Harman, Graham, "The Problem with Metzinger," *Cosmos and History* 7/1 (2011): 7–36.

Harman, Graham, *The Quadruple Object* (Winchester: Zero Books, 2011).

Harman, Graham, "Quentin Meillassoux: A New French Philosopher," *Philosophy Today* 51/1 (2007): 104–17.

Harman, Graham, *Quentin Meillassoux: Philosophy in the Making* (2nd edn, Edinburgh: Edinburgh University Press, 2015).

Harman, Graham, *The Third Table/Der dritte Tisch* (Ostfildern: Hatje Cantz, 2012).

Harman, Graham, "Time, Space, Essence, and Eidos: A New Theory of Causation," *Cosmos and History* 6/1 (2010): 1–17.

Harman, Graham, *Tool-Being: Heidegger and the Metaphysics of Objects* (Chicago: Open Court, 2002).

Harman, Graham, *Towards Speculative Realism: Essays and Lectures* (Winchester: Zero Books, 2010).

Harman, Graham, "Undermining, Overmining, and Duomining: A Critique," pp. 40–51 in *ADD Metaphysics*, ed. Jenna Sutela (Aalto, Finland: Aalto University Digital Design Laboratory, 2013).

Harman, Graham, *Weird Realism: Lovecraft and Philosophy* (Winchester: Zero Books, 2012).

Harman, Graham, "Whitehead and Schools X, Y, and Z," pp. 231–48 in *The Lure of Whitehead*, ed. Nicholas Gaskill and A. J. Nocek (Minneapolis: University of Minnesota Press, 2014).

Meillassoux, Quentin, *After Finitude: Essay on the Necessity of Contingency*, trans. R. Brassier (London: Continuum, 2008).

Meillassoux, Quentin, "Appendix: Excerpts from *L'Inexistence divine*," trans. Graham Harman, pp. 224–87 in Harman, *Quentin Meillassoux: Philosophy in the Making* (2nd edn, Edinburgh: Edinburgh University Press, 2015).

Meillassoux, Quentin, "Iteration, Reiteration, Repetition: A Speculative Analysis of the Meaningless Sign", unpubd version, trans. R. Mackay, 2012, https://cdn. shopify.com/s/files/1/0069/6232/files/Meillassoux_Workshop_Berlin.pdf ["The Berlin lecture"].

Meillassoux, Quentin, *The Number and the Siren: A Decipherment of Mallarmé's Coup de Dés*, trans. R. Mackay (Falmouth: Urbanomic, 2012).

Meillassoux, Quentin, "Spectral Dilemma," *Collapse* IV (2008): 261–75.

Works by Others

Aristotle, *Metaphysics*, trans. J. Sachs (Santa Fe, NM: Green Lion Press, 1999).

Aristotle, *Poetics*, trans. A. Kenny (Oxford: Oxford University Press, 2013).

Ayache, Elie, *The Blank Swan: The End of Probability* (Hoboken, NJ: Wiley, 2010).

Badiou, Alain, *Being and Event*, trans. O. Feltham (London: Continuum, 2007).

Badiou, Alain, *Deleuze: The Clamor of Being*, trans. L. Burchill (Minneapolis: University of Minnesota Press, 1999).

Badiou, Alain, *Logics of Worlds: Being and Event II*, trans. A. Toscano (London: Continuum, 2009).

Barad, Karen, *Meeting the Universe Halfway: Quantum Physics and the Entanglement of Matter and Meaning* (Durham, NC: Duke University Press, 2007).

Barbour, Julian, *The End of Time: The Next Revolution in Physics* (Oxford: Oxford University Press, 2001).

Baudrillard, Jean, *Symbolic Exchange and Death*, trans. I. H. Grant (London: Sage, 1993).

Bergson, Henri, *Matter and Memory*, trans. N. M. Paul (New York: Zone Books, 1990).

Berkeley, George, *A Treatise Concerning the Principles of Human Knowledge* (Indianapolis: Hackett, 1992).

Bhaskar, Roy, *A Realist Theory of Science* (London: Verso, 2008).

Bogost, Ian, *Unit Operations: An Approach to Videogame Criticism* (Cambridge, MA: MIT Press, 2008).

Bowie, Andrew, "Friedrich Wilhelm Joseph von Schelling," *The Stanford Encyclopedia of Philosophy*, ed. E. Zalta (Fall 2016 edn), https://plato.stanford. edu/archives/fall2016/entries/schelling/.

Bryant, Levi R., *The Democracy of Objects* (Ann Arbor, MI: Open Humanities Press, 2011).

Burnyeat, Myles, "Idealism and Greek Philosophy: What Descartes Saw and Berkeley Missed," *Philosophical Review* 91/1 (1982): 3–40.

Caputo, John D., "For Love of the Things Themselves: Derrida's Phenomenology of the Hyper-Real," pp. 37–59 in *Fenomenologia hoje: significado e linguagem*, ed. R. Timm de Souza and N. Fernandes de Oliveira (Porto Alegre, Brazil: EDIPUCRS, 2002).

Chalmers, David, *The Conscious Mind: In Search of a Fundamental Theory* (Oxford: Oxford University Press, 1997).

Cogburn, Jon, *Garcian Meditations: The Dialectics of Persistence in* Form and Object. (Edinburgh: Edinburgh University Press, 2017).

DeLanda, Manuel, *Intensive Science and Virtual Philosophy* (London: Continuum, 2002).

Deleuze, Gilles, *Bergsonism*, trans. H. Tomlinson and B. Habberjam (New York: Zone Books, 1990).

Deleuze, Gilles, *Difference and Repetition*, trans. P. Patton (New York: Columbia University Press, 1995).

Derrida, Jacques, *Of Grammatology*, trans. G. Spivak (Baltimore: Johns Hopkins University Press, 1997).

Dupuy, Jean-Pierre, "Some Pitfalls in the Philosophical Foundations of Nanoethics," *Journal of Medicine and Philosophy* 32 (2007): 237–61.

Eddington, Arthur Stanley, *The Nature of the Physical World* (New York: Macmillan, 1929).

d'Espagnat, Bernard, *On Physics and Philosophy* (Princeton, NJ: Princeton University Press, 2006).

Fried, Michael, "Art and Objecthood," pp. 148–72 in Fried, *Art and Objecthood: Essays and Reviews* (Chicago: University of Chicago Press, 1998).

Gabriel, Markus, *Fields of Sense: A New Realist Ontology* (Edinburgh: Edinburgh University Press, 2015).

Gratton, Peter, *Speculative Realism: Problems and Prospects* (London: Bloomsbury, 2014).

Hegel, G. W. F., *Phenomenology of Spirit*, trans. A. V. Miller (Oxford: Oxford University Press, 1977).

Heidegger, Martin, *Being and Time*, trans. J. Macquarrie and E. Robinson (New York: Harper, 2008).

Heidegger, Martin, *Contributions to Philosophy: Of the Event*, trans. R. Rojcewicz and D. Vallega-Neu (Bloomington: Indiana University Press, 2012).

Heidegger, Martin, *Der deutsche Idealismus (Fichte, Hegel, Schelling) und die philosophische Problemlage der Gegenwart* (2nd edn, Frankfurt: Vittorio Klostermann, 2011).

Heidegger, Martin, *Fundamental Concepts of Metaphysics: World–Finitude–Solitude*, trans. W. McNeill and N. Walker (Bloomington: Indiana University Press, 2001).

Heidegger, Martin, *History of the Concept of Time: Prolegomena*, trans. T. Kisiel (Bloomington: Indiana University Press, 2009).

Heidegger, Martin, "Insight into That Which Is," pp. 3–76 in *Bremen and Freiburg Lectures*, trans. A. Mitchell (Bloomington: Indiana University Press, 2012).

Heidegger, Martin, *Kant and the Problem of Metaphysics*, trans. J. Churchill (Bloomington: Indiana University Press, 1962).

Heidegger, Martin, *Towards the Definition of Philosophy*, trans. T. Sadler (London: Continuum, 2008).

Heidegger, Martin, *What is Called Thinking?*, trans. J. G. Gray (New York: Harper, 1968).

Heidegger, Martin, "What is Metaphysics?" and "On the Essence of Ground," pp. 82–135 in *Pathmarks*, ed. W. McNeill (Cambridge: Cambridge University Press, 1998).

Hibbs, Darren, "On the Possibility of Pre-Cartesian Idealism," *Dialogue* 48 (2009): 643–53.

Hilbert, David, "Über das Unendliche," *Mathematische Annalen* 95/1 (1926): 161–90.

Husserl, Edmund, *Logical Investigations*, 2 vols, trans. J. N. Findlay (London: Routledge & Kegan Paul, 1970).

Israel, Jonathan, *Radical Enlightenment: Philosophy and the Making of Modernity, 1650–1750* (Oxford: Oxford University Press, 2002).

Kant, Immanuel, *Critique of Judgment*, trans. W. Pluhar (Indianapolis: Hackett, 1987).

Kant, Immanuel, *Critique of Practical Reason*, trans. M. Gregor and A. Reath (Cambridge: Cambridge University Press, 2015).

Kant, Immanuel, *Critique of Pure Reason*, trans. N. K. Smith (New York: St Martin's Press, 1965).

Kant, Immanuel, *Prolegomena to Any Future Metaphysics*, trans. J. Ellington (Indianapolis: Hackett, 2001).

Kauffman, Stuart, *The Origins of Order: Self-Organization and Selection in Evolution* (Oxford: Oxford University Press, 2000).

Kierkegaard, Søren, *The Essential Kierkegaard*, ed. H. Hong and E. Hong (Princeton, NJ: Princeton University Press, 2000).

Kripke, Saul, *Naming and Necessity* (Cambridge, MA: Harvard University Press, 1996).

Lacan, Jacques, *The Sinthome: The Seminar of Jacques Lacan, Book XXIII*, trans. A. R. Price (Cambridge: Polity, 2016).

Ladyman, James, and Don Ross (with David Spurrett and John Collier), *Every Thing Must Go: Metaphysics Naturalized* (Oxford: Oxford University Press, 2009).

Lakatos, Imre, *The Methodology of Scientific Research Programmes* (Cambridge: Cambridge University Press, 1980).

Laruelle, François, *Anti-Badiou: On the Introduction of Maoism into Philosophy*, trans. R. Mackay (London: Bloomsbury, 2013).

Laruelle, François, *Philosophies of Difference: A Critical Introduction to Non-Philosophy*, trans. R. Gangle (London: Bloomsbury, 2011).

Laruelle, François, *Philosophy and Non-Philosophy*, trans. T. Adkins (Minneapolis: Univocal, 2013).

Laruelle, François, *Principles of Non-Philosophy*, trans. N. Rubczak and A. P. Smith (London: Bloomsbury, 2013).

Latour, Bruno, *An Inquiry into Modes of Existence: An Anthropology of the Moderns*, trans. C. Porter (Cambridge, MA: Harvard University Press, 2013).

Latour, Bruno, "Irreductions," trans. J. Law, pp. 151–236 in *The Pasteurization of France: War and Peace of Microbes*, trans. A. Sheridan and J. Law (Cambridge, MA: Harvard University Press, 1988).

Latour, Bruno, "On the Partial Existence of Existing and Nonexisting Objects," pp. 247–69 in *Biographies of Scientific Objects*, ed. L. Daston (Chicago: University of Chicago Press, 2006).

Latour, Bruno, *Pandora's Hope: Essays on the Reality of Science Studies* (Cambridge, MA: Harvard University Press, 1999).

Latour, Bruno, *We Have Never Been Modern*, trans. C. Porter (Cambridge, MA: Harvard University Press, 1993).

Leibniz, G. W. von, "Monadology," pp. 213–25 in *Philosophical Essays*, trans. R. Ariew and D. Garber (Indianapolis: Hackett, 1989).

Levinas, Emmanuel, *Existence and Existents*, trans. A. Lingis (Dordrecht: Kluwer, 1988).

Ligotti, Thomas, *The Conspiracy Against the Human Race: A Contrivance of Horror*, with a foreword by Ray Brassier (New York: Hippocampus Press, 2010).

Locke, John, *An Essay Concerning Human Understanding*, 2 vols (New York: Dover, 1959).

Lovecraft, H. P., *Tales* (New York: Library of America, 2005).

Luhmann, Niklas, *Social Systems*, trans. J. Bednarz Jr (Stanford, CA: Stanford University Press, 1996).

Lyotard, Jean-François, *The Inhuman: Reflections on Time*, trans. G. Bennington and R. Bowlby (Stanford, CA: Stanford University Press, 1992).

Lyotard, Jean-François. *Libidinal Economy*, trans. I. H. Grant (Bloomington: Indiana University Press, 1993).

Metzinger, Thomas, *Being No One: The Self-Model Theory of Subjectivity* (Cambridge, MA: MIT Press, 2004).

Milton, John, *Paradise Lost* (Oxford: Oxford University Press, 2008).

Morrison, Toni, *Beloved* (New York: Vintage, 2004).

Morton, Timothy, *The Ecological Thought* (Cambridge, MA: Harvard University Press, 2010).

Morton, Timothy, *Ecology Without Nature: Rethinking Environmental Aesthetics* (Cambridge, MA: Harvard University Press, 2009).

Morton, Timothy, *Hyperobjects: Philosophy and Ecology After the End of the World* (Minneapolis: University of Minnesota Press, 2013).

Morton, Timothy, *Realist Magic: Objects, Ontology, Causality* (Ann Arbor, MI: Open Humanities Press, 2013).

Nietzsche, Friedrich, *Twilight of the Idols*, trans. R. Polt (Indianapolis: Hackett, 1997).

Omnès, Roland, *Quantum Philosophy* (Princeton, NJ: Princeton University Press, 1999).

Peck, Jamie, *Constructions of Neoliberal Reason* (Oxford: Oxford University Press, 2013).

Peden, Knox, "Ray Brassier, *Nihil Unbound: Enlightenment and Extinction*," *Continental Philosophy Review* 42/4 (2010): 583–9.

Plato, "Timaeus," in *Timaeus and Critias*, trans. R. Waterfield (Oxford: Oxford University Press, 2009).

Plotinus, *The Six Enneads*, trans. S. MacKenna and B. S. Page (CreateSpace Independent Publishing Platform, 2017).

Priest, Graham, *Beyond the Limits of Thought* (Oxford: Oxford University Press, 2002).

Rovelli, Carlo, "Halfway Through the Woods," pp. 180–223 in *The Cosmos of Science: Essays of Exploration*, ed. J. Earman and J. Norton (Pittsburgh: University of Pittsburgh Press, 1998).

Sellars, Wilfrid, "Philosophy and the Scientific Image of Man," pp. 369–408 in *In the Space of Reasons: Selected Essays of Wilfrid Sellars*, ed. K. Scharp and R. Brandom (Cambridge, MA: Harvard University Press, 2007).

Shakespeare, William, *Macbeth* (London: Bloomsbury, 2015).

Shaviro, Steven, *The Universe of Things: On Speculative Realism* (Minneapolis: University of Minnesota Press, 2014).

Shelley, Mary, *Frankenstein* (New York: W. W. Norton, 2012).

Simondon, Gilbert, *L'Individuation à la lumière des notions de forme et d'information* (Grenoble: Editions Jérôme Millon, 2005).

Skrbina, David, *Panpsychism in the West* (Cambridge, MA: MIT Press, 2007).

Smith, Anthony Paul, *François Laruelle's* Principles of Non-Philosophy*: A Critical Introduction and Guide* (Edinburgh: Edinburgh University Press, 2016).

Smolin, Lee, *The Life of the Cosmos* (Oxford: Oxford University Press, 1999).

Sparrow, Tom, *The End of Phenomenology: Metaphysics and the New Realism* (Edinburgh: Edinburgh University Press, 2014).

Stanislavski, Konstantin, *An Actor's Work: A Student's Diary*, trans. J. Benedetti (New York: Routledge, 2008).

Stove, David, *The Plato Cult and Other Philosophical Follies* (Oxford: Blackwell, 1991).

Uexküll, Jakob von, *A Foray into the World of Animals and Humans: With A Theory of Meaning*, trans. J. O'Neil (Minneapolis: University of Minnesota Press, 2010).

Vernes, Jean-René, *Critique de la raison aléatoire, ou Descartes contre Kant* (Paris: Aubier, 1982).

Watkins, Christopher, *Difficult Atheism: Post-Theological Thinking in Alain Badiou, Jean-Luc Nancy and Quentin Meillassoux* (Edinburgh: Edinburgh University Press, 2011).

Whitehead, Alfred North, *Process and Reality* (New York: Free Press, 1979).

Williams, Alex, and Nick Srnicek, "#ACCELERATE MANIFESTO for an Accelerationist Politics," Critical Legal Thinking blog, May 14, 2013, http://criticallegalthinking.com/2013/05/14/accelerate-manifesto-for-an-accelerationist-politics/.

Wolfendale, Peter, *Object-Oriented Philosophy: The Noumenon's New Clothes* (Falmouth: Urbanomic, 2014).

Žižek, Slavoj, *Less Than Nothing: Hegel and the Shadow of Dialectical Materialism* (London: Verso, 2012).

Žižek, Slavoj, and Glyn Daly, *Conversations with Žižek* (Cambridge: Polity, 2004).

Zubíri, Xavier, *On Essence*, trans. A. R. Caponigri (Washington, DC: Catholic University of America Press, 1980).

Index